Emerson Manaloto combines biblical p
concerns to address the pressing ne
priorities from programs to people. He competently and accurately sketches
the profile of the New Testament church and then suggests ways that vision
might be carried out in the Filipino church that he is so familiar with.

Douglas J. Moo, PhD
Kenneth T. Wessner Professor of Biblical Studies,
Wheaton College, Wheaton, Illinois, USA
Chair, Committee on Bible Translation

The "house church" is not a new invention. It goes all the way back to the
apostolic era of the early New Testament church. In the contemporary church
age, "small groups" have made a significant impact upon the maturity, growth
and discipleship of the church. While much literature has been published,
Pastor Emerson Manaloto's vital contribution lies in two significant ways. He
presents a keen survey of the biblical, theological and sociological ramifications
of small groups and house churches, as well as a practical assessment of the
effective implementation of this pertinent church dynamic to the Filipino
church. We can certainly learn from it!

Rev Edmund Chan
Leadership Mentor, Covenant Evangelical Free Church, Singapore
Founder, Global Alliance of Intentional Disciplemaking Churches

One of the great delights in contemporary theologizing is to hear the ever-
increasing voices from the Majority World. And one of the persistent challenges
in global Christianity is to wrestle with what it means to be the gathered people
of God in a world where traditions and institutions are increasingly being
questioned. This questioning is also occurring within the church. How can
we more fully shape our life together in the light of the biblical story as a way
of worship, formation and service to the world? In this very readable text, Dr
Manaloto gives us some answers from within a Southeast Asian context for
being church as community rather than as institution.

Charles Ringma, PhD
Adjunct Faculty, Asian Theological Seminary, Manila, Philippines
Emeritus Professor, Regent College, Vancouver, Canada
Honorary Research Associate Professor, Studies in Religion,
University of Queensland, Brisbane, Australia

I am grateful for the publishing of Dr Emerson Manaloto's book, *Let the Church Meet in Your House!* Having studied small group ministry myself and having lived for years in the Filipino context, I have followed this study as it developed in our church. Many here in Asia have copied the latest small group models from North and South America, South Korea, and Singapore, but this is a Filipino model fit for the Filipino context, based on the historical and biblical perspective of the New Testament church. All of this is foundational for further theological and practical development of small group ministry for the future. I highly recommend this book!

Frank Pardue, DMin
Asia Director, WorldVenture

What makes this book an important contribution to the study of small groups is its specific consideration of both the New Testament and the Filipino contexts. We have a saying in Filipino, *Ang hindi marunong lumingon sa pinanggalingan ay hindi makararating sa paroroonan* (Those who do not know how to look back from where they came will never reach their destination). The book surveys the relevant works on small groups and growth groups, but does not stop there. Instead, Dr Manaloto goes back to his own history and culture in order to understand the challenges confronting Filipinos in the application of New Testament principles. The result is the much-needed contextual interpretation of the biblical teaching of home/house groups.

Federico Villanueva, PhD
Asia Regional Commissioning Editor, Langham Publishing
Scholar Care Coordinator, Asia, Langham Scholars

Global Perspectives Series

Let the Church Meet in Your House!

Langham

GLOBAL LIBRARY

Let the Church Meet in Your House!

The Theological Foundation of the New Testament House Church

Emerson T. Manaloto

Langham
GLOBAL LIBRARY

© 2019 Emerson T. Manaloto

Published 2019 by Langham Global Library
An imprint of Langham Publishing
www.langhampublishing.org

Langham Publishing and its imprints are a ministry of Langham Partnership

Langham Partnership
PO Box 296, Carlisle, Cumbria, CA3 9WZ, UK
www.langham.org

ISBNs:
978-1-78368-720-6 Print
978-1-78368-721-3 ePub
978-1-78368-722-0 Mobi
978-1-78368-723-7 PDF

Emerson T. Manaloto has asserted his right under the Copyright, Designs and Patents Act, 1988 to be identified as the Author of this work.

British Library Cataloguing-in-Publication Data
A catalogue record for this book is available from the British Library

ISBN: 978-1-78368-720-6

Cover & Book Design: projectluz.com

This work is dedicated
to my *house*, my loving and ever supportive wife, Dyan, and
to our children, Paul Emerson and John Emerson, and
to my *church,* Greenhills Christian Fellowship, and its small groups.

CONTENTS

List of Figures

List of Tables

Foreword

This scholarly research, I believe, is on the road to becoming one of the most important textbooks in ministry, particularly for those who are praying for the saturation of the gospel in any given sphere or location. The book also affirms the vision and direction of the evangelical church in the Philippines to saturate the whole country, all cities and all spheres of society, with the gospel of Jesus Christ. Where conventional and traditional church-planting strategies cannot reach, the church must go back to the strategy of the apostles in the book of Acts to see the discipleship of the Filipino people here and everywhere around the world.

The last one hundred years in the Philippines saw the explosive growth of the number of disciples and the multiplication of churches in the Philippines. In 1974, denominations and church leaders gathered together to evaluate the growth of the church over the last century. It was reported that there were 600,000 evangelical born-again Christians and 5,000 local churches in the country at that time. That meeting also gave birth to a new cooperative discipleship and church-planting program in the country called *Discipling a Whole Nation* or DAWN 2000 Philippines, that aims to accelerate church growth by planting a church in every barangay[1] in the country.

At the end of the DAWN 2000 program, the count of the number of churches grew from 5,000 in 1974 to 51,300 in 2000. But it was noted that after the program, that there were still 20,000 barangays in the country unchurched and unreached. This is true especially in places where traditional church-planting approaches are restricted, including many tribal places and hundreds of temporary dwelling sites.

Thus there was a realization that new strategies and creative mission approaches must be applied. In the last twenty years, simple churches and house churches have mushroomed in the country that include discipleship movements, house churches, simple churches that meet in business establishments, campus churches, jail churches, groups that meet in police and army camps, basketball courts, etc. What is left undone and unreached can be done through the house-church strategy employed in the book of Acts.

> And they devoted themselves to the apostles' teaching and the fellowship, to the breaking of bread and the prayers. And awe came

---

1. Barangay - the smallest administrative division in the Philippines.

upon every soul, and many wonders and signs were being done through the apostles. And all who believed were together and had all things in common. And they were selling their possessions and belongings and distributing the proceeds to all, as any had need. And day by day, attending the temple together and breaking bread in their homes, they received their food with glad and generous hearts, praising God and having favor with all the people. And the Lord added to their number day by day those who were being saved. (Acts 2:42–47 ESV)

Church history tells us that when restrictions erupted in China in the late 1940s, pastors and bishops were arrested, churches were padlocked, and Bibles were confiscated. During this period, it was reported that churches went underground and scattered. Even in the absence of pastors and bishops, and with places of worship not available, the number of disciples grew in China through countless churches that met in homes.

Today, it is reported that there are more than 65 million Christians in China,[2] although Bible translators say that there are more than 130 million Christians in the country, making the Chinese church the largest and fastest growing in the world. All these are attributed to the exponential growth happening through churches that meet in homes.

Crucial to the quantitative and explosive growth of Christian churches is the qualitative growth of every believer. Studies show, especially among those who belong to mega-churches, that belonging to small groups is key not only to connectivity of individuals but to the spiritual growth of believers. There is more transparency and intimacy in the house-church setting than those in the larger groups. In this era of Internet, fast speed communication, one stop-shops, mega-churches and fake news, one can be easily lost in the crowd. Loving, caring and real relationships are better found in small groups.

Churches that meet in homes are not an alternative program or approach in missions and discipleship – they must be parallel with and complement all the ministries that reach the entire population and all spheres of society.

Bishop Noel A. Pantoja
National Director, Philippine Council of Evangelical Churches (PCEC)
President, Philippine Relief and Development Services

---

2. https://www.huffpost.com/entry/china-largest-christian-country_n_5191910.

Preface

This book is not intended to promote a house church network that regards itself as the only biblical model compared to other churches. It is written, rather, to introduce, from an evangelical point of view, a small group movement which traditional churches tend to neglect due to their engagement with programs designed primarily for large group gatherings. It is not overstating or idealizing that movement, being aware that houses were not, and *are* not, the only venue for church gatherings. Basically, this research simply aims to present what the twenty-first-century Filipino small group can learn from the first-century New Testament house church.

In this work (which is based on the updated edition of my doctoral dissertation[1]), I critically analyze the house church in terms of its concepts in the first century, its context in the Greco-Roman world, the content of its practices in the New Testament, and its implications for the small group's concepts in the twenty-first century in the context of the Philippines and with the content of contemporary theology. To analyze these areas, I will go through the following process: introduction, investigation, interpretation, integration, implication, and implementation.

Chapter 1 is the introduction of the contemporary Filipino small group, its problems, proposed solutions, and the anticipated results based on my ministry need and description. Chapter 2 constitutes the following process: (1) the introduction of the concepts of the first century church; (2) the investigation and interpretation of the context of the Greco-Roman house churches; and (3) the integration of the concept of the New Testament house church with the context of Greco-Roman house churches and the content of New Testament house church practices.

Furthermore, chapter 3 involves the following process: (1) the introduction of the concepts of the twenty-first century church and small group; (2) the investigation and interpretation of the context of Filipino small groups; and (3) the integration of the content of New Testament house church practices with the content of contemporary small group theology. Chapter 4 is the presentation of my research findings regarding the New Testament house

---

1. Emerson T. Manaloto, "A Critical Analysis of the New Testament House Church and Its Implications for the Contemporary Filipino Small Group" (DMin diss., Southwestern Baptist Theological Seminary, 2011).

church and its implication for the pressing concerns of contemporary Filipino small groups. Finally, chapter 5 concludes the book with recommendations for further research and future plans of implementation in my Growth Group Ministry at Greenhills Christian Fellowship (GCF).

Acknowledgments

Because of its importance to the GCF mission of making disciples, our former Senior Pastor, the late Dr Luis Pantoja Jr., encouraged me to provide a solid biblical basis for the growth group in my doctoral dissertation. With profound gratitude, I recognize Pastor Luis as the one who counseled me throughout my studies, and, most importantly, mentored me throughout my ministry as a pastor at GCF.

I thank my home church at GCF for the financial support of the scholarship grant that allowed me to pursue doctoral studies and reach this far in my professional pursuits. My church family is the inspiration behind, and the immediate beneficiaries of, this research's full implementation. This book is my contribution to the advancement of the breadth and depth of its Growth Group Ministry.

I acknowledge the all-out support and guidance of my faculty supervisors at Southwestern Baptist Theological Seminary, Dr Waylan Owens and Dr Robert W. Bernard, including the Acting Associate Dean for the Professional Doctoral Program, Dr Terry L. Wilder, without which this work would not have reached its conclusion.

I'm deeply grateful to my wife, Dyan, for her fervent belief and steadfast faith in my doctoral studies. She is the one who rooted for me when the road was still long and cheered me on when the end was finally in sight. She is, and always will be, my partner in life and in ministry.

Most especially, I give thanks and praise to the Almighty God for entrusting me with this work and for providing me with everything necessary to reach its completion. To God be the glory!

1

Introduction

It all started with my passion for small groups, which have been proven to be an effective church planting strategy in the Philippines. This book was borne out of my conviction that forming and developing healthy "reproducing small groups"[1] expedites the birthing of daughter churches. At present, however, it can be observed that small groups in the Philippines are slow to grow and rarely multiply. The common determining factors that cause this lack of growth in small groups are (1) the scarcity of leaders, (2) the exclusivity of members, (3) the superficiality of curricula, and (4) the unsuitability of venues.

A careful study of the New Testament house church, however, reveals that such should not be the case. The book of Acts and the Pauline epistles, which all contain common practices of the early church that typically met in houses, point to the following: (1) a volunteer-based ministry of small group leaders from the laity, (2) a home-focused community of small group learners at each level, (3) a Bible-centered study of small group lessons that change one's life, and (4) a Spirit-directed strategy for small group locations in every locality.

A. Background of the Study

Subsequent to the presentation of my ministry need is the short ministry description of my "missionary journey." I am currently serving as associate pastor of a forty-one-year-old church, Greenhills Christian Fellowship (GCF), assigned as the Ministry Head of the Disciple-Making Groups, with eight pastoral staff serving under my supervision. These Disciple-Making Groups include the demographic cluster of small groups from the following ministries: Children, International Christian School (ICS), Youth, Young Adults/Sports, Connect (BPO), Men/Women, and Couples/Seniors; as well as the geographic

---

1. Small group reproduction means the ability of small groups to grow exponentially, resulting in new church starts.

cluster of small groups in Ortigas Center, Quezon City, San Juan, and other cities in the metropolis.

Located along the eastern border of Metro Manila in Ortigas Center, Pasig City, which is a central business district, GCF has an average attendance of 2,250 and 181 small groups. Since its inception, this burgeoning church was envisioned to be reaching out to the Filipinos who have the resources, influence, and leadership to spread the good news of salvation nationwide and beyond. GCF was officially launched on 14 February 1978 in Greenhills, San Juan City (where the church got its name). As it grew, the worship gathering was held in different locations until it finally moved into its own building in 1990, where it is situated hitherto. Eventually, it spawned twenty-two daughter churches nationwide (which are now mostly independent GCF affiliates), and six in Canada, all using growth groups as their primary strategy in church planting and church growth.

Prior to my homecoming to the mother church as a church planter in 2015, I served for two years as an assistant pastor in the pioneering ministry at GCF East, Taytay, Rizal in 1999, then I moved up to northern Luzon to assist the pastor at GCF San Fernando, Pampanga, in 2001–2004. All these daughter churches were planted strategically through the use of "growth groups." I also initially headed the Growth Group Ministry of GCF Ortigas Center for one year way back in 2005, and worked with a nine-member ministry team and twenty-seven cluster shepherds[2] to strengthen the 133 growth groups situated in six districts of Metro Manila, which eventually led to the birth of new daughter churches. Years later, I served as a satellite pastor down south at GCF Sta. Rosa, Laguna, for almost four years in 2006–2009. Thereafter, I continued my pioneering ministry up north at GCF Northeast in Fairview, Quezon City, for five years in 2009–2014. These two churches were likewise developed through the concerted effort of the four to five small groups from the satellites of GCF South and GCF North, respectively.

With its mission of "making disciples of Christ in the Philippines and beyond" and vision of "lives and communities transformed through Christ,"[3] GCF's use of growth groups remains its "key ministry strategy"[4] in reaching these goals. According to GCF's *Growth Group Manual*:

---

2. A cluster shepherd oversees four to six small groups in a given area.

3. Greenhills Christian Fellowship's *By-Laws and Constitution* (as approved by GCF members on 28 July 2013), 1.

4. Note GCF's three key strategies: (1) Every worshiper in a growth group; (2) every growth group a multiplier; and (3) every church a planter.

The Growth Group Ministry plays an important role in church development. Many years ago, the Spirit led our church leaders to organize small groups to answer the need for nurture among members of a burgeoning congregation. "Care Groups" were formed. After a few years, these evolved into "Discipleship Groups." In 1994, these small groups began to be regarded as microcosms of the church and were renamed "Growth Groups." Since our congregation has grown so big, Growth Group became the venue for people to experience church life in a smaller and more personal level.[5]

Consequently, GCF's Growth Group Ministry's Mission reemphasizes that "we will develop every member of Greenhills Christian Fellowship into maturing and multiplying disciples of the Lord Jesus Christ within the relational context of small groups."[6] As the "microcosm" of the church, every small group gathering is intended to GROW growth group members in **G**od's Word, **R**elationships, **O**utreach and **W**orship, which is true also of the big church gathering.

In the last two decades of my ministry at GCF, however, I have made some observations about the small group ministry and the need to address certain issues in order for it to remain as an effective key strategy for church planting. In my personal assessment, GCF as a whole has not developed its growth groups to their full potential in the following areas: leadership, membership, curriculum, and community. As a result, the growth groups are slow to grow and rarely multiply, thereby affecting the development of the church and its "spiritual potency" to reproduce new daughter churches.

Notably, I observe that some growth groups assign small group leadership to clergy only, which causes a scarcity in small group shepherds. Others prefer their small group learners to be limited to adults, which brings about exclusivity in the small group sheep. Still others tend towards curriculum over-dependence in preparing their small group lessons, which results in the superficiality of small group study. The rest have a perspective of meeting anywhere in terms of their small group locations, which leads to the unsuitability of small group sites. These attitudes and preferences, I believe, are immensely contributory to the stunting of small group growth and the deterring of new church starts.

Having witnessed these tendencies, I am constrained to find ways to address and resolve these major issues by revitalizing the GCF growth groups in the following areas: leaders, learners, lessons, and locations. I solely believe

---

5. Greenhills Christian Fellowship, *Growth Group Manual*, 1.

6. Greenhills Christian Fellowship, 1.

that, in terms of teaching, reproof, correction, and training, the Scripture, as the inspired Word of God, is profitable for all of these things (2 Tim 3:16). A good starting point is revisiting the Lord's Great Commission to all his disciples, thus bringing the church back to its ultimate mission:

> And Jesus came up and spoke to them, saying, "All authority has been given to me in heaven and on earth. Go therefore and make disciples of all the nations, baptizing them in the name of the Father and the Son and the Holy Spirit, teaching them to observe all that I commanded you; and lo, I am with you always, even to the end of the age." (Matt 28:18–20)

As mandated by the Lord, the mission of the church is to "make disciples of all nations"[7] through the following process: "going, baptizing, and teaching."[8] In Acts 1:8 Jesus unveiled to the apostles the scope of mission and strategy: "You will receive power when the Holy Spirit has come upon you; and you shall be My witnesses both in Jerusalem, and in all Judea and Samaria, and even to the remotest part of the earth." When the promised Spirit was sent, the Apostle Peter preached the gospel with power. Subsequently, about three thousand accepted his word, were baptized, counted to the number, and devoted themselves continually "to the apostles' teaching . . . fellowship . . . breaking of bread, and to prayer" (Acts 2:41–42). Luke described how the early believers grew in number as they met daily in the temple courts and broke bread "from house to house . . . taking their meals together with gladness and sincerity of heart, praising God, and having favor with all the people" (Acts 2:46–47). The disciples continued to increase in number because the apostles were persistent even in the midst of persecution: "Every day, in the temple and from house to house, they kept right on teaching and preaching Jesus as the Christ" (Acts 5:42–6:1a).

Finally, Paul's instruction to Timothy to be a multiplying disciple is evident in his letter, "the things which you have heard from me in the presence of many witnesses, entrust these to faithful men who will be able to teach others also" (2 Tim 2:2). This is how the spiritual multiplication in the New Testament happened. As the discipleship expert Edmund Chan defines it, "Disciplemaking is the process of bringing people into a right relationship

---

7. The main verb μαθητεύσατε is in the imperative mood.

8. Πορευθέντες, βαπτίζοντες, and διδάσκοντες are all verbal participles; see Aland et al., *Greek New Testament*, 117.

with God, and developing them to full maturity in Christ, through intentional growth strategies, that they might multiply the entire process in others also."[9]

B. Thesis Statement

It is my conviction that going back to the Bible in order to examine how early Christians used house churches to obey the Great Commission of making disciples is urgently needed. Many important things can be learned from the practices of the early Christians who met in private homes, whose task was focused on the *mobilization of laity*, whose target was aimed at every *generation in the family*, whose goal was set for *conversion through study*, and whose strategy was concentrated on the *penetration of the city*.

Therefore, the main thesis of this book is that the examination of the New Testament house church and the appropriation of its common practices – such as the sharing of leadership, shepherding of families, searching of Scriptures, and saturating of cities[10] – to the contemporary Filipino small group will develop (1) a *volunteer-based* ministry of small group leaders from the laity, (2) a *home-focused* community of small group learners at each level, (3) a *Bible-centered* study of small group lessons that change one's life, and (4) a *Spirit-directed* strategy for small group locations in every locality.

C. Purpose of the Study

This work is intended to start a small group movement in the Philippines and beyond. The background of the study described earlier has compelled me to take interest in small groups and put into writing the house church practices that can be learned from the New Testament so that other churches with small groups can also benefit from this book. The purposes of this study are (1) to present the value of Filipino small groups today in church planting

---

9. Chan, *Certain Kind*, 51.

10. To saturate is "to fill completely with something that permeates or pervades (e.g. water saturated with salt; or an overwhelming concentration of military forces or firepower)" (Mish, *Merriam-Webster's Collegiate Dictionary*, 1035). Note that when the NT house church is said to have a common practice of "saturating the city" with the gospel, it only means that it was able to fill the city completely or cover it with the knowledge of the Lord. How was it that the number of Christians, which started small, reached about half of the population of the Roman Empire within just three hundred years? Only by saturating the city with Christians in house churches which resulted in communities saturated by the Gospel. In the same way, this book believes that contemporary small groups, as the scattered church, can collaborate to use the same strategy to gradually impact a city with the gospel of Jesus Christ (for further discussion, see 59–64, 147–157).

and the problems they are facing, (2) to pursue investigation of the use of houses from the early first century during the time of Jesus in the Gospels, the apostles in Acts, and Paul in his epistles, (3) to use non-biblical sources in tracing the origin of house churches during the first century in order to shed light where the social data is sparse in the New Testament and to show its general development until the Constantinian introduction of the basilica in the third century, (4) to set forth the first-century house church practices and evaluate them in light of the twenty-first century small group; and, (5) to offer recommendations regarding the appropriation of New Testament house church practices to contemporary small groups in the Philippines, particularly the GCF growth groups.

D. Research Methodology

This book utilizes both the research methods of data collection (with the Bible as the primary source and textbooks, journal articles, student dissertations, and websites as secondary data sources) and data analysis in studying the first-century house church and the twenty-first-century small group. The daunting task of describing the early church is like painting a picture. The paint is the Scripture, the canvass is the social setting, and the brush is theology. To reproduce a "work of art" will take both the exegetical-theological and socio-historical approaches in working with the *early house church* model that originated and was developed in the first century. One has to look first into Scripture, particularly the New Testament, for the literary data and then utilize archaeology and sociology. This study combines archaeological, socio-historical, and textual material in studying the first-century concepts, context, and components of house churches, as well as the content of New Testament house church practices. The entire process is done, however, with exact diligence and utmost care.

In his book *Christian Theology*, Millard J. Erickson explains that "in making the Bible the primary or supreme source of our understanding, we are not completely excluding all other sources. In particular, if God has also revealed himself in general ways in such areas as nature and history (as the Bible itself seems to teach), then we may also fruitfully examine these for additional clues to understanding the principal revelation. But these will be secondary to the Bible."[11] He further states, "If God has revealed himself in two complementary and harmonious revelations, then at least in theory something can be learned

---

11. Erickson, *Christian Theology*, 37.

from the study of God's creation. General revelation will be of value when it sheds light upon the special revelation or fills it out at certain points where it does not speak."[12] In short, the use of non-biblical sources in this book serves the purpose of confirming and affirming the veracity of the biblical data and not in contesting or contradicting it.

After a thorough survey and critical analysis of the early church and the house churches in the first century, the same process is repeated for the next section on the church and small groups in the twenty-first century. This book also studies the concepts and context of the church today and of the contemporary small groups. Thereafter, the major segment of the ministry plan compares and analyzes the New Testament house churches and the contemporary Filipino small groups based on their given concepts, contexts, and components (leaders, learners, lessons, and locations). The last step applies the content of the New Testament house church practices to revitalize the Filipino small groups of today.

The study concludes with some recommendations for future research and plans for ministry application through the implementation of the research findings in my immediate Filipino church context, that is, the church and small groups at GCF in Ortigas Center, Pasig City, Philippines.

E. Limitations of the Study

The focus of this study is delimited in the following ways:

First, it is beyond the scope of this work to discuss in detail the post-modern viewpoint of house church networks that affirms the house church as the only biblical model and disregards the traditional church. However, what the author says about house churches today does arise from the need to address the post-modern house church movement's limited understanding of the social setting of early Christianity. Since there is no consensus on house churches in conservative, evangelical scholarship, the scope of this study is to identify a more conservative, Baptist evangelical view.

Second, though οἶκος and οἰκία occur several times in the Bible, only a few verses in the New Testament give a substantial description of the house church. These references are predominantly in Acts and the Pauline epistles, which is central in the exegetical and biblical studies of this book. The use of non-biblical sources is delimited to tracing the origin of house churches and features only the Greco-Roman houses, households, and house-cults in the

---

12. Erickson, 72.

first century. Since the use of domestic spaces continued to be the norm for the first three centuries, this study will also focus on the general development of house churches from the first century substructure of *oikos* to the third century superstructure of the basilica introduced by Constantine.

Third, as the book stresses the four components of a small group – namely leaders, learners, lessons, and locations – the corresponding study of Filipino cultural context zeroes-in on the following categories: leading, grouping, studying, and planning.

Fourth, while there may be many other house church practices in the New Testament, this work merely concentrates on the most common ones such as the sharing of leadership, the shepherding of families, the searching of Scriptures, and the saturating of cities.

Finally, the study of the concepts and principles of the small group is vast, and this book only covers home groups with an emphasis on the growth group model. Moreover, as this work formulates a theology of the small group – focusing on volunteer-based ministry, home-focused community, Bible-centered teaching, and Spirit-directed mission – it highlights the role of laity as small group leaders, the role of family as small group learners, the role of Scripture in small group lessons, and the role of Spirit in small group locations, respectively.

F. Literature Review (Condensed and Updated)

A multitude of books, and some journal articles, dissertations, and internet resources – spanning the decades from the 1980s to the present-day – were chosen as references for this work based on their contribution to the study of house churches and small groups and their relationships to contemporary Filipino culture.

1. House Churches

The study of the New Testament house church used to be rare until, in 1931, pieces of evidence were discovered in the Dura-Europos, a third-century Syrian garrison town that became "the most convincing archaeological site testifying to an early Christian *domus ecclesiae*."[13] Then, in 1939, Floyd V. Filson published his seminal article on "The Significance of the Early House Churches" which serves as the classic foundational study of house churches. All subsequent

---

13. Blue, "Acts and the House Church," 166.

writings about house churches refer back to this article. Filson believed that an examination of the "actual physical conditions under which the first Christians met and lived" and, particularly, careful consideration of "the importance and function of the house church" would shed better light in understanding the New Testament church.[14] In his study on house churches, Filson lists five findings that could enrich our understanding of the early church:

> (a) The house church enabled the followers of Jesus to have a distinctively Christian worship and fellowship from the very first days of the apostolic age.

> (b) The large part played by the house churches affords a partial explanation of the great attention paid to family life in the letters of Paul and in other Christian writings. It must not be forgotten that both in Jewish and Gentile life religious observance had been largely centered in the home.

> (c) The existence of several house churches in one city goes far to explain the tendency to party strife in the apostolic age.

> (d) A study of the house church situation also throws light upon the social status of the early Christians. . . . The apostolic church was more nearly a cross section of society than we have sometimes thought.

> (e) The development of church polity can never be understood without reference to the house churches. The host of such a group was almost inevitably a man of some education, with a fairly broad background and at least some administrative ability . . . The house church was the training ground for the Christian leaders who were to build the church after the loss of "apostolic" guidance, and everything in such a situation favored the emergence of the host as the most prominent and influential member of the group.[15]

Nonetheless, little attention was shown to Filson's admonition in the four decades that followed. In 1980, however, there was a renewal of interest in house churches among the majority of biblical scholars. In his book *House Church and Mission* (a resource central to this study), New Testament scholar and author Roger W. Gehring declares that it was in 1980 that scholars finally took on the challenge of confronting the issues concerning house churches,

---

14. Filson, "Significance of the Early House Churches," 105–106.
15. Filson, 109–112.

with literature on the subject beginning to flourish and a greater number of books and articles published in subsequent years.[16]

Some of the significant texts on early Christian households and house churches referenced in this study – from the 1980s onwards – include Robert J. Banks' *Paul's Idea of Community: The Early House Churches in Their Historical Setting* (1981); Hans-Josef Klauck's "The House-Church as Way of Life" (1982); John H. Elliot's "Philemon and House Churches" (1984); Wayne A. Meeks' *The First Urban Christians: The Social World of the Apostle Paul* (1983); Bradley B. Blue's "Acts and the House Church" (1994); and Carolyn Osiek and David L. Balch's *Families in the New Testament World: Households and House Churches* (1997).

There are other essential non-literary sources (using early architecture and archaeology) on the existence and functions of the first-century house, such as Paul C. Finney's review article on "Early Christian Architecture: The Beginnings" (1988); Bradley Blue's study on "Early Church Architecture" (1997); and Peter Oakes' more recent archaeological research in his book *Reading Romans in Pompeii: Paul's Letter at Ground Level* (2013).

Finally, while several works have explored the modern house church network in the past forty years, some of them consider the house church as the only biblical model, such as Robert Fitts' *The Church in the House, A Return to Simplicity* (2001) and Rad Zdero's *The Global House Church Movement* (2004). Though this study does not concur with all these authors' suppositions and conclusions, their materials are nevertheless useful in describing the house church movement today.

On the other hand, J. D. Payne's book on *Missional House Churches: Reaching our Communities with the Gospel* comes from a more conservative Baptist evangelical view. Being a Southern Baptist Theological Seminary professor, Payne writes from the perspective of correcting existing house churches from going to the extreme (e.g. discarding pastors, isolating themselves from other churches, etc.) and, at the same time, cites what "traditional" churches can learn from missional house churches (e.g. "simplicity, rapid multiplication, [the] value of small groups, and biblical and missiological principles of indigenous church planting").[17] This resource material is key to this study.

---

16. Gehring, *House Church and Mission*, 5.

17. Payne, *Missional House Churches*, 121, 130.

2. Small Groups

Much Christian literature has been written on various models of small groups, particularly cell groups and home groups which are both necessary for the comparative study of this book. Some of the major works are Ralph W. Neighbour's book, *Where Do We Go from Here? A Guidebook for the Cell Group Church* (1990); David L. Finnell's *Cell Group Basic Training* (1993); and Joel T. Comiskey's dissertation on "Cell-Based Ministry: A Positive Factor for Church Growth in Latin America" (1997). Other studies were based on C. Kirk Hadaway, Stuart A. Wright and Francis M. DuBose's *Home Cell Groups and House Churches* (1987) and Sammy Elliot's project on "Building Community through Koinonia Home Groups" (2004). Also, a specific kind of home group utilized at GCF is the growth group, which is discussed thoroughly in *The Growth Group Manual* (1998), a key material for this study.

Likewise, the writings that address various issues related to small groups are many. To list a few, we have Neal F. McBride's handbook on *How to Lead Small Groups* (1990), Gareth Weldon Icenogle's primer on *Biblical Foundations for Small Group Ministry: An Integrational Approach* (1994), Darin Kennedy's article on "A Theology of Small Groups" (1996), Carl F. George's *Nine Keys to Effective Small Group Leadership* (1997), Randy Fujishin's study on *Discovering the Leader Within: Running Small Groups Successfully* (1997), and Bill Donahue and Russ Robinson's *Building a Church of Small Groups* (2001). While many studies have been done on small groups in general, the publications on a volunteer-based ministry of small group leaders, a home-focused community of small group learners, a Bible-centered study of small group lessons, and a Spirit-directed strategy for small group locations – appropriating the New Testament house church practices of sharing leadership, shepherding families, searching Scriptures, and saturating cities, respectively – are rare.

Finally, understanding Filipino cultural values is very important to small group leaders in making their leadership and teaching ministry suitable to the group members' context and in reaching out to the immediate community where the small group is situated. For general references on culture, the following resource materials are helpful in developing a biblical and culturally relevant curriculum for small groups. Worthy of consideration are Timothy J. Keller's book *Center Church: Doing Balanced, Gospel-Centered Ministry in Your City* (2012) and the three Lausanne documents (1974, 1989, 2011), which are all central to this study. Another reference is Rodrigo Tano's *Theology in the Philippine Setting* (1981) and Melba P. Maggay's book on *Communicating Cross-Culturally: Towards a New Context for Missions in the Philippines* (1989).

Other essential works include Teodoro Agoncillo and Milagros Guerrero's *History of the Filipino People* (1977), Rogelia Pe-pua's *Filipino Psychology: Theory, Method, and Application* (1982), Virgilio Enriquez's *From Colonial to Liberation Psychology: The Philippine Experience* (1994), and F. Landa Jocano's books on *Towards Developing a Filipino Corporate Culture* (1988), *Filipino Value System* (1997) and *Filipino Worldview* (2001).

The general and particular references on culture and values are wide-ranging, but the literature on leading small groups in the Philippine context which takes Filipino cultural values into consideration are few. Most of the curriculum materials being used in weekly Bible studies are Western. This, then, will be the contribution of this study to the Philippine literature as the above-mentioned works are surveyed, serving as tools in developing a small group ministry which is biblical and also considers the context of small group members and their surrounding community.

The literature review on both house churches and small groups shows that this book is unique since there is not yet any study of the New Testament house church which analyzes it for the sole purpose of relating it to contemporary small groups in four areas – leaders, learners, lessons, and locations – in the context of Filipino culture. This indicates that there is a need for this work and its contrasting approach to the broad perspective of most of the studies surveyed. It is the intent of this book to add a needed viewpoint to the literature.

G. Theological Foundation of the NT House Church (Overview)

Theology, as defined by Erickson, is "that discipline which strives to give a coherent statement of the doctrines of the Christian faith, based primarily upon the Scriptures, placed in the context of culture in general, worded in a contemporary idiom, and related to the issues of life."[18] Theology, therefore, must be both biblical and contemporary. By being biblical, Erickson means taking the Old and the New Testament as the principal basis for content and using biblical research methods and tools. It also uses the contributions of other avenues of truth which are all part of God's general revelation.[19] By being contemporary, Erickson points to the use of "language, concepts, and thought

---

18. Erickson, *Christian Theology*, 21.
19. Erickson, 21.

forms that make some sense in the context of the present time."[20] However, he cautions to not go to the extent of distorting the biblical materials.[21]

So, in its study of the early church, this book looks into the Scripture, particularly the New Testament, for literary data and also makes use of extra-biblical sources. With utmost care, the research integrates archaeological, socio-historical, and textual material in studying the concepts and context of the first century οἶκος with the aim of defining the New Testament concept of house church and identifying the content of its practices in four areas: house church leaders, lessons, learners, and locations. This material also studies the concepts of the church, the house church today, and the contemporary small group before comparing the first-century Greco-Roman house church with the twenty-first century Filipino small group in their given contexts. Having surveyed and critically analyzed the early church, focusing particularly on the house church in the first century, this work will take on the challenge of appropriating the common practices of the first-century house church for the twenty-first century Filipino small group with the goal of formulating a contemporary small group theology in four aspects: small group ministry, community, teaching, and mission.

Following Erickson's theological framework, this study of the first-century house church highlights the four areas of theological studies: biblical, historical, doctrinal, and practical.[22] The first half of this book, which deals with "The Church and House Churches in the First Century," concentrates on biblical and historical studies; whereas the last half, which tackles "The Church and Small Groups in the Twenty-First Century," culminates in the doctrinal and practical aspects of theological study.

---

20. Erickson, 21.
21. Erickson, 21–22.
22. Erickson, 23.

2

The Church and House Churches in the First Century

What are the different concepts of ἐκκλησία and οἶκος in the first century and how are they related? What are the various functions of οἶκος in the Greco-Roman context based on archaeological, sociological, historical, and biblical data? Did house churches really exist in the first century or were they merely household (fellowship) groups? What is the New Testament concept of a house church and what is the content of its practices? These key questions will be answered in the first part of this book.

A. Concepts of a Church and a House Church

To understand the house church it is necessary to first understand what a church is. What is ἐκκλησία and how was it used in the first century?

1. First-Century Church

Etymologically speaking, as G. W. Kirby points out, "[t]he English word 'church' with its cognate form, 'kirk,' is derived from the Greek word *kyriakós* [κύριακός] signifying 'the Lord's' or 'belonging to the Lord' [Κύριος]. [But] the New Testament equivalent *ekklēsía* [ἐκκλησία] was originally employed by the Greeks."[1] Ernest Best further explains that in the Septuagint, the two main words used to refer to the people of God are assembly [ἐκκλησία] and synagogue [συναγωγή]. First-century Jews used the term συναγωγή, and for that reason the first Greek-speaking Christians opted to use ἐκκλησία to trace

---

1. Kirby, "Church," 845.

their ties to the Old Testament and their lineage to the Old Testament people of God.[2]

a. Meaning of ἐκκλησία in the first century

In the LXX, the Greek word ἐκκλησία (occurring about one hundred times[3]) represents absolutely the Hebrew קָהֵל ("assembly") which according to Peter T. O'Brien "could describe assemblies of a less specifically religious or nonreligious kind, for example, the gathering of an army in preparation for war (1 Sam 17:47; 2 Chr 28:14). . . . However, particularly significant are those instances of ἐκκλησία (rendering *qāhāl*) which denote the congregation of Israel when it assembled to hear the Word of God on Mt. Sinai (Deut 4:10)."[4] The Septuagint use of the word ἐκκλησία does not reflect the New Testament meaning of the word "church" but is a common term for an "assembly."

Nonetheless, in the Gospels, the word ἐκκλησία appears only twice, in Matthew 16:18 and 18:17. The context of the former is that of Jesus talking to Peter about the church that he will build in the future, whereas the latter refers to the issue of church discipline. As to the reason why ἐκκλησία is rare in the Gospels, L. Coenen explains, "all the early Christian writers use *ekklēsia* only for those fellowships which come into being after the crucifixion and resurrection of Jesus. [Hence] it is not used for the period of the historical Jesus or to describe the disciples who gathered around him."[5] Erickson stresses that "the fact that Luke never uses ἐκκλησία in his Gospel but employs it twenty-four times in Acts is also significant. It would seem that he did not regard the church as present until the period covered in Acts. . . . We conclude that the church originated at Pentecost . . . [and] those who were part of Israel prior to Pentecost have been incorporated in the church."[6]

Finally, in the Book of Acts and the apostolic epistles the term ἐκκλησία is frequently used. As Best points out, "[the] 'church' always denotes a group of people, either all the Christians in a city (Acts 14:23; 1 Cor 1:2; 2 Cor 1:1) or those gathered for worship in a particular house (Rom 16:5; 1 Cor 16:19; [also Col 4:15 and Phlm 2]) or all Christians in all the churches, the whole church

---

2. Best, "Church," 168.

3. Coenen, "Church, Synagogue," 292.

4. O'Brien, *Colossians and Philemon*, 57–58.

5. Coenen, "Church, Synagogue," 298.

6. Erickson, *Christian Theology*, 1048. Erickson argues that the church does not start until Pentecost because Luke does not use the word "church" in his Gospel but uses it twenty-four times in Acts. If the church existed before Pentecost, he reasons, why did Luke not speak of it before that time? Jesus's use of the word "church" (ἐκκλησία) twice in Matthew's Gospel (16:18 and 18:17) pertains to the future church.

(Eph 1:22)."[7] In his book *Systematic Theology*, Wayne Grudem correctly argues that "we should not make the mistake of saying that only a church meeting in the house expresses the true nature of the church, or only a church considered at a city-wide level can rightly be called a church, or only the church universal can rightly be called by the name 'church.' Rather, the community of God's people considered at any level can be rightly called a church."[8]

So the common concept of ἐκκλησία, as used in the Jewish sense, is an assembly or congregation of people in general. As O'Brien clearly emphasizes, ἐκκλησία originally was not rendered as an "organization" or "society"; it has no inherently religious meaning and was quite secular in character, except in the occurrences when Israel gathered to listen to God's Word.[9] In the Christian sense, however, the concept of ἐκκλησία in the New Testament is a gathering of believers for worship both locally and universally. Hence, the word ἐκκλησία was used in the entire New Testament neither to refer to a building for public worship nor to a denomination. It is not even a continuation of the Jewish synagogue. Kirby explains that the word "church" is principally used to refer to people (body of believers), and not used with reference to a building where public worship is held. Generally, the word is used to describe "the company of the faithful throughout all the world."[10]

Three elements must be present in the term ἐκκλησία: (1) people (the "who"); (2) purpose (the "why"); and (3) place (the "where"). First, the kind of *people* gathering is specific. It is not *gathering anyone* (or people in general), as in the case of evangelistic campaigns. It should be the gathering of Christians predominantly. Second, the *purpose* of people gathering is also particular. It is not the *gathering anyhow* of Christians for the sake of gathering (or it will be a mere social gathering); rather, the sole purpose is for worship and fellowship. Lastly, the *place* of gathering (or house of God's people) is also specific (local ἐκκλησία). It is not the *gathering anywhere* of Christians. Rather, it should be at only one location where God's people are geographically situated. On the other hand, it must be clarified that the "place of worship" (or house of God) is general (universal ἐκκλησία). It is the *worshipping anywhere* of Christians everywhere. It could be at any one location since "God is spirit, and . . . must [be] worship[ed] in spirit and truth" (John 4:24). Moreover, "[He] does not dwell in houses [or any building] made by human hands" (Acts 7:48).

---

7. Best, "Church," 168.

8. Grudem, *Systematic Theology*, 857–858.

9. O'Brien, *Colossians and Philemon*, 58.

10. Kirby, "Church," 846.

Therefore, the Christian ἐκκλησία or the New Testament church is the gathering of specific people, of *Christians primarily*, for the specific purpose of *worship alone*, both locally (in the place to gather people specifically at only one location) and universally (in the place to worship God generally at any one location). In short, the term ἐκκλησία in the New Testament is God's *people* meeting together for the *purpose* of worship locally in one *place* and universally in any *place*.

b. Nature of ἐκκλησία in the New Testament

The New Testament metaphorically describes the nature of the church in various ways. Kirby declares that there are a number of metaphorical images of the Church in the New Testament, each one emphasizing a particular facet of its nature.[11]

1) House/household images

The most common of all the range of biblical metaphors are the house (building) and household (family) images. As a *spiritual building*, the church is pictured as "God's house [οἶκός]" (Heb 3:6) or "God's spiritual house [οἶκος πνευματικός]" (1 Pet 2:5). As a spiritual house, Grudem qualifies, "the church is . . . not built with literal stones but built with Christian people who are 'living stones' (1 Pet 2:5) built up on the 'cornerstone' who is Christ Jesus (1 Pet 2:4–8)."[12] Second, Paul also calls the church in Corinth "God's building [Θεοῦ οἰκοδομή]" (1 Cor 3:9) and refers to the saints at Ephesus as a building undergoing construction, that is "being built together [συνοικοδομέω] into a dwelling of God in the Spirit" (Eph 2:22). Third, the church is viewed architecturally as "the pillar and support of the truth [στῦλος καὶ ἑδραίωμα τῆς ἀληθείας]" (1 Tim 3:15). Kirby explains that "the implication is that the Church is the guardian of God's truth and the defender of it. The Church is grounded on the truth, and is the citadel of it."[13] So the church is metaphorically and not literally referred to as a building since the idea of a church as a physical building is nowhere to be found in the entire Bible.

As a *spiritual family*, the church is described by Paul as "the household of God [ἐν οἴκῳ Θεοῦ]" (1 Tim 3:15). Elsewhere, the phrase "the household of God" in Ephesians 2:19 denotes "the company of the redeemed."[14] The church is

---

11. Kirby, 847.

12. Grudem, *Systematic Theology*, 858.

13. Kirby, "Church," 847.

14. Vine, Unger, and White, *Vine's Complete Expository Dictionary*, 313.

also referred to as "the household of the faith [οἰκείους τῆς πίστεως]" (Gal 6:10). Kirby points out that what is important is that "Christians have been born into God's family, and therefore stand in a special relationship to Him as well as to one another. Knowing the same Father, they should recognize themselves to be brothers and sisters in Christ."[15] Second, the church is depicted as a "family of God" (1 Tim 5:1–2). In these verses, Paul instructs Timothy "to act as if all the church members were members of a larger family."[16] Moreover, Paul says, "and I will be a father to you, and you shall be sons and daughters to me" (2 Cor 6:18). Third, the church is commonly regarded as "the bride of Christ" (Rev 19:7; 21:2). According to Grudem, "a somewhat different family metaphor is seen when Paul refers to the church as the bride of Christ. He says that the relationship between a husband and wife 'refers to Christ and the church' (Eph 5:32), and he says that he brought about the engagement between Christ and the church at Corinth and that it resembles an engagement between a bride and her husband-to-be (2 Cor 11:2)."[17]

2) Other biblical metaphors

Other metaphors of the church present in the New Testament which are useful in this study are as follows: "the temple of the Holy Spirit/God" (1 Cor 3:16–17; 6:19; Eph 2:21–22); "holy/royal priesthood" (1 Pet 2:5, 9); "the body of Christ" (1 Cor 12:12–13, 25, 27; Eph 1:22–23; Col 1:18; 2:19); "the people of God" (2 Cor 6:16; Rom 9:24–26); "the new/heavenly Jerusalem" (Rev 3:12; 21:2; Heb 12:22); and "sheep/flock" (1 Pet 2:25; 5:2–4; Heb 13:20).

Thus, it is noteworthy that the New Testament predominantly pictures the church as a house or a household. One possible reason would be that "the house or family is the fundamental unit of the church, and the church is a social structure patterned after the household."[18] The church as God's household then, is like a big family.

2. First-Century House Church

According to Webster's dictionary, the word "house" is defined in a wider sense as "a *building* in which people live . . . a *family*, including ancestors and descendants. . . . [It] is generally applied to a *structure* built for one or two

---

15. Kirby, "Church," 847.

16. Grudem, *Systematic Theology*, 858.

17. Grudem, 858.

18. Verner, *Household of God*, 1–2, 127, cited in Gehring, *House Church and Mission*, 7.

families or *social units*."[19] Hence, a house today is understood both in the structural and social sense. How was the house understood in the first century? The two Greek words used for house, particularly in the New Testament, are οἶκος and οἰκία.

a. Meaning of οἶκος and οἰκία in the first century

Are *oikos* and *oikia* the same or different from each other? In the secular sense, J. Goetzmann indicates,

> *oikos* is attested as early as Mycenaean Greek and has been handed down from Homer on. It means both the dwelling place and the structure. *Oikia*, from Herodutus on, denotes the dwelling, the house. Originally the two words were differentiated in meaning, in that *oikia* denoted the dwelling place, and *oikos* the whole house, the premises, the family property, and even the inhabitants of the house. . . .
>
> In popular speech *oikos* meant any kind of house, but frequently also a particular house and even a temple. In such cases the divine name attached to *oikos* indicated the god to whom the temple was dedicated. But the word was also used in the metaphorical sense. It denoted the family, the property and other similar concepts connected with the house itself.[20]

Furthermore, the Greek words *oikos* [οἶκος] and *oikia* [οἰκία] commonly appear in the Septuagint to render the Hebrew word *bayith* [בַּיִת].[21] Vine, Unger, and White cite that "*Bayit* [בַּיִת] appears about 2,048 times in biblical Hebrew (44 times in Aramaic) and in all periods."[22] The word בַּיִת which is translated "house" in the Old Testament can also mean "buildings, daughter,

---

19. Costello, *Random House Webster's College Dictionary*, 650. Italics added.

20. Goetzmann, "House, Build, Manage, Steward," 247.

21. Goetzmann, 247.

22. Vine, Unger, and White, *Complete Expository Dictionary*, 117. This reference textbook further elucidates that "this noun [בַּיִת] denotes a fixed, established structure made from some kind of material [Gen 19:2; 33:17; 2 Sam 16:21; 1 Chr 9:23; Ps 132:3] . . . (especially when the word is joined to the word God) *bayith* represents a place of worship or 'sanctuary' [Exod 23:19; 1 Kgs 6:5; Ezek 41:7]. . . . [It] can signify rooms and/or wings of a house . . . and also the inside of a building or some other structure as opposed to the outside [Gen 6:14]. . . . [It] sometimes refers to the place where something or someone dwells or rests [Exod 26:29; Job 17:13; Eccl 12:5; Neh 2:3; Isa 3:20; 1 Kgs 18:32; Prov 8:2; Job 39:6] . . . [and it] is often used of those who live in a house, i.e., a 'household' [Gen 7:1; 50:4; Exod 2:1; Josh 7:14; 1 Sam 20:16; 2 Sam 2:4]. . . . In a few passages *bayith* means 'territory' or 'country' [Hos 8:1; 9:15; Jer 12:7; Zech 9:8]" (Vine, Unger, and White, 117–118).

dungeon, family, hall, harem, holders, home, homeborn, household, palace, place, residence, room, shrine, temple, tomb, and treasury."[23]

In the Christian sense, the concept of οἶκος and οἰκία in the New Testament are identical and both have a similar array of meaning in the secular Greek and in the LXX. Their common usage is literally that of a "house" (e.g. Matt 2:11; 7:24–27; 9:7; Mark 7:30) and metaphorically of a "family" or "household" (e.g. Matt 13:57; Mark 6:4; John 4:53; 1 Cor 1:16; 16:15; 2 Tim 1:16; 4:19).[24]

New Testament scholars, however, vary in their stand on whether the word pairs are really synonymous or not. One example is Elliott who translated οἰκία as "house" or "building" and οἶκος as "groups of persons," although the difference was flexible to him.[25] Similarly, Klauck asserts that "both Greek words for house (οἶκος, οἰκία) keep a double meaning throughout Greek history: (a) dwelling and (b) family, clan. The meshing of these two meanings can connote *household*."[26] As Klauck further explains,

> In the first sense, the house-church was the assembly of Christians in a private house, a group of 10–40 people. In the second sense (the inhabitants of the house) we think of the typical ancient family: the master of the house with his dependents. These might include women, children, slaves, free servants, relatives. The two senses are not mutually exclusive, for a gathering in a dwelling-house included the family, and these in turn often formed the kernel of the house-church.[27]

Thus, despite some disagreements, the majority of exegetes believe that οἶκος and οἰκία are simply used interchangeably in the New Testament. For instance, Paul switches from οἰκία in 1 Corinthians 11:22 to οἶκος in 11:34; and then in 1 Corinthians 16:15 he uses οἰκία but οἶκος in 1:16 and 16:19. Likewise, Luke also used the word pair synonymously as in the case of the centurion's house (Luke 7:6, 10), Jairus's house (Luke 8:41, 51), the house of the man of peace (Luke 10:5), and the Philippian jailer's house (Acts 16:31, 32, 34).

Nevertheless, this study discovers that Luke consistently used the term οἶκος six times when referring to Cornelius's house/household in Acts 10:2,

---

23. Thomas, *New American Standard Exhaustive Concordance*, 1497.

24. Goetzmann, "House, Build, Manage, Steward," 248.

25. John H. Elliott, *A Home for the Homeless: A Sociological Exegesis of 1 Peter, Its Situation and Strategy* (Philadelphia: Fortress Press, 1981), 188 fn. 110–112, 252 fn. 112, quoted in Gehring, *House Church and Mission*, 8.

26. Klauck, "House-Church as Way of Life," 153.

27. Klauck, 154.

22, 30; 11:12–14, whereas he used οἰκία four times for the house of Simon the tanner where Peter was staying in Acts 10:6, 17, 32; 11:11. Luke's consistency in his usage of the terms is significant. Furthermore, Gehring validly contends that "even though οἶκος appears 112 times and οἰκία 94 times in the NT, we encounter οἶκος 4 times in connection with ἐκκλησία (Rom 16:5; 1 Cor 16:19; Phlm 2; Col 4:15) and οἰκία not once."[28] L. Michael White suggests that the discrepancy on defining the terms can be resolved through a new lexicographical work on οἶκος and οἰκία.[29] Even so, this book focuses only on οἶκος.

b. Functions of οἶκος in the first century

Conceptually, like the first-century ἐκκλησία in the Christian sense, οἶκος in the New Testament also has these three basic elements present: the *place* (the "where"); the *people* (the "who"); and the *purpose* (the "why"). As for a place, it is *where* the *oikos* is structurally. As for a people, it is *who* the *oikos* is socially. And as for a purpose, it is *why* the *oikos* is spiritually. What are the various functions of οἶκος in the Greco-Roman context based on archaeological, sociological, historical, and biblical data? The specific functions of οἶκος in the first century are as follows: *house* in the structural sense, *household* in the social sense, and *house church* in the spiritual sense.

B. Context of Greco-Roman House Churches

As Meeks narrates, within the ten years after the crucifixion of Jesus, Palestinian village culture was superseded by the Greco-Roman city and became the major setting for the Christian movement.[30] According to Banks,

> relatively new trends in social organization began to flourish and attract an increasing number of people. Traditionally there had been two main types of community with which people might associate themselves: *politeia,* the public life of the city or nation-state to which people belonged; and *oikonomia,* the household order into which they were born or to which they were attached. For some, involvement in communities of both types could be a very full and satisfying affair.[31]

---

28. Gehring, *House Church and Mission*, 8 fn. 45.

29. L. Michael White, "Domus," 568 fn. 195, quoted in Gehring, *House Church and Mission*, 9.

30. Meeks, *First Urban Christians*, 11.

31. Banks, *Paul's Idea of Community*, 19.

Filson, on the other hand, pioneered the research on the early Christians' physical conditions in house churches which functioned as their dwelling and meeting place.[32] Moreover, M. J. Selman points out that the "architectural information in the Bible has been supplemented considerably by the results of archaeological excavation."[33] Such architectural data will lead to the reconstruction of the sociological and ecclesiological aspects of the house church ambiguously described in the New Testament. Thus, to understand the concept of the New Testament οἶκος, this book studies the first-century Greco-Roman house churches both from the biblical and non-biblical perspectives. This study combines archaeological, historical, and biblical material in analyzing the functions of οἶκος in the first-century Greco-Roman world.

1. Archaeological Perspective

Marilyn M. Schaub correctly observes that "the Bible offers numerous references to specific parts of houses, such as roofs, upper rooms, doors, courtyards, but it gives no full description of a typical house."[34] Is there a way to know what kind of housing the early Christians used in their gathering? Schaub notes that while there is archaeological evidence that allows us to trace the overall development and description of the Palestinian house, such data is inadequate for every era and is only based on remaining structures such as foundations and walls in ruins.[35]

a. Greco-Roman houses

In their book *Families in the New Testament World: Households and House Churches*, Carolyn Osiek and David Balch assert that all the evidence suggests that residential structures were the original venues used for the assembly of the early church.[36] The Greco-Roman houses, regarded as cultural artifacts, were assumed to be the major context for Pauline house churches. Michele George focuses in her journal article on diverse house types from Pompeii and Ephesos to learn about family structures and social relations in the Roman world using the existing architectural evidence.[37] George affirms the wide-

---

32. Filson, "Significance of the Early House Churches," 105–106.

33. Selman, "House," 487.

34. Schaub, "House," 409.

35. Schaub, 409.

36. Osiek and Balch, *Families in the New Testament World*, 32.

37. George, "Domestic Architecture and Household Relations, 7–25.

ranging evidence found in Pompeii in terms of the number of houses – which is over four hundred – and the range in their size and quality.[38] Consequently, this author points out that "the remarkable and unique plenitude of Pompeian houses does offer the best possibility of recovering some understanding of family life within the context of built space in the Roman era."[39]

It is also critical to establish the probability of whether the early believers – if housed in residential buildings – would be more likely to be located in elite houses, which were bigger in size, or merely non-elite apartments with limited spaces. In his more recent work, Oakes draws on the rich archaeological finds of the Pompeian excavations that shed light on the life of a hypothetical Roman house church. Being convinced that the non-elite house church model (which would have been quite small) is the one appropriate for most study of Pauline texts, Oakes surmises that

> scholars have generally been looking at the wrong houses when looking for types of houses in which a typical early Christian group would have met. The elite were a tiny percentage of society. They must have formed an even lower percentage of house-church members. The majority of house churches are unlikely to have included members of the elite, in which case they will not generally have met in elite houses . . . . [Hence] most early Christians who met in houses probably did so in non-elite houses, [and] this breaks down the main social contrast usually drawn between churches based in houses and those based in apartments. If our house church is hosted by a craftworker, the social structure of the group that meets there is unlikely to be radically different from that of a church hosted by a similar craftworker in a space in an apartment block.[40]

Nonetheless, this author continues to use the term "house church" in describing the early Christian groups, even when he strongly believes they gathered in apartment blocks.[41]

Additionally, being predominantly gentiles, many members of the Pauline churches were likely craftworkers.[42] This is supported by Paul's instruction to "work with your hands" (1 Thess 4:11) and the apostle himself being known for

---

38. George, 11.

39. George, 11.

40. Oakes, *Reading Romans in Pompeii*, 70.

41. Oakes, 92.

42. Oakes, 76.

his own trade as a tent-maker – a trade through which he met Prisca and Aquila (Acts 18:2–3), possible craftworking house church hosts.[43] In his article "Prisca and Aquila: Traveling Tentmakers and Church Builders," Jerome Murphy-O'Connor puts the business-couple in Rome "in a ground-floor workshop with mezzanine living accommodation and estimates that they would be able to host a house-church of between 10 and 20."[44] Hence, Oakes confirms that "the nature of the Pompeian evidence, and the prominence of craftworkers in the general scholarly view of Pauline Christianity, mean that a craftworker [non-elite] house church looks most likely to provide a fruitful model for an initial attempt to use the Pompeian archaeological evidence to help us understand the text of Romans."[45]

Subsequently, Oakes tries to reconstruct the possible size of a typical house church gathering in a medium-sized, non-elite Pompeian craftworker's house that fits the socio-economic profile evidenced by a survey of Pompeian housing.[46] "The Cabinet-Maker's house shows that someone non-elite, a craftworker, could have space to host a meeting of a fair-sized house church. Forty or so people could fit into the garden, portico and rear-facing dining rooms – as long as they did not mind stepping over boxes of tools and work in progress."[47] Oakes also came up with a hypothetical group designed to be representative of the likely social composition of craftworker house churches in Rome, thirty people in total, comprising

> a craftworker who rents a fairly large workshop (c. 45 m²) and some separate living accommodation, his wife, children, a couple of (male) craftworking slaves, a (female) domestic slave, a dependent relative; a few other householders renting lesser space; a couple of members of other families, slaves, free or freed dependents of people, homeless people, and a few other people renting space in shared rooms.[48]

---

43. Oakes, 44–45.

44. Jerome Murphy-O'Connor, "Prisca and Aquila: Traveling Tentmakers and Church Builders," *Bible Review* 8, no. 6 (1992): 49, quoted in Oakes, *Reading Romans in Pompeii*, 93.

45. Oakes, *Reading Romans in Pompeii*, 79.

46. Oakes, 86–87.

47. Oakes, 44; cf. Oakes, 81. Similarly, as mentioned earlier, Klauck believes that "the house-church was the assembly of Christians in a private house, a group of 10–40 people" (Klauck, "House-Church as Way of Life," 154).

48. Oakes, *Reading Romans in Pompeii*, 96.

Therefore, based on some archaeological data gathered in the remains of Greco-Roman houses, this study concludes that the domestic buildings, though limited in size, were the first sites for Christian gatherings.

b. Greco-Roman households

Studying the archaeological evidence for the existence of Greco-Roman houses provides new insights into family structures and social relations. According to Osiek and Balch, "The first step toward understanding the ancient Christian family is to take a look at the physical environment in which such families lived, for the arrangement and use of space can be telling indicators of how people behaved and related."[49] Having critically examined the Greco-Roman houses, this book now investigates the social aspects of four areas of the ancient Christian household: gender, family, education, and religion.

(1) Gender

Osiek and Balch observe that cultures have diverse ways of viewing honor and shame. Specifically, they cite that in the Greco-Roman world male honor entailed protecting one's reputation or status from any form of external threats, hence fierceness and manliness, and also being sexually potent and prolific, were highly valued.[50] How was male honor shown? Osiek and Balch explain,

> The patron functions as a kind of surrogate father, and the patronage system is a way of replicating systems. The patron must provide some material benefits to the client, but most important, benefits for social advancement. The complementary role of the client is proper deference toward the patron, the pouring on of attributed honor, and the performance of certain actions that contribute to the support of the patron, especially help in any way that the patron might need.[51]

On the other hand, the honor of women was in their sexual purity. Great importance was placed on a woman's virginity prior to marriage. A woman who had been seduced "pollute[d] the honor of the family" and had to be removed by a male family member in order to regain honor.[52] As Osiek and Balch point out, "The positive aspect of shame is generally seen as sensitivity

---

49. Osiek and Balch, *Families in the New Testament World*, 5.

50. Osiek and Balch, 38.

51. Osiek and Balch, 39.

52. Osiek and Balch, 39.

to one's honor. The person who lacks this sensitivity, and will therefore act in a dishonorable fashion, is 'shameless.'"[53]

Females in the Greco-Roman culture were regarded as inferior to males. An ancient Mediterranean man would only consider another man of comparable education and social standing as his equal. A man's only equal was another man and a woman's equal was only another woman.[54] Such a worldview placed women in a very disadvantaged position. As Osiek and Balch unveil,

> In both Greek and Roman systems, theoretically women could not administer their own property without the male guardianship. . . . All women were expected to be under the legal guardianship of a male relative, whether father, husband, or next of kin. Without his consent, a woman could not make major decisions about her own property, whether that of inheritance or dowry.[55]

Additionally, in terms of space, a dividing line separated the two genders. In Greek culture, women ate separately from men and did not participate in their public social gatherings or those that took place at home. Only in private family meals were the women, along with their children, allowed to dine with men.[56] Generally, a man's world revolved around his activities in the public space and what he could do agriculturally and politically; whereas a woman's sphere contained only the private space and the things she could do domestically and within her family.[57] As Osiek and Balch state,

> In the arrangement of domestic space . . . the Roman architect Vitruvius characterizes the Greek house as having a front area for the men and their social activities, while the back part of the house is reserved for the women and for family activities. While the male head of the house dominates in the front, the more public space, his wife dominates the domestic activities of the more private women's quarters, subject always to his ultimate authority.[58]

---

53. Osiek and Balch, 39.
54. Osiek and Balch, 41.
55. Osiek and Balch, 57.
56. Osiek and Balch, 59.
57. Osiek and Balch, 41.
58. Osiek and Balch, 44.

(2) Family

How was the family comprised in the Greco-Roman world? In their discussion on "Defining the Family" Osiek and Balch cite this comprehensive description: "The family in a traditional Mediterranean society can be understood as a diachronic and synchronic association of persons related by blood, marriage, and other social conventions, organized for the dual purpose of enhancement of its social status and legitimate transfer of property. The major means of achieving these ends are marriage and child-raising."[59] Based on this definition, a family in the Greco-Roman setting was composed primarily of three elements: parents, children, and property.

(a) **Parents.** Similar to most Asian families, Greco-Roman parents exercised authority over their children through a family-arranged marriage where parents matched their children (especially their daughters) with partners of their own choice.[60] Greco-Roman mothers doted on their sons since they were crucial to their own standing in their husband's family.[61] Consequently, married males found themselves more attached to their mothers than to their own wives. Osiek and Balch state that "in virilocal marriages, the bride enters the realm of her husband's family and must often live under the tyranny of a demanding mother-in-law."[62] The fathers, on the other hand, have both legal and social power over their entire household and property.[63] Significantly, Osiek and Balch mention that "under Greek law, it was possible for a father to relinquish his paternal authority in favor of a son. . . . In Roman Law, the legal term is *patria potestas*, viewed by ancient writers as a unique degree of legal power."[64]

(b) **Children.** Childrearing in the Greco-Roman context was largely the responsibility of mothers who nurtured their young children in the women's quarters.[65] At the age of puberty girls got married, whereas boys entered adulthood, but their emotional ties to their mothers lingered.[66] As a result, the daughter-in-law always experienced conflict with her mother-in-law as she competed for her husband's love and affection.[67] Osiek and Balch add, "Once

---

59. Osiek and Balch, 41.
60. Osiek and Balch, 61.
61. Osiek and Balch, 43.
62. Osiek and Balch, 43.
63. Osiek and Balch, 57.
64. Osiek and Balch, 57.
65. Osiek and Balch, 42.
66. Osiek and Balch, 42.
67. Osiek and Balch, 43.

thrust into the male world, sons found themselves subject to stern discipline and testing from their fathers in order to prepare them for the anticipated ordeals of adult manhood. The dynamic between demanding father with high expectations of his son, and son who must strive to meet those expectations, a major force in most cultures, is highly charged here."[68] The bottom-line here is that the Greco-Roman children were considered investments in the family's future and had to live up to their family's expectations.[69]

(c) **Property.** Lastly, concerning Greco-Roman family assets and possessions Osiek and Balch report:

> Property was kept in the family from generation to generation. The family's most precious possessions were therefore its children, who were socialized to assume their place in the next generation according to established gender roles: Boys to preserve the family property, protect their women, and beget sons; girls to contract good marriages, assure favorable alliances between families, and produce sons. In many situations, therefore, endogamous marriages, that is, with the closest kin allowable by law or custom, are preferred.[70]

Hence, the transfer of property to the next generation was secured through marriage which was a legal and social contract between two families; whereas the property agreements, including the relationship between two families, were severed upon the request of one of the marriage partners for divorce.[71]

(3) Education

For Greco-Romans who valued home schooling, "education is more important than birth, wealth, reputation, beauty, health, or strength."[72] Since several Greco-Roman couples desired their children to be their heirs and their caregivers at old age, education was deemed essential in maturing them and eventually making them responsible adults.[73] As Albert Craig et al. recount,

> Education was entirely the responsibility of the family, the father teaching his own son at home. It is not clear whether in early times girls received any education, though they certainly did later on.

---

68. Osiek and Balch, 43.
69. Osiek and Balch, 165.
70. Osiek and Balch, 42.
71. Osiek and Balch, 42.
72. Osiek and Balch, 68.
73. Osiek and Balch, 64.

The boys learned to read, write, and calculate, and they learned the skills of farming. They memorized the laws of the Twelve Tables, Rome's earliest code of law; learned how to perform religious rites; heard stories of the great deeds of early Roman history and particularly those of their ancestors; and engaged in the physical training appropriate for potential soldiers. This course of study was practical, vocational, and moral. It aimed at making the boys moral, pious, patriotic, law-abiding, and respectful of tradition.[74]

According to Osiek and Balch, "Between seven and sixteen or seventeen the father and often a tutor (*paedagogus*) took over education of the children, until the time when the upper-class son would be given the adult toga and might study with a rhetorician or a philosopher."[75] Eventually, the education of children at home necessitated the establishment of schools as Romans were exposed to Greek language, literature, and philosophy. As Osiek and Balch continue: "After 200 BCE Greek influence grew in Rome, which sometimes meant special schools apart from the home. The child learned reading, writing, and arithmetic early, then in the final three or four years of home schooling, he might be taught language and poetry by a grammarian (*grammaticus*). Even in Rome, these subjects were often taught in Greek by Greeks, so that such Romans were bilingual."[76] Craig et al. further narrate that

> by the last century of the Roman Republic, the new Hellenized education had become dominant. Latin literature had come into being along with Latin translations of Greek poets, and these formed part of the course of study, but Roman gentlemen were expected to be bilingual, and Greek language and literature were still central to the curriculum. Many schools were established, and the number of educated people grew extending beyond the senatorial class to the equestrians and outside Rome to the cities of Italy.[77]

(4) Religion

It was the Greeks who influenced Roman religion at its very onset, with the Romans naming their gods with Greek counterparts and adapting Greek

---

74. Craig et al., *Heritage of World Civilizations*, 139–140.

75. Osiek and Balch, *Families in the New Testament World*, 67.

76. Osiek and Balch, 67.

77. Craig et al., *Heritage of World Civilizations*, 140.

mythology as their own.[78] Osiek and Balch point out that "among the many forms that religion took in the Greco-Roman city, family religion played an important part. This importance of household and family religion would translate easily into household assemblies for Christians."[79] As Elliott observes, "Small wonder that house and home were . . . social centers for pagan house cults and Jewish house synagogues as well as for Christian house churches."[80] In his discussion on the history of religions, Klauck presents a significant summary of Greco-Roman pagan practices and house-cults which consisted of the private cult of Philadelphia in Lydia, the Orgeones at Athens, and the Serapis-cult.[81] Others also include the springing up of Jewish house synagogues in the Greco-Roman world:

> The closest model for early Christianity, however, was Judaism. Jewish household worship was extremely important, but its details are little known. Significant features included daily prayer, meal blessings and Sabbath worship, all culminating in the Pasch. On this day, according to Philo, every house was a temple and the whole people priests. And when public worship was made difficult, the home could take over its functions. . . .
>
> The synagogue itself arose out of separation from the Temple during the Exile. The oldest synagogues were created by altering private houses and villas. Not far from the Christian house-church in Dura-Europos is a synagogue fashioned from a dwelling, with a wing occupied by the builder or donor.[82]

This study finds that the spiritual (or religious) function of a house in the Greco-Roman – and also Jewish – context had a long history which could have been the setting for the origin and development of house churches. Klauck affirms that the house church "resembled contemporary private cult-associations and competed successfully with them by offering a genuine message of fellowship. In the house-church there was 'neither Jew nor Greek, slave nor free, male nor female' (Gal 3:28)."[83]

---

78. Craig et al., 138.

79. Osiek and Balch, *Families in the New Testament World*, 83.

80. Elliott, "Philemon and House Churches," 150.

81. Klauck, "House Church as Way of Life," 156.

82. Klauck, 156.

83. Klauck, 156–157.

More importantly, Klauck also discovers that the house church finds its direct Christian prototype in the Jewish house synagogue.[84] Likewise Meeks notes, "Because Christianity was an offshoot of Judaism, the urban Christian groups obviously had the diaspora synagogue as the nearest and most natural model."[85] It is very likely, then, that the house church of the Christians must have evolved from the house synagogue of the Jews. As Meeks further elucidates,

> The practice of meeting in private houses was probably an expedient used by Jews in many places as it was for the Pauline Christians, to judge from the remains of synagogue buildings at Dura-Europos, Stobi, Delos, and elsewhere that were adapted from private dwellings. In the cities where Paul founded congregations, however, the Jews had probably already advanced to the stage of possessing buildings used exclusively for the community's functions. The sorts of activities in the meetings were also probably similar, including scripture reading and interpretation, prayers, common meals.[86]

Therefore, studying households in the Greco-Roman world – and their perception of gender, family, education, and religion – is foundational in understanding house churches in the first century. The obvious reason is that the family is the basic unit of the church and the church is a social structure patterned after the family. Pieter F. Craffert emphasizes in his journal article that "the household structure provided the basic social setting both for the expansion and for the assembly of Pauline communities in the cities of the Greco-Roman Empire. Existing households serve as nuclei for the expansion of the movement as well as for the assembly of these communities."[87] So the family and the church are mutually related. While the house church is composed of households, the household is a pattern of how a house church should function.

c. Greco-Roman house churches
Based on the overall physical evidences gathered from the remaining structures of Greco-Roman houses and the reconstructed households' social setting, this book affirms the existence of Greco-Roman house churches in the first century. The archeological data from the Greco-Roman houses proves that the earliest church structures were domestic residences which were eventually

---

84. Klauck, 156–157.

85. Meeks, *First Urban Christians*, 80.

86. Meeks, 80.

87. Craffert, "Pauline Household Communities," 325.

renovated as the early Christians grew in number. Filson states, "Archaeology suggests the process by which the small group meeting in a private house developed into a larger body requiring more space than a private residence could offer."[88] Likewise, according to Blue, "recent archaeological evidence suggests that the early Christian groups gathered in domestic residences which could accommodate their needs, sometimes renovating these private homes so that they no longer served the needs for which they were originally constructed."[89] This structural change of the house church building as its needs and size grew, as well as the implications of this change, will be discussed further and addressed historically in the next section of this study.

2. Historical Perspective

In his review article "Early Christian Architecture: The Beginnings," Paul C. Finney states that Richard Krautheimer's seminal research is the starting point for the historical study of early Christian architecture in its initial stage.[90] Krautheimer's essay on "The Beginning of Early Christian Literature" first introduced the three-stage structural development of the church from a house to a basilica.[91] This was later followed by Lloyd Michael White as he made some major advancements on Krautheimer's work. According to Krautheimer, the early Christian period (AD 50–313) can roughly be divided into three sections that correspond to the church's structural development: *The House Church* (c. 50–150); *The Domus Ecclesiae* (c. 150–250); and *The Aula Ecclesiae* (c. 250–313).[92]

a. The house church, c. 50–150.

The early church's history of structural development begins from its use of unaltered domestic architecture in the first century. In Krautheimer's first stage (c. 50–150), where Christianity was rapidly growing, the early believers were depicted as congregating in residential spaces owned by individual members –

---

88. Filson, "Significance of the Early House Churches," 109.

89. Blue "Acts and the House Church," 124.

90. Finney, "Early Christian Architecture," 329.

91. Richard Krautheimer, "Beginning of Early Christian Literature," *RR* 3 (1939): 127–148, cited in Finney, "Early Christian Architecture," 329, and in Blue, "Acts and the House Church," 124. The original essay was reprinted in Richard Krautheimer, *Studies in Early Christian, Medieval, and Renaissance Art* (New York: New York University Press, 1969), 1–20.

92. Finney, "Early Christian Architecture," 329–331; Blue, "Acts and the House Church," 124–125.

spaces commonly known as house churches.[93] Krautheimer is convinced that several Christians who met in private apartments were specifically gathering in the dining area, where they tailored their Eucharistic rituals based on the existing domestic structure.[94] Apparently, according to Krautheimer's study, "the earliest Christian attitudes toward real places to be utilized for worship were motivated in great degree by practical considerations, such as the size of the community, its organization and its financial resources."[95]

Even so, Finney declares that the surviving archaeological data is insufficient to give direct proof of Christian beginnings.[96] Likewise, Blue finds it problematic to deal with house churches archaeologically because "domestic architecture is rarely well preserved [and] even when domestic architecture is found it is seldom possible to determine whether the residence was used for non-domestic use, such as a meeting place for believers."[97] Additionally, in his other study on "Early Church Architecture," Blue points out that "since house churches did not demand architectural alterations, their archaeological remains are undetectable unless they were subsequently incorporated into a *domus ecclesiae* and/or an *aula ecclesiae*."[98]

b. The *domus ecclesiae*, c. 150–250.

In this next stage of the early church architecture, its structural development emerges. When the house was found to be functionally insufficient for the church's needs, as the practices of the assembly developed, structural adjustments were made to improvise.[99] Accordingly, the church eventually transitioned from the *house church* (substructure) – and its use of unconverted domestic residences in the first century – to the *church house* ("sprouting" structure), having refurbished the original house buildings in the second century. Finney explains that, according to Krautheimer, this period – where the interiors of apartments and houses were remodeled to be conducive for worship – is characterized under the title *domus ecclesiae*.[100] The term *domus ecclesiae* is translated as a "community center or meeting house."[101] During this

---

93. Blue, "Acts and the House Church," 124.
94. Finney, "Early Christian Architecture," 330.
95. Finney, 330.
96. Finney, 330.
97. Blue, "Acts and the House Church," 125–126.
98. Blue, "Architecture, Early Church," 94.
99. Blue, "Acts and the House Church," 189.
100. Finney, "Early Christian Architecture," 330.
101. Blue, "Acts and the House Church," 127.

second stage, which covered the years c. 150–250, there was a remodeling of domestic structures to fit the early believers' needs.[102] According to Finney, "In Rome such structures are commonly denominated *tituli,* which means they are identified by the names of the putative former owners who are thought to have donated their once private properties to the church for architectural conversion and use as a place of worship."[103]

Some significant examples of *domus ecclesiae* include the remains at Dura-Europos and Capernaum (the location of Peter's former house). As Blue reports, the 1931 discovery of Dura-Europos (a third-century garrison town in Syria) became the most convincing archaeological evidence affirming the early Christian *domus ecclesiae.*[104] Klauck states that the excavations "revealed a private house that had been adapted (about AD 240) as a house-church by enlarging the living room to accommodate some 60 persons and decorating a small room as a baptistry [that] thus shows a transitional stage between the private dwelling which doubled as a Christian meeting-place and the public church building."[105] Moreover, Blue also suggests that based on "the archaeological excavations at Capernaum . . . the former house of Peter was later transformed into a *domus ecclesiae* and may well be the most ancient evidence of an original house church. [However,] unlike the remains at Dura-Europos, the remains at Capernaum do not allow an unambiguous reconstruction of the original building and its history of structural development."[106]

c. The *aula ecclesiae,* c. 250–313.

Having traced the history of the early church's first and second stage of structural development (*substructure and "sprouting" structure*) in the first and second century, this study proceeds to the third stage where the church moved from domestic residences to public buildings (*simple structure*). According to Blue, "The last stage c. 250–313, saw the introduction of larger buildings and halls (both private and public) before the introduction of basilical architecture by Constantine."[107] Blue indicates that White (not Krautheimer) introduced the term *aula ecclesiae,* "a larger building (which may have already functioned as a *domus ecclesiae*)."[108] Furthermore, according to White, *aula ecclesiae* "was

---

102. Blue, 124–125.

103. Finney, "Early Christian Architecture," 330–331.

104. Blue, "Acts and the House Church," 166.

105. Klauck, "The House-Church as Way of Life," 153.

106. Blue, "Architecture, Early Church," 94.

107. Blue, "Acts and the House Church," 125.

108. Blue, 129.

designated as a large rectangular hall, but with none of the formal features of basilical architecture."[109] As Blue states, "Basilica S. Crisogono (*Titulus Chrysogoni*) is an indisputable example of an *aula ecclesiae* in Rome. It is located on the ancient *Via Aurelia*, and the basilica was constructed by incorporating a large, preexisting rectangular hall. This particular hall dates to the beginning of the fourth century (c. 310)."[110]

The flow chart below, based on Krautheimer's work, conceptually summarizes the early church's three-stage structural development:

---

1. THE CHURCH IN UNALTERED HOUSES (House Church: c. 50–150)

2. THE CHURCH IN RENOVATED HOUSES (*Domus Ecclesiae*: c. 150–250)

3. THE CHURCH IN PUBLIC BUILDINGS (*Aula Ecclesiae*: c. 250–313)

Figure 2.1 A flow chart based on Krautheimer's three-stage development of early church architecture[111]

The church in larger public buildings (*simple structure*) later evolved into the church as monumental basilical buildings (*superstructure*) which were officially introduced by Constantine. In their book, *Two Kingdoms: The Church and Culture through the Ages*, Robert Clouse, Richard Pierard, and Edwin Yamauchi mention the legalization of Christianity under Constantine: "In 313 Constantine and his eastern colleague Licinius agreed to grant toleration to Christians and restore property that had been confiscated from them. This is commonly known as the 'Edict of Milan' . . . [where] Constantine . . . legalized bequests to churches, began the construction of basilicas – the first public structures to be used as church buildings."[112] Nonetheless, White emphasizes the essential point that "while monumental basilicas were springing up at Rome and elsewhere under the aegis of Constantine, at the same time other churches were being founded on the tradition of the *domus ecclesiae* and *aula ecclesiae*."[113]

---

109. L. Michael White, *Domus Ecclesiae*, 29, quoted in Blue, "Acts and the House Church," 129.

110. Blue, "Architecture, Early Church," 95.

111. Cf. Blue, "Architecture, Early Church," 92–95; Blue, "Acts and the House Church," 124–130; and Finney, "Early Christian Architecture," 329–331.

112. Clouse, Pierard, and Yamauchi, *Two Kingdoms*, 63–64.

113. White, *Domus Ecclesiae*, 32, quoted in Blue, "Acts and the House Church," 130.

Krautheimer's three-stage development receives a helpful clarification from White. Using Krautheimer's work as his foundation, White creates a five-fold model of architectural development which is conceptually summarized in the chart below:

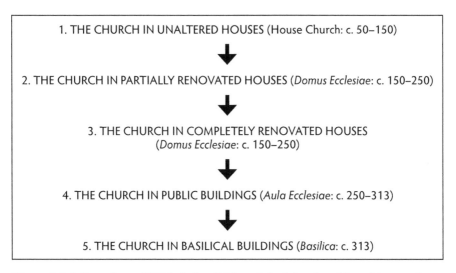

Figure 2.2 A flow chart of White's five-fold model of the church's architectural development[114]

Finney comments that White's significant contribution to architectural origins "is his emphasis on a developmental model which underscores the gradual transformation of already existing architectonic spaces and places. This incremental approach clearly squares with the archaeological evidence."[115] Blue also recognizes White's major advancements on Krautheimer's three-stage development: "First, he makes finer, more accurate demarcations in the periods of development. . . . Second, he demonstrates that the development was *not consistently felt in all areas.* The amassed evidence indicates that while in later periods certain communities were meeting in public halls, believers elsewhere were still meeting in house churches."[116]

It can be argued, then, that the assembly of Christians in domestic spaces (including the renovated homes) "continued to be the norm until the early decades of the fourth century when under the tutelage of Constantine, the

114. Cf. White, *Domus Ecclesiae*, 25–40, 475–519, cited in Finney, "Early Christian Architecture," 334–335.

115. Finney, "Early Christian Architecture," 335.

116. Blue, "Acts and the House Church,"125.

Christians began erecting the first basilicas."[117] As Clouse, Pierard, and Yamauchi point out, "In fact, for the better part of three centuries the Christians assembled in homes, not in public structures."[118] In her article "House-Churches in Rome," Joan M. Petersen also reasonably argues "that large 'purpose-built' churches were not erected until the adoption of Christianity as the official religion made them necessary for the greatly increased congregations."[119] Church life, therefore, was simpler when the early believers were just meeting in residential houses. But, inevitably, they were constrained to embrace the complexity of church life in the name of "development and growth." In the course of time, the basis of growth gradually shifted to the size of their massive church building and attendance, which unwittingly, is also the trend in most of the present-day "mega-churches" (the modern-day basilicas). Consequently, Osiek and Balch recount that because of architectural transformation,

> what was once a private house became a building devoted to Christian religious use. . . . The separation of Eucharist from meal and the growing numbers of believers necessitated the removal of worship from the venue of the private dwelling, and thus from the family setting. From then on, Christian worship was conducted according to the profile of public liturgy and no longer took place in a family environment. The growing authority of the bishop concentrated more and more power in the hands, not of local leaders, but of centralized authority figures responsible for larger and larger groups of believers.[120]

Therefore, this shows how the architectural evolution of the early church building took place from *substructure* (domestic architecture) to *superstructure* (basilical architecture) at the time of Constantine. From the initial spiritual focus of the early church as the believers gathered in small domestic spaces (house church), they moved to structural development by building huge public spaces (basilical church). This also explains why the church is subsequently understood as a place (building) rather than as a people (believers).

---

117. Blue, 124.

118. Clouse, Pierard, and Yamauchi, *Two Kingdoms*, 39.

119. Petersen, "House-Churches in Rome," 266.

120. Osiek and Balch, *Families in the New Testament World*, 35.

3. Biblical Perspective

Did house churches really exist in the first century or were they merely household (fellowship) groups? What is the New Testament's concept of a house church? The New Testament is the primary literary source for the existence of house churches. This section focuses on the spiritual function of the house as used as a meeting place for believers in the time of Jesus and his disciples, as recorded in the Gospels, and the time of the apostles, as recorded in Acts and the Pauline epistles.

a. The use of houses in the Gospels

In the Synoptic Gospels, Jesus's ministry was portrayed as both public and private. The Lord's teaching ministry was conducted not only in open-air settings but also in enclosed venues where the Jews gathered for worship (synagogues) and even the ordinary residential homes of different people at that time.[121]

Since the Jews in the early first century belonged to a synagogue community, Jesus predominantly utilized that strategic venue to minister to people.[122] Consequently, several scholars tend to believe that (aside from open spaces) the Jewish places of enclosed gathering (synagogues) were the only venues that Jesus used for ministry.[123] Such is not the case. Jesus also utilized domestic houses in his ministry. As Gehring argues,

> First, in the ancient Jewish, Christian, and Hellenistic world, a private home often provided the meeting place for religious and intellectual dialogue and instruction. Particularly in the Jewish and Christian setting, domestic houses were viewed as 'the basic cell for the assemblies of the master with his disciples.' . . . Second, as we consider the central economic and social significance of the *oikos* in the ancient world generally and in Palestine or Galilee specifically, it should not surprise us to discover that houses played a central role in the life and ministry of Jesus. Third, synagogues may well have been widespread in 70 C.E. and earlier, not only in the Diaspora but in Palestine as well, primarily in the form of house synagogues, that is, private homes that served with or

---

121. Gehring, *House Church and Mission*, 29.

122. Here is the list of synagogues used by Jesus in the Gospels: Matt 4:23; 9:35; 12:9; 13:54; Mark 1:21, 23, 29, 39; 3:1; 6:2; Luke 4:15–16, 20, 28, 33, 38, 44; 6:6; 13:10; John 6:59; 18:20. Cf. Young, *Analytical Concordance to the Bible*, 951.

123. Gehring, *House Church and Mission*, 29.

without architectural alteration as the place of assembly for a synagogue community. . . . All of this is evidence that Jews of the first century were accustomed to meeting for worship in private homes, which in turn would apply also to Jesus and his disciples.[124]

The Gospel of Mark records five key verses (Mark 1:29, 33; 2:1; 3:20; 9:33) that show how Jesus used the ordinary house of Peter in Capernaum, where he temporarily stayed (cf. Matt 17:24–27), to serve as a meeting place to minister to people through healing and teaching.[125] Next to Nazareth, Capernaum became the second home of Jesus and served as his center for ministry operation. From Capernaum, Jesus's itinerant ministry reached also the area surrounding the Sea of Galilee and beyond the "evangelical triangle" (Capernaum, Chorazin and Bethsaida, cf. Matt 11:21/Luke 10:13–15) by traveling from village to village, which implies from house to house.[126]

Like the house of Peter in Capernaum, the house of Martha (or Lazarus) in Bethany was also implied to function as a meeting place and teaching facility (John 11:19, 31; 12:1–9; Luke 10:38–42).[127] Eventually, the disciples appear to also follow the pattern set by their Master in using houses as a base of operations for reaching the cities (Luke 10:1–12).[128] Thus, domestic houses were used by Jesus and the disciples for ministry to the people and as a mission strategy for reaching a town or city. Gehring describes such "house mission" as "likely the embryonic form of house-to-house missional outreach and church development practiced after Easter."[129]

b. The use of houses in Acts

Similar to the Lord's approach, the apostles' and early believers' ministries in Acts were also depicted as both public and private. Their assembly was not only in open spaces but in synagogues' enclosed structures and ordinary houses as well (cf. Acts 20:20).

On the one hand, the synagogue building was used as a gathering place by the church in Jerusalem (Acts 8:1–3; 22:19–20; 26:10–11) and the believers in Damascus (Acts 9:1–2). Paul used the synagogues to proclaim the gospel primarily in his missionary journeys (Acts 9:20; 13:5, 14–16, 43; 14:1; 17:1, 10,

---

124. Gehring, 29–30.
125. Gehring, 36–37.
126. Gehring, 38–39, 42.
127. Gehring, 43–44.
128. Gehring, 53.
129. Gehring, 58.

17; 18:4, 19; 19:8), and Apollos did as well (Acts 18:26).[130] On the other hand, the Jewish and Gentile Christians predominantly met in domestic houses. The first meeting place of the first Christians was in the upper room in Jerusalem (Acts 1:12–15). Eventually, the church in Jerusalem assembled in other private homes (Acts 2:1–2; 42–47; 5:42). While the church also gathered together in the "temple courts," the meeting "from house to house" or in various private homes became very necessary in order for the early Christians to grow, as is evident in the verses below:

> Day by day continuing with one mind in the temple, and breaking bread *from house to house*, they were taking their meals together with gladness and sincerity of heart, praising God and having favor with all the people. And the Lord was *adding to their number* day by day those who were being saved. (Acts 2:46–47)
>
> And every day, in the temple and *from house to house*, they kept right on teaching and preaching Jesus as the Christ. Now at this time while the disciples were *increasing in number* . . . the word of God kept on spreading; and the *number* of the disciples *continued to increase greatly* in Jerusalem, and *a great many* of the priests were becoming obedient to the faith. (Acts 5:42–6:1a, 7)[131]

In addition, Luke records how the church in Jerusalem purposefully used the domestic spaces when a great persecution arose against it. Saul of Tarsus ravaged the church as he entered "house after house" to drag and imprison both the believing men and women (Acts 8:1, 3). After his conversion, the Apostle Paul cited how he taught the elders in Ephesus not only publicly but also "from house to house" (Acts 20:20). As Filson clarifies,

> Outside of Jerusalem, no temple served as a partial center of attention for the Christians. Whenever the synagogue was closed to Christian propaganda – and this seems to have occurred early in the development of Paul's work in the cities he visited – the house church dominated the situation. Only rarely could a public assembly hall be obtained (Acts 19:9). With the exception of such limited use as could be made of the market place and other public areas of the city, the regular setting for both Christian meetings and evangelistic preaching was found in the homes of believers.[132]

---

130. Young, *Analytical Concordance to the Bible*, 951.

131. Emphasis added.

132. Filson, "Significance of the Early House Churches," 106.

The Christian households whose names are mentioned in Acts (except one) are the house of Cornelius in Caesarea (Acts 10:2, 22, 30; 11:12–14); the house of Simon the Tanner in Joppa (10:6, 17, 32; 11:11); the house of Mary in Jerusalem (Acts 12:12–17); the house of Lydia in Philippi (Acts 16:14–15, 40); the house of Jason in Thessalonica (Acts 17:5–9); the house of Titius Justus in Corinth (Acts 18:7); the house of Crispus in Corinth (Acts 18:8); the house of Philip in Caesarea (21:8–9); and the house of the unnamed jailer in Philippi (Acts 16:31–34). The long list of families recorded in the book of Acts alone is significant. Elliott remarks,

> Even when contact with the Jerusalem Temple and Jewish synagogues was still maintained, it was nevertheless the household which serves as the new and vital center for social networks, worship, interprovincial communication, recruitment, baptizing and instruction in the faith, the hosting of travelling missionaries, and the material support essential to the sustenance and growth of the movement across the Roman Empire.[133]

So, while the early church gathered in the temple (also in Solomon's portico, John 10:23; Acts 3:11; 5:12) and house synagogues, the house was the structure primarily used for church meetings, the reasons for which are summarized by Blue:

> (1) The "upper rooms" and domestic residences were immediately available.

> (2) The domestic structure provided a relatively inconspicuous meeting place. Although the house setting was not a guarantee against persecution (see Acts 8:3), in the early years when persecution was a threat, Christians used discretion in their choice of meeting place.

> (3) The Jews in Palestine and the Diaspora assembled in house synagogues. Since most of the early believers were Jews and God-fearers, it is not difficult to envisage the Christian communities adopting Jewish patterns, particularly since many of the activities in the house church resembled those of the house synagogue.

---

133. Elliott, "Philemon and House Churches," 147.

(4) The "house" provided the necessities of a Christian gathering, most importantly, the facilities needed for the preparation, serving and eating of the Lord's Supper.[134]

Finally, in regards to the predominant and purposeful use of house churches in the first century, Abraham Malherbe significantly observes that "house churches in the mission field appear to have been the rule rather than the exception. . . . It would be the normal thing for the church in any particular city to be made up initially of one congregation meeting in a home. . . . A number of household churches would exist in a particular location after an extended period of missionary activity even if a plurality is not explicitly mentioned."[135]

c. The use of houses in the Pauline epistles

In the Pauline epistles, there are four significant occurrences of the phrase "the church that is in someone's house/household" (ἡ κατ᾿ οἶκον ἐκκλησία) in the apostle's greetings: (1) Aquila and Prisca's οἶκος in Ephesus: "Aquila and Prisca greet you heartily in the Lord, with the church that is in their house" (1 Cor 16:19); (2) Prisca and Aquila's οἶκος in Rome: "Greet Prisca and Aquila, my fellow workers in Christ Jesus . . . also greet the church that is in their house" (Rom 16:5); (3) Philemon's οἶκος in Colossae: "To Philemon our beloved brother and fellow worker . . . and to the church in your house" (Phlm 1–2); and (4) Nympha's οἶκος in Laodicea: "Greet . . . also Nympha[136] and the church that is in her house" (Col 4:15).

The two possible meanings of οἶκος used in Paul's four epistolary greetings could either refer to a *quarter* where one lives or a *household* that one is in charge of.[137] Is Paul then referring to οἶκος as a place of meeting for a Christian group or the people inside the house – the household group? Banks replies that the occurrence of domestic baptisms in Acts 10:48 and 11:14, and the usage of

---

134. Blue, "Architecture, Early Church," 92.

135. Malherbe, "The Household of God," 15–16.

136. Several modern translations (NASB, ESV, HCSB, NIV, and RSV) prefer the feminine "Nympha" than the masculine "Nymphas" (used only in ASV and KJV). This is the preference of the UBS *Greek New Testament*, based on the weight of B 6 424ᶜ 1739 1877 1881 syrʰ· ᵖᵃˡ ᵐˢ copˢᵃ Origen (Aland et al., *The Greek New Testament*, 703 fn. 2). As O'Brien argues, "Since the earliest manuscripts had no accents by which the masculine and feminine forms might be distinguished, the only ancient evidence lies in the personal pronoun which follows: 'in her/ his/their house' (κατ᾿ οἶκον αὐτῆς/αὐτοῦ/αὐτῶν). The manuscripts vary inconsiderably, but on balance it appears preferable to understand the reference to a woman and render the whole phrase: 'Nympha and the church that is in her house'" (O'Brien, *Colossians and Philemon*, 256). This research, therefore, takes the feminine translation.

137. Banks, *Paul's Idea of Community*, 45.

oikos in reference to the extended family – probably slaves – in the Pastorals (1 Tim 3:12; cf. 3:5 and 5:14), implies the latter reading.[138] However, in reference to 1 Cor 16:19, Banks declares, "It is nowhere stated in Acts, and their Jewish convictions make it unlikely, that Aquila and Prisca had a household of this kind. While *oikos* does sometimes refer to slaves, it does not necessarily have that meaning. It is to their home then that the term *oikos* refers."[139]

While Banks renders *oikos* as a place (house), Meeks, on the other hand, takes the other possible translation of *oikos* as referring to people (household) and not merely to the place (house). Meeks's position is to translate the phrase ἡ κατ᾽ οἶκον ἐκκλησία (in Col 4:15) as "the assembly at N.'s [Nympha] household"[140] based on a two-fold argument:

> An intimate connection with existing households is also suggested by 1 Cor 1:16, where Paul says he baptized the "house [*oikos*] of Stephanas," and later in the same letter (16:15f.), where he commends the Stephanas household (*oikia*) as the "firstfruits of Achaia," who have "devoted themselves to service for the saints." The conversion of a person "with (all) his/her house" is mentioned several times in Acts as well [Acts 16:15 (Lydia); 16:31–34 (Philippian jailer); 18:8 (Crispus, the archi-synagogos of Corinth)]. The letters also mention other groups, not necessarily founded by members of the Pauline circle, that are identified by the households to which their members belong (Rom 16:10–15; 1 Cor 1:11; Phil 4:22). The local structure of the early Christian groups was thus linked with what was commonly regarded as the basic unit of the society. . . .
>
> Paul probably uses *kat' oikon* to distinguish these individual household-based groups from "the whole church" (*holē hē ekklēsia*), which could also assemble on occasion (1 Cor 14:23; Rom 16:23; cf. 1 Cor 11:20), or from the still larger manifestations of the Christian movement, for which he used the same term, *ekklēsia*. The *kat' oikon ekklēsia* is thus the "basic cell" of the Christian movement, and its nucleus was often an existing household.[141]

---

138. Banks, 45.
139. Banks, 45.
140. Meeks, *First Urban Christians*, 75.
141. Meeks, 75.

This book, however, aims to look into the possibility that the noun οἶκος in Paul's four greetings (in 1 Cor 16:19; Rom 16:5; Phlm 1–2; Col 4:15) may refer to both the "place" (house) and "people" (household), which is the common understanding of the term in the first century. The author's presupposition is based on the way various modern translations of the Bible and some New Testament scholars vary in their translations of the Pauline expression ἡ κατ' οἶκον ἐκκλησία as presented below:

1.

"the church that meets in your house" (Phlm 2 – HCSB, O'Brien[142])
"the church that meets in your home" (Phlm 2 – NIV)
"the church that meets in their home" (Rom 16:5 – HCSB;
   1 Cor 16:19 – HCSB, Patterson[143])
"the church that meets at their house" (Rom 16:5 – NIV, Stott[144];
   1 Cor 16:19 – NIV)

2.

"the church in your house" (Phlm 2 – NASB, ESV, RSV)
"the church in thy house" (Phlm 2 – ASV, KJV)
"the church in her house" (Col 4:15 – ESV, HCSB, NIV, RSV,
   O'Brien[145])
"the church which is in his house" (Col 4:15 – KJV)
"the church in their house" (Rom 16:5 – ESV, RSV; 1 Cor 16:19 –
   ESV, RSV)
"the church of their house" (Rom 16:5, Moo[146])
"the church that is in their house" (Rom 16:5 – ASV, KJV, NASB;
   1 Cor 16:19 – NASB, ASV, KJV; Col 4:15 – ASV)

The first group has the sense of translating the phrase as "the church's meeting place is at someone's house (place)"; whereas the second group appears to render it as "the church is in someone's house (place) or household (people)." Banks's rendering of ἡ κατ' οἶκον ἐκκλησία as referring to a place concurs with the stance of most of the New Testament scholars and modern translations, since it appears to be the most common understanding of the four given texts. Following Meeks's position, however, inevitably raises this question: Would it

---

142. O'Brien, *Colossians and Philemon*, 271.

143. Patterson, *Troubled Triumphant Church*, 320.

144. Stott, *Message of Romans*, 393.

145. O'Brien, *Colossians and Philemon*, 245.

146. Moo, *Epistle to the Romans*, 916.

make sense, then, for Paul's expression to mean that the ἐκκλησία (people) is in someone's οἶκος – that is, both in a house (place) and a household (people)?

Since nothing is for certain here, a proper understanding of the prepositional phrase κατ᾽ οἶκον, particularly the use of κατά with the accusative, will be essential. In his discussion on "The Nature of Prepositions," Daniel Wallace points out that, "[i]n general, the prepositions that take accusative and dative case objects function adverbially."[147] Of the six basic uses of the specific preposition κατά with the accusative,[148] the two possible adverbial usages in the four given texts are in the sense of manner and location, or distributive and locative.

Should κατ᾽ οἶκον be translated, then, in the distributive or locative sense? If the former, it would be rendered "the church that establishes itself in a house-like manner."[149] By "distributive," Wallace means that it is referring to "the division of a greater whole into individual parts."[150] As Gehring explains, "Klauck supports this distributive translation with lexical argumentation. He lists Josephus and several papyri and appeals to the authority of Moulton-Milligan, W. Bauer, and G. Delling."[151] Klauck argues that both forms, the small house churches and the whole church as a unit at that location, existed side by side in early Christianity.[152] According to Klauck, there is a distinction between house churches and the assembly of the whole church. Similarly, Meeks understands it in the same way when he mentions earlier in his arguments that "Paul probably uses *kat' oikon* to distinguish these individual household-based groups from 'the whole church' (*holē hē ekklēsia*) [1 Cor 14:23; Rom 16:23; cf. 1 Cor 11:20]."[153]

However, with regard to corporate worship and individual religious life, Klauck explains that the same elements can be observed to be present in both forms. In one of his theological journals, Klauck writes that the house church during the early centuries was the "base for mission, assembly-place for the

---

147. Wallace, *Greek Grammar Beyond the Basic*, 357.

148. Wallace, 377. Note that Wallace enumerates the six basic uses of the specific preposition κατά with the accusative: (1) Standard; (2) Spatial; (3) Temporal; (4) Distributive; (5) Purpose; and (6) Reference/Respect.

149. Hans-Josef Klauck, *Hausgemeinde*, 19, 21, quoted in Gehring, *House Church and Mission*, 25, 155.

150. Wallace, *Greek Grammar Beyond the Basics*, 377.

151. Hans-Josef Klauck, *Hausgemeinde*, 19, 20 fn. 23, cited in Gehring, *House Church and Mission*, 155.

152. Gehring, *House Church and Mission*, 25.

153. Meeks, *First Urban Christians*, 75.

Lord's Supper, prayer and catechesis, locus of Christian fellowship."[154] But Klauck qualifies that such "understanding of the transition from house church to whole church needs to be kept as open as possible."[155]

Taking the opposite stand, Gehring, on the other hand, cites another New Testament scholar, Marlis Gielen, who is convinced that κατ᾽ οἶκον is to be understood in a locative sense. According to Gielen, it is unlikely for the four texts to refer to the manner of church assembly since "the extension of the prepositional phrase κατ᾽ οἶκον with a possessive pronoun locates the church in the house of the aforementioned persons."[156] Gielen supports her locational translation "by the observation that in Koine, κατ᾽ οἶκον is documented as a standing phrase for ἐν οἴκῳ. In addition, there are references already in classical Greek for the use of κατά with the accusative in the sense of location. In time it eventually became interchangeable with ἐν."[157] Gielen also contends that the house churches did not exist separate or alongside the local church in any given city. Gielen believes "that for Paul ἡ κατ᾽ οἶκον ἐκκλησία and ἡ ἐκκλησία ὅλη do not stand in opposition to one another; instead, he uses ὅλη in both cases (Rom 16:23; 1 Cor 14:23) for text-pragmatic reason only."[158] For Gielen, as Gehring elucidates, "the expression ἡ κατ᾽ οἶκον ἐκκλησία refers to local churches, that is, to the whole church at that location or in that town and so all passages, that are held by other scholars to refer to so-called house churches refer in reality only to houses. They would thus not be house churches in the full sense but merely household fellowship groups."[159]

Nonetheless, Gehring reasonably presupposes that both the distributive and locative sense is possible in the four texts cited. Hence, Gehring raises the question of "how a distributive understanding of the phrase could be expressed in a translation in any way other than locationally and whether a locational translation necessarily excludes a distributive nuance."[160] Gehring argues that while, on the one hand, κατά with accusative denotes an individualization and is, consequently, to be rendered not distributively but locationally, on the other hand, an individualization of the church as a whole into separate

---

154. Klauck, "House-Church as Way of Life," 157.

155. Hans-Josef Klauck, *Hausgemeinde*, 36–39, cited in Gehring, *House Church and Mission*, 26 fn. 140.

156. Marlis Gielen, "Zur Interpretation," 112, cited in Gehring, *House Church and Mission*, 156.

157. Gielen, 112, cited in Gehring, 156.

158. Gielen, 110–118, cited in Gehring, 25.

159. Gehring, *House Church and Mission*, 25.

160. Gehring, 156.

congregations warrants that it must also be translated distributively.[161] Thus, Gehring concludes, "The locational and the distributive interpretations of the Pauline expression κατ' οἶκον do not mutually exclude one another, even though from a purely grammatical perspective it must be determined as locational."[162]

Arguing against Gielen, Gehring further contends that positing such an expression as referring to the local church alone is untenable. As a result, he believes that "it is legitimate to understand the two expressions ἡ κατ' οἶκον ἐκκλησία and ἐκκλησία ὅλη as being in opposition to one another and to assume that the coexistence of house churches alongside the local church as a whole does not have to be excluded a priori as a possibility for exegetical reasons."[163] In support of his argument, Gehring states that "a plurality of house churches was demonstrated with certainty for Rome, probably for Thessalonica, and possibly for Ephesus, Philippi, and Laodicea, and the coexistence of a number of house churches alongside the local church as a whole was demonstrated for Corinth."[164] Therefore, this book notes Gehring's analysis that Paul's standard expression in his four epistolary greetings implicitly indicates a plurality of house churches within the local church as a whole.[165]

d. Meaning of house church in the NT

Having critically analyzed the meaning and functions of the first-century οἶκος as a house, household, and house church in the Greco-Roman world based on the archaeological, historical, and biblical perspective, what, then, is the meaning of house church in the New Testament?

New Testament scholars vary in their definition of what a house church is. In his study of house church, Blue adopts this definition: "A domestic residence which is architectonically unaltered and is used (occasionally) by the local Christian community (or a part thereof)."[166] A house church according to Kirby is "a small company of Christians meeting together in a house for worship and edification."[167] Coenen describes house churches as the "small groups in individual houses [which] are called *ekklēsia*."[168] Meeks refers to a house church as an "individual household-based group . . . the 'basic cell' of the Christian

---

161. Gehring, 156–157.
162. Gehring, 159.
163. Gehring, 159.
164. Gehring, 159.
165. Gehring, 157.
166. Blue, "Acts and the House Church," 125.
167. Kirby, "Church," 846.
168. Coenen, "Church, Synagogue," 301.

movement, and its nucleus was often an existing household."[169] Lastly, Gehring suggests a working definition: "A *house church* is a group of Christians that meets in a private home."[170] According to Gehring, it is a "Christian [household] fellowship group that [was] formed in and/or around an *oikos.*"[171]

Which, then, is the right definition of a house church? In his article "The Church in the House," Hans-Ruedi Weber contends, "If the house-church is 'church' in the full sense of this word, all the constituent elements of the church can and must be present within the house-church."[172] This study finds Gehring's proposal in determining what constitutes a house church helpful. Most scholars concur with his three-fold criteria:

> (a) A group exists that has developed its own religious life, including regular gatherings for worship. (b) The content of these regular gatherings for worship includes evangelistic and instructional proclamation, the celebration of baptism and communion, prayer, and fellowship. (c) Elements such as (unclearly defined) organizational structures can be considered further indications of a house church in the full sense.[173]

Before defining a house church based on the given criteria, this book defines first what it is not. A house church is not gathering anyone, anywhere, and anyhow. The people, place, and purpose must, then, be specific. As in the case of the term ἐκκλησία which was discussed earlier, the same three elements must also be present in a house church: (1) people (the "who"); (2) place (the "where"); and (3) purpose (the "why").

First, the kind of *people* gathering is specific. It is not *gathering anyone* (or people in general) as in the case of evangelistic campaigns. Primarily, it should be the gathering of a Christian assembly. Second, the *place* of gathering is also particular. It is not the *gathering anywhere* of Christians. Rather, it should be at one location at a time, where God's people are geographically situated, such as at someone's domestic residence. Lastly, the *purpose* of people gathering is also definite. It is not the *gathering anyhow* of Christians for the sake of gathering, or it will be a mere social gathering. The purpose must be clear and that purpose is to observe only the common practices of the early church.

---

169. Meeks, *First Urban Christians*, 75.

170. Gehring, *House Church and Mission*, 27.

171. Gehring, 119.

172. Weber, "Church in the House," 13.

173. Gehring, *House Church and Mission*, 27.

Therefore, the meaning of house church in the New Testament is the regular gathering of a small Christian assembly (people) in someone's domestic residence (place) where the common practices of the early church are observed (purpose). These practices include the sharing of leadership, shepherding of families, searching of Scriptures, and saturating of cities. To know more about the purpose of gathering in a house church setting, this study now proceeds to its discussion of the content of house church practices which are extant primarily in the biblical literature, particularly the New Testament.

C. Content of New Testament House Church Practices

While methods change over the course of time, principles do not as they are timeless and trans-cultural. As the first part of this book culminates, the principles derived from the four New Testament house church practices will be tackled and, in the last section, will be appropriated for contemporary small groups in the Philippine context.

Who were the leaders of the house churches in the New Testament and what lessons were they teaching their members? What defined the house church learners in the New Testament and how were these members described in Scripture in terms of their status, gender, and number? How strategic were the locations of the house churches? These questions on house church leaders and learners (people), house church lessons (purpose), and house church locations (place) will be answered in the discussion of the four New Testament house church practices below – namely the sharing of leadership, shepherding of families, searching of Scriptures, and saturating of cities.

1. House Church Leaders: Sharing of Leadership

Is there a way to trace the leadership of the house churches and their practices in the New Testament? As Malherbe explains,

> Our information on the organizational relationship between these house churches in one location is not unambiguous. On the one hand, in Jerusalem the leaders of the church had responsibility for the whole church in the area. The same situation is also reflected in Crete, where elders were to be appointed in every town (Titus 1:5). On the other hand, on the first missionary journey Paul and

Barnabas appointed elders in every church they had established (Acts 14:23).[174]

The leadership of the Jerusalem church by the apostles, particularly Peter and James, is apparent in the book of Acts, as are the leadership roles Paul bestowed on the elders of the Greco-Roman churches as recorded, primarily, in his epistles. As Aubrey Malphurs and Will Mancini recount, "At that time the apostles and others were in the beginning stages of constructing the church and thus building their leadership-development processes."[175] However, since the church planting of Paul's missionary journeys was done predominantly in domestic residences, it is noteworthy to ask whether the apostle's appointed elders could also be the householders. In the words of Filson, "The house church was the training ground for the Christian leaders who were to build the church after the loss of 'apostolic' guidance, and everything in such a situation favored the emergence of the host as the most prominent and influential member of the group. The strong leader of one such group might assume leadership throughout a city or section."[176] Likewise Meeks cites that the household head, as usually expected by the society, had a certain power over the group including some legal responsibility.[177] Accordingly, it is possible that some of the elders could have been the householders with whom Paul practiced the *sharing of leadership* within the house setting of the church through his apostolic letters and visits.

If the presupposition of this book is correct, the *sharing of leadership* would be a common practice in the New Testament house church. The transient apostles shared the local leadership of individual house churches with the ordinary volunteer workers and, practically, with the trained householders who even included women. Osiek and Balch point out that the *domus* owners, regardless of their gender, had absolute authority over anyone residing or worshiping within their premises.[178] The two authors further expound that

> mostly in the Pauline letters and in Acts . . . a number of people have an *oikos* in which a Christian group can meet, which presupposes a certain economic and social level: the mother of John Mark in Jerusalem (Acts 12:12), Prisca and Aquila at Rome and/or Ephesus (Rom 16:5; 1 Cor 16:19), Nympha (Col 4:15),

---

174. Malherbe, "Household of God," 16.
175. Malphurs and Mancini, *Building Leaders*, 95.
176. Filson, "Significance of the Early House Churches," 112.
177. Meeks, *First Urban Christians*, 76.
178. Osiek and Balch, *Families in the New Testament World*, 215.

Philemon (Philemon 2), and the merchant Lydia (Acts 16:15, 40). In these cases, the host or hostess of the group became patron of the group, with all the social expectations accompanying patronage of groups. The patron provided material subvention, including in this case regular hospitality and social protection and advancement, while clients owed honor and gratitude.[179]

The obvious practical reason is that the apostles could not do the awesome tasks by themselves with their very limited number and presence. Thus, there was a need to delegate or share the leadership of the house church with qualified members. How is the leadership formation of the lay people (non-apostles) depicted in the Pauline epistles? The leadership formation in Pauline house churches in Thessalonica appears to pertain to "those who labor diligently [κοπιάω] . . . and have charge over [προΐστημι] . . . and give instruction [νουθετέω]" (1 Thess 5:12–14). Likewise, in Corinth Paul refers to "everyone who helps in the work [συνεργέω] and labors [κοπιάω]" (1 Cor 16:15–16). In Colossae, the apostle calls "Philemon [a] fellow worker [συνεργός] . . . and Archippus [a] fellow soldier [συστρατιώτης]" (Phlm 1–2). Lastly, in Philippi he addresses "the overseers and deacons [ἐπισκόποις καὶ διακόνοις]" in his letter (Phil 1:1) which is an example of the "plurality of bishops at one location." Gehring emphasizes that the "organizational structures [such as the one indicated in Phil 1:1] can be considered further indications of a house church in the full sense."[180] It can be observed, then, that the hierarchical leadership structure is absent in many house churches. Gehring, however, emphasizes that leadership in its social sense as a homeowner had social power and authority.[181]

In addition, several women were tapped for leadership functions in the Pauline house churches in Cenchreae, Rome, Laodicea, and Philippi. Paul called Phoebe "a servant [or helper] of the church which is at Cenchreae" (Rom 16:1–2). In Rome, the apostle regards Prisca, Mary, Tryphaena, Tryphosa, and Persis as "workers in the Lord" and Junia[182] as a "fellow prisoner" (Rom 16:3–7,

---

179. Osiek and Balch, 97.

180. Gehring, *House Church and Mission*, 27.

181. Gehring, 284.

182. Some versions (NASB, ASV, RSV, and NIV) prefer the masculine form "Junias," whereas others (ESV, HCSB, and KJV) prefer the feminine name "Junia." One cannot be definite in identifying whether the Greek word *Iounian* refers to a man or a woman. But as Moo argues, it is more likely that "Junia" is the correct rendering since the masculine name is much more rare than the feminine one. Like Prisca and Aquila, Andronicus and Junia were perhaps a husband-and-wife team, commissioned as a missionary couple (Moo, *Encountering the Book of Romans*, 196). Furthermore, Stott points out that Ἰουνίαν "could be the accusative of either Junias (masculine) or Junia (feminine). Commentators are agreed that the latter is much more

12). Julia and again Prisca were addressed as hosts of the saints/church in Rome (Rom 16:3, 5, 15). The same applies to Nympha as a host in Laodicea (Col 4:15) and Lydia in Philippi (Acts 16:14–15, 40). Finally, Euodia and Syntyche were described as women who "shared [Paul's] struggle in the cause of the gospel" in Philippi (Phil 4:2–3). Alexander Faivre states, "The services performed by women were sufficiently important for them to be regarded as true ministries, even though they had no precise title or status. These women ministers did not constitute a clergy or a caste, but continued simply to be part of the people."[183] As Paul declared to the Galatian Christians: "There is neither Jew nor Greek, there is neither slave nor free man, there is neither male nor female; for you are all one in Christ Jesus" (Gal 3:28).

2. House Church Learners: Shepherding of Families

Who comprised the house church learners in the New Testament and how were these members described in Scripture in terms of their status, gender, and number? The *shepherding of families* is another common practice in the New Testament house church due to the value of the household to Christianity which Jesus himself exemplified. As Christopher J. H. Wright writes, "It is clear from the Gospels that Jesus had a positive appreciation of the family, both in terms of marriage, children and the responsibilities of parenthood."[184] Furthermore, the predominant biblical image of a church as a "household" depicts the significance of family and how the church should function as a spiritual family. Some of the biblical references are as follows: "the household of the faith" (Gal 6:10); "the household of God" (1 Tim 3:15; Eph 2:19; 1 Pet 4:17); "house/household of Christ" (Heb 3:6, see HCSB); "family of God" (1 Tim 5:1–2; Eph 3:14; 2 Cor 6:18; Rom 12:10; Matt 12:49–50); and "the bride of Christ" (Eph 5:22–32; 2 Cor 11:2–3; Rev 19:7–9; 21:2–11). This is so because the church is a social structure patterned after the household. As Wright points out, "The use of family and household imagery for the local churches was, of course, greatly facilitated by the historical fact that many of them originated as converted households and met in homes."[185] That explains then why the leaders leading the spiritual households are required to manage their own households well (1 Tim 3:4–5; Titus 1:6).

---

likely to be correct, since the former name is unknown elsewhere" (Stott, *Message of Romans*, 396). This study, thus, takes the feminine translation.

183. Faivre, *Emergence of the Laity in the Early Church*, 12.

184. Wright, *Old Testament Ethics*, 356.

185. Wright, 359.

The early households were also essential in Paul's ministry. Filson states that "the large part played by the house churches affords a partial explanation of the great attention paid to family life in the letters of Paul . . . both in Jewish and Gentile life religious observance had been largely centered in the home."[186] As each of the households is properly shepherded by the house church leader and grows spiritually, they can also repeat the same process with other neighboring families until their influence is felt in the entire community. The individual household as defined by Meeks "was the basic unit in the establishment of Christianity in the city, as it was, indeed, the basic unit of the city itself."[187] The change in a city begins in the change of individual families.

There are records of some families in the New Testament who appear to be involved in house churches: the household of Prisca and Aquila (Rom 16:3, 5; 1 Cor 16:19); the household of Aristobulus (Rom 16:10); the household of Narcissus (Rom 16:11); the household of Stephanas (1 Cor 1:16; 16:15–18); the household of Philemon and Apphia (Phlm 1–2); the household of Nympha (Col 4:15); the household of Caesar (Phil 4:22); and the household of Lydia (Acts 16:14–15, 40).[188] Additionally, there are also New Testament references to certain individuals believing in God along with their *oikos* or family members, as in the case of the Philippian jailer (Acts 16:31–34); synagogue ruler Crispus (Acts 18:8); and also Onesiphorus (2 Tim 1:16; 4:19).[189] Malherbe surmises that Paul appears to strategically utilize households as centers for the longevity of his missionary work since each family is a captive audience for his preaching and as a result is saved by the gospel as a whole.[190] As Elliott concludes, "It was the context of the household and the family which served as the chief locus, focus, and basis of early Christian ministry and mission."[191]

Finally, what constituted a family in a house church and what was the focus of shepherding in every household? In his other writing, Malherbe explains that in the New Testament times the household was recognized as a basic social unit, and it comprised not only members of the immediate family, but also slaves, freedmen, servants, laborers and sometimes business associates and tenants.[192] Likewise, Oakes believes that "many of the likely relationships between people in the group would [be that of a] friend, neighbor, relative,

---

186. Filson, "Significance of the Early House Churches," 109.

187. Meeks, *First Urban Christians*, 29.

188. Young, *Analytical Concordance to the Bible*, 500.

189. Osiek and Balch, *Families in the New Testament World*, 97–98.

190. Malherbe, "Household of God," 14.

191. Elliott, "Philemon and House Churches," 150.

192. Malherbe, *Social Aspects of Early Christianity*, 69.

customer, supplier, casual employee, (informal) client."[193] Such is the case because in a Greco-Roman house there is no distinction in the use of space for domestic (family) and public (work) use. Best further remarks,

> The members of the church were drawn from all levels of society. Some were wealthy enough to own slaves (Phlm 15–16), to have positions of importance in the secular community (Acts 13:12; 17:12, 34; Rom 16:23), and to have houses large enough for meetings to be held in them (Acts 18:7; Rom 16:5; 1 Cor 16:19; Col 4:15). These were a minority, however (1 Cor 1:26). Many Christians were slaves (1 Cor 7:20–24; Col 3:22–25; Eph 6:5–9; 1 Pet 2:18–25), but it would be wrong to assume the majority were. . . . Although Jesus' disciples had all been Jews, by the end of the first century the vast majority in the churches were Gentiles.[194]

In addition, Filson writes, "On many occasions entire households, including, no doubt, slaves in some instances, came into the church as a unit (cf. Acts 16:33). The natural result was special attention to proper family relationships among Christians."[195] Thus, the household structures in the New Testament are evident in Colossians 3:18–4:1 and Ephesians 5:21–6:9, and corresponding instructions on family relationships were written, particularly, for "the husbands and wives relationship" in Colossians 3:18–19 and Ephesians 5:21–33; "the parents and children relationship" in Colossians 3:20–21 and Ephesians 6:1–4; and "the masters and slaves relationship" in Colossians 3:22–4:1 and Ephesians 6:5–9. Such instructions given by Paul to the family members through his Colossian and Ephesian epistles were intended to guide them, which is an important aspect of shepherding the flock through feeding, leading, and caring for them using God's Word (cf. John 10:11, 15–16, 27; 21:15–17; Acts 20:28; Heb 13:20; 1 Pet 2:25; 5:2–4).

As each of the families in the New Testament gathered together in homes to devote themselves to the apostles' teaching, it can be assumed that the children were also present and were probably participating in the spiritual activities led by their parents. Stott states, "We know that they [Roman believers] met in houses or household churches, for Paul probably refers to such six times (Rom 16:5, 10, 11, 14, 15; cf. 23). How was the membership of these determined? We cannot suppose that they met according to sex or rank, so that there were

---

193. Oakes, *Reading Romans in Pompeii*, 93.
194. Best, "Church," 169–170.
195. Filson, "Significance of the Early House Churches," 109–110.

> Now I praise you because you remember me in everything and hold firmly to the traditions, just as I delivered them to you. (1 Cor 11:2)

> So then, brethren, stand firm and hold to the traditions which you were taught, whether by word of mouth or by letter from us. (2 Thess 2:15)

> Was it from you that the word of God first went forth? Or has it come to you only? If anyone thinks he is a prophet or spiritual, let him recognize that the things which I write to you are the Lord's commandment. But if anyone does not recognize this, he is not recognized. (1 Cor 14:36–38)

It is important to note then, that the apostles "understood that their own teaching was handed down from the Lord as authentic 'tradition,' and made it clear to their listeners and readers that they themselves were held responsible to heed apostolic teaching as from the Lord."[202] As Del Birkey defines, "The *apostles' tradition* is simply all the teachings of Jesus formed into the apostles' teaching or doctrine so that essential truth and practices are summarized and 'handed down' for understanding, experience and edification."[203]

It is the apostles' duty to search and teach the "pure" Word of God to the household leaders who in return will reiterate the same process among their own family members. The preservation of the gospel tradition is crucial prior to its propagation. The faithful and proper handling of God's Word is a serious responsibility that every household teacher must undertake. It can either make or break one's family ministry and was proven to be the best defense against false teachings proliferating in early Christian households. Filson notes that "the party strife in the apostolic age [was primarily caused by] the deep doctrinal differences which divided one group from another in Corinth and other centers."[204] Searching and teaching a sound doctrine was a deterrent against false teachers. At the same time, it was both for promoting order and pursuing godliness in the household of faith: "All Scripture is inspired by God and profitable for teaching, for reproof, for correction, for training in righteousness; so that the man of God may be adequate, equipped for every good work" (2 Tim 3:16–17).

---

202. Birkey, *House Church Book*.
203. Birkey.
204. Filson, "Significance of the Early House Churches," 110.

4. House Church Locations: Saturating of Cities

Cities are perceived negatively by many Christians as bringing out the worst of human nature while Scripture sees it differently. How does God's Word view the city and the mission to saturate it with the gospel? Beginning in the Old Testament, the book of Genesis pictures cities as places of violence, rebellion and perversion (e.g. Cain the murderer and first city-builder in chapter 4; Tower of Babel in 11:1–9; and Sodom and Gomorrah in chapter 19). On the other hand, cities are also depicted as places of refuge and peace (cf. Num 35:6; Ps 107:4–8). In his book *Center Church: Doing Balanced, Gospel-Centered Ministry in Your City*, Timothy J. Keller describes the city as a walled place and protected space of safety (Num 35:6), diversity (Acts 13:1), and productivity (cf. Gen 4:11).[205] As Keller points out, "the city form, in service to God, actually fulfills the will of God for human life."[206]

The Bible even references a vision of the City of God (cf. Heb 11:8–10). If the Tower of Babel was erected "to make a name for ourselves" (Gen 11:4); the City of Jerusalem is built as the dwelling place for God's Name (1 Kgs 14:21): "God's city is different from human cities (like Babel) where skyscrapers are designed for their builders' own prosperity and prominence. By contrast, God's city is 'the joy of the whole earth' (Ps 48:2) . . . [so] the urban society in God's plan is based on service, not on selfishness."[207] Thus, while cities can be provocative instruments to instigate human uprising against God, they can also be a positive means of social transformation for his name's sake.

Furthermore, in his sermon on Mars Hill, Paul proclaims to the Athenians, "He made from one man every nation of mankind to live on all the face of the earth, having determined their appointed times and the boundaries of their habitation, that they would seek God, if perhaps they might grope for Him and find Him, though He is not far from each one of us" (Acts 17:26–27). Since the earth has been lovingly crafted as a dwelling place for people, God undoubtedly anticipated the development of the city.[208] Thus, based on the New Testament's perspective, urban growth should not be mistaken as utterly evil since providentially that has been a part of God's redemptive purpose so

---

205. Keller, *Center Church*, 136–138.

206. Keller, 140.

207. Keller, 140–141.

208. Dawson, *Taking Our Cities for God*, 44.

"men should seek Him and reach out for Him."[209] Indeed, God is ultimately the architect of the city and is actively involved in it. Where there is a city there are people whom God desires to redeem. Finally, when the promised Holy City (the new Jerusalem) comes down out of heaven, God's people can be completely home at last and will worship him there forever. Thus, while God's salvation plan started in the garden (Gen 3:21–24), it will culminate in a city (Rev 3:12; 21:2; Heb 12:22).

Having established that the Bible in general has a high regard for the city, would saturating it with the gospel be a good strategy in reaching the world for Christ? Why is there a need to concentrate primarily on cities and not suburbs? As Best observes, "The first churches were all in cities; it was some time before Christianity spread into rural areas."[210] Similarly, Keller believes that "the early church was largely an *urban* movement that won the people of the Roman cities to Christ, while most of the rural countryside remained pagan. Because the Christian faith captured the cities, however, it eventually captured the ancient Greco-Roman world."[211] Lastly, Bob Roberts Jr. also concurs that "the spread of the gospel has historically always been tied to the cities. From there it spreads out across the rest of the world. Cities are linked in almost every way."[212] Hence, "it is easy to see that the *mission strategy of the early church was to evangelize the city.* It is no exaggeration to say that in Acts the church is almost exclusively associated with the city."[213] John Elliott enumerates the following cities, recorded in the book of Acts and the Pauline letters, where the progression of the Christian mission can be followed from the households of Jerusalem in the East to those of Rome in the West:

> Jerusalem and Judea (Acts 1:12–14; 2:1–4, 42–47; 4:23–31; 5:42;
>   8:3; 9:43; 12:12–19)
> Caesarea (Acts 10:1–11:18)
> Damascus (Acts 9:10–19)
> Philippi (Acts 16:11–15, 25–34)
> Thessalonica (Acts 17:5–6)

---

209. Roger Greenway, "World Urbanization and Missiological Education," in *Missiological Education for the Twenty-First Century: The Book, the Circle, and the Sandals,* ed. J. Dudley Woodberry, Charles Van Engen, and Edgar J. Elliston (Maryknoll, NY: Orbis, 1996), 145–146, cited in Keller, *Center Church,* 160.

210. Best, "Church," 170.

211. Keller, *Center Church,* 149.

212. Roberts, *Multiplying Church,* 130.

213. Leland Ryken, James C. Wilhoit, and Tremper Longman III, eds., *Dictionary of Biblical Imagery* (Downers Grove, IL: InterVarsity Press, 1998), 153, cited in Keller, *Loving the City,* 130.

Corinth: The three households of Stephanas (1 Cor 1:16; 16:15–18),
    Gaius (1 Cor 1:14; Rom 16:23), and Crispus (Acts 18:8; 1 Cor
    1:14)

Cenchreae: The patron Phoebe (Rom 16:1–2)

Troas (Acts 20:7–12)

Ephesus (1 Cor 16:19; 2 Tim 4:19)

Colossae: Philemon's household

Laodicea (Col 4:15)

Rome: The five households of Aquila and Prisca (Rom 16:3–5;
    Acts 18:2), Aristobulus (Rom 16:10), Narcissus (Rom 16:11),
    and the groups mentioned in Rom 16:14–15.[214]

As demonstrated by this network of households, it is evident that the *saturating of cities* was a common practice for the New Testament house church. This appears to be in utter obedience to what Jesus told His apostles to do: "You will receive power when the Holy Spirit has come upon you; and you shall be my witnesses both in Jerusalem, and in all Judea and Samaria, and even to the remotest part of the earth" (Acts 1:8). Based on the Lord's Great Commission in Matthew 28:18–20, Rodney Stark points out that "if the goal is to 'make disciples of all nations,' missionaries need to go where there are many potential converts, which is precisely what Paul did. His missionary journeys took him to major cities such as Antioch, Corinth, and Athens, with only occasional visits to smaller communities such as Iconium and Laodicea."[215]

Likewise, Osiek and Balch affirm that "Paul's mission was an urban one, and much effort has been expended . . . to understand the Pauline house churches in the context of a Greco-Roman city."[216] Filson postulates "that when Paul began missionary work in a city, one of his first objectives was the winning of a household which could serve as the nucleus and center of his further work."[217] As mentioned earlier, Paul's house church learners were undoubtedly a family, as that was the focus and primary strategy in his urban ministry. Moreover, Filson notes that, as a missionary, Paul's practical means for attaining a venue

---

214. Elliott, "Philemon and House Churches," 149. Oakes also notes, "'The assembly in the house' of Prisca and Aquila (16:5) is a craftworker-led house church. 'The brothers and sisters with' Asyncritos et al. (16:14) are presumably another house church, as are 'all the holy ones with' Philologos, Julia and the others (16:15). 'Those belonging to Aristobulus' (16:10) sounds like predominantly slave house church, as does 'those who belong to Narcissus who are in the Lord' (16:11)" (Oakes, *Reading Romans in Pompeii*, 79).

215. Stark, *Cities of God*, 25–26.

216. Osiek and Balch, *Families in the New Testament World*, 5.

217. Filson, "Significance of the Early House Churches," 111.

in a city "was to win a household with a home large enough to serve as a center of Christian activity. . . . He had a place and a function for the man of means."[218] That the Apostle Paul's ministry seems to be intentionally centered around creating house churches to gain access to the city is explicated by Gehring:

> An integral part of his center missional outreach usually consisted of a prolonged stay in someone's house at a given location (cf. Corinth, Ephesus). These houses played an important role in the context of Paul's evangelistic ministry by naturally opening the door to a whole network of relationships. Householders were able to create an immediate audience for Paul by inviting their friends, relatives, and clientele. As the guest of the head of the household, Paul was automatically an insider and as such enjoyed the trust not only of the householder but of the entire household and everyone connected with it as well. Thus, within a very short time after becoming the guest in someone's home, Paul had a relatively large number of high-quality contacts for one-on-one conversations and his evangelistic meetings.[219]

The cities with demonstrable house churches in the New Testament are as follows: Philippi (Acts 16:11–15, 25–34), Thessalonica (Acts 17:1–9), Corinth (Acts 18:1–11), Troas (Acts 20:6–12), Ephesus (1 Cor 16:19), Rome (Rom 16:3, 5), Colossae (Phlm 1–2, 21–22), Laodicea (Col 4:15), and – it's implied – Cenchreae (Rom 16:1–2). Is it remarkable, then, that Paul's missionary journeys, as he was guided by the Spirit, did not revolve aimlessly around the major cities of Roman Empire? Roland Allen notes that "all the cities . . . in which he [Paul] planted churches were centers of Roman administration, of Greek civilization, of Jewish influence, or of some commercial importance."[220] Athens in particular was an *intellectual* center (Acts 17), Corinth a *commercial* center (Acts 18), Ephesus a *religious* center (Acts 19), and Rome itself a *political* and *military* center (Acts 28). John Stott observes that "it seems to have been Paul's deliberate policy to move purposefully from one strategic city-center to the next."[221]

As Keller further explains, "By reaching the city, Paul reached all segments of society. . . . This suggests that if the gospel is unfolded at the urban center,

---

218. Filson, 111.

219. Gehring, *House Church and Mission*, 188.

220. Allen, *Missionary Methods*, 13.

221. John R. W. Stott, *The Message of Acts: The Spirit, the Church, and the World* (Downers Grove, IL: InterVarsity Press, 1994), 293, cited in Keller, *Loving the City*, 130.

you can effectively reach the region and the surrounding society."[222] Keller is also convinced that "Paul and other Christian missionaries went to great cities because when Christianity was planted there, it spread regionally (cities were the centers of transportation routes); it also spread globally (cities were multiethnic, international centers, and converts took the gospel back to their homeland); and finally it more readily affected the culture (the centers of learning, law, and government were in the cities)."[223] Thus, the genius of the Pauline strategy in saturating cities helped Christianity propagate widely until its followers had grown to almost half the population of the Roman Empire in just three centuries.[224] Indeed, saturating cities with the gospel is the best approach in winning more lost for Christ! As Stark ultimately upholds:

> Christianity did not grow because of miracle working in the marketplaces (although there may have been much of that going on), or because Constantine said it should, or even because the martyrs gave it such credibility. It grew because Christians constituted an intense community. . . . And the primary means of its growth was through the united and motivated efforts of the growing numbers of Christian believers, who invited their friends, relatives, and neighbors to share the "good news."[225]

Overall, this study, therefore, finds that the concept of *oikos* in the New Testament as a house or household has not only architectural and sociological importance but also ecclesiological significance (as a house church) in terms of the expansion of Christianity in the Greco-Roman world during the early centuries. The first-century οἶκος was intentionally used by the Lord for his ἐκκλησία due to its convenience, suitability, availability, security and privacy – and for its being strategic, foundational, and timeless.[226] As Filson concludes,

> It thus appears that the house church was a vital factor in the church's development during the first century, and even in later generations. It provided the setting in which the primitive Christians achieved a mental separation from Judaism before the actual open break occurred. It gave added importance to the effort to Christianize family relationships. It explains in part the

---

222. Keller, *Center Church*, 149.

223. Keller, 154.

224. Stark, *Rise of Christianity*, 7–9.

225. Stark, 208.

226. Castillo, "Church in Thy House," 56–57.

proneness of the apostolic church to divide. It helps gain a true understanding of the influential place of families of means in what has sometimes been regarded as a church of the dispossessed. It points us to the situation in which there were developed leaders to succeed apostolic workers.[227]

227. Filson, "Significance of the Early House Churches," 112.

3

The Church and Small Groups in the Twenty-First Century

After focusing on biblical and historical studies in chapter 2 (the first half of this book), chapter 3 (the second half) culminates with doctrinal and practical aspects of this theological study.

What are the various concepts of the church today and of the contemporary small group? How is the context of the first-century Greco-Roman house church similar to and different from the context of twenty-first century Filipino small groups? How can the content of New Testament house church practices be appropriated for the twenty-first century small group? What is the content of contemporary small group theology? These are the key questions that will be answered in the concluding part of this chapter.

A. Concepts of a Church and a Small Group

To understand properly what a small group is, we begin first with the proper understanding of what a church is in the twenty-first century.

1. Twenty-First Century Church

Erickson correctly observes that "the church is at once a very familiar and a very misunderstood topic."[1] Most Christians today understand "church" almost exclusively as a church building when in fact the entire New Testament never uses the term in that sense. Some Christian leaders even compromise their belief and drift away from the biblical teaching for the sake of promoting

---

1. Erickson, *Christian Theology*, 1026.

their church (the church building) more than Christ. John F. MacArthur Jr. notices that

> the church has changed a great deal over the centuries. It has become complex and businesslike. Today it is a massive organization with denominations, commissions, committees, councils, boards, and programs. It quite often functions like a business rather than a body, a factory rather than a family, and a corporation rather than a community. Churches have become entertainment centers, giving performances to placid piles of unproductive churchgoers. Almost all such devices are geared to get people into the church but don't do anything with them once they come.[2]

Why is this happening today? What are the contributing factors that led to the major shift from the concept of church as "*believers* gathering together to worship" to a "*building*" where people merely attend the service? Erickson offers an explanation to such a phenomenon:

> Part of this misunderstanding results from the multiple usages of the term *church*. Sometimes it is used with respect to an architectural structure, a building. Frequently it is used to refer to a particular body of believers; we might, for example, speak of the First Methodist Church. At other times, it is used to refer to a denomination, a group set a part by some distinctive; for instance, the Presbyterian church or the Lutheran church. In addition to the confusion generated by the multiple usages of the term *church*, there is evidence of confusion at a more profound level – a lack of understanding of the basic nature of the church.[3]

Consequently, the churches of today grow and multiply slowly. Missionary researcher Todd M. Johnson reports, "At the end of the 20th century, just over 33% of the world's population professes to be Christians. Contrary to the optimistic outlook 100 years ago of a 'Christian century,' this percentage is actually slightly lower than it was in 1900."[4] Have the first two decades of the twenty-first century seen any significant progress in this regard?

---

2. MacArthur, *Master's Plan for the Church*, 83.

3. Erickson, *Christian Theology*, 1026.

4. Johnson, "Christianity at 2000," 33. Todd Johnson is a full-time missionary researcher and is presently Director of the World Evangelization Research Center (WERC) in Richmond, Virginia, USA. All statistics in his article are documented in D. Barrett, G. Kurian, and T.

One of the most startling accounts of early Christian effectiveness is reported by Stark in his book *The Rise of Christianity*. He details how the early Christian movement grew from several thousand followers to some thirty million – about half the population of the Roman Empire – within just three hundred years.[5] This is the exact opposite of what is currently happening among churches. There is a huge difference between early Christianity and today's Christianity in terms of growth. What is urgently needed now is to go back to the ancient *Word* instead of focusing too much on making it relevant to the postmodern *world*. Any departure of the church from what is right and true will only result in the church's regress and death. As Hans-Ruedi Weber bluntly expresses,

> Our terminology betrays us: We speak of "going to church," our traditional evangelism is an invitation "to come to church," and in our common understanding "church workers" are those whose work is especially linked with the church building or church institution. Even the use of the term "laity" has been affected by this church-building-centered teaching: too often a "good, active layman" is understood to mean nothing else than a man or woman who spends much time, money and energy in and on church buildings and church organizations.[6]

In his book *Total Church Life: How to Be a First Century Church in a 21st Century World*, Darrell W. Robinson writes, "Our world has all but forgotten what church is all about – to have many churches. The greatest need in our time is for 'the church to be the church,' a first-century church in a twenty-first-century world. It is time that the church returned to the principles of the New Testament. Let the church be the church getting a vision from God for its life and mission."[7] Hence, there is a need today to shift from "doing" church to "being" the church that Christ wants us to be.

The New Testament church in the book of Acts presents a significant contrast when compared to today's church:

> They were continually devoting themselves to the apostles' teaching and to fellowship, to the breaking of bread and to prayer. Everyone kept feeling a sense of awe; and many wonders and signs

---

Johnson, *World Christian Encyclopedia: A Comparative Survey of Churches and Religions in the Modern World*, 2nd ed., Oxford: Oxford University Press, 2001.

5. Stark, *Rise of Christianity*, 7–9.

6. Weber, "Church in the House," 10.

7. Robinson, *Total Church Life*, 9.

were taking place through the apostles. And all those who had believed were together and had all things in common; and they began selling their property and possessions and were sharing them with all, as anyone might have need. Day by day continuing with one mind in the temple, and breaking bread from house to house, they were taking their meals together with gladness and sincerity of heart, praising God and having favor with all the people. And the Lord was adding to their number day by day those who were being saved. (Acts 2:42–47)

It is apparent from the passage above how the church today has drifted from the New Testament distinctive. There was a sudden shift from a people-to-people setting to a program-to-people agenda when the church started to focus more on meeting in church buildings rather than private homes. The bottom line of all this is a wrong understanding of what a church should be as defined in Scripture. Consequently, there is a need to define the church theologically from a conservative, evangelical point of view based on the New Testament concept of ἐκκλησία.

a. Meaning of church today

(1) Theological definition

In the words of Erickson, a tentative theological definition of the church is "the whole body of those who through Christ's death have been savingly reconciled to God and have received new life."[8] According to Grudem it is "the community of all true believers for all time."[9] In the doctrinal statement on "The Church" as contained in *The 2000 Baptist Faith and Message*, the church is described comprehensively in the following way:

> A New Testament church of the Lord Jesus Christ is an autonomous local congregation of baptized believers, associated by covenant in the faith and fellowship of the gospel; observing the two ordinances of Christ, governed by His laws, exercising the gifts, rights, and privileges invested in them by His Word, and seeking to extend the gospel to the ends of the earth. Each congregation operates under the Lordship of Christ through democratic processes. In such a congregation each member is responsible and accountable to Christ as Lord. Its scriptural officers are pastors and deacons.

---

8. Erickson, *Christian Theology*, 1034.
9. Grudem, *Systematic Theology*, 853.

While both men and women are gifted for service in the church, the office of pastor is limited to men as qualified by Scripture. The New Testament speaks also of the church as the Body of Christ which includes all of the redeemed of all the ages, believers from every tribe, and tongue, and people, and nation.[10]

(2) New Testament concept

While there were various biblical metaphors used earlier in this study to describe a church, the New Testament predominantly depicts the church as "God's house" (Heb 3:6); "God's spiritual house" (1 Pet 2:5); "God's building" (1 Cor 3:9; Eph 2:22); "the pillar and support of the truth" (1 Tim 3:15); "the household of God" (1 Tim 3:15; Eph 2:19); "the household of the faith" (Gal 6:10); "family of God" (1 Tim 5:1–2; 2 Cor 6:18); and "the bride of Christ" (Eph 5:32; 2 Cor 11:2; Rev 19:7; 21:2). The reason for this is that the church is a social structure patterned after the household. The nature of the church is best expressed in a family-like setting since the most conducive and common meeting place during the first century to gather God's people for the purpose of worship was in a residential house.

The church in the New Testament, as cited previously, "always denotes a group of people, either all the Christians in a city (Acts 14:23; 1 Cor 1:2; 2 Cor 1:1) or those gathered for worship in a particular house (Rom 16:5; 1 Cor 16:19; [also Col 4:15 and Phlm 2]) or all Christians in all the churches, the whole church (Eph 1:22)."[11] The common concept of ἐκκλησία as used in the Jewish sense is an assembly or congregation of people in general. In the Christian sense, however, the concept of ἐκκλησία in the New Testament is a gathering of believers for worship locally and universally. It is apparent, then, that the New Testament ἐκκλησία was never referred to in Scripture as a "building" but as a "body of believers."

b. Models of churches today

Of the various models of churches today, the three major ones are the traditional church, cell church, and house church.

---

10. Southern Baptist Convention, "The 2000 Baptist Faith and Message." The doctrinal statement on "The Church" is based on the following Scripture references: Matt 16:15–19; 18:15–20; Acts 2:41–42, 47; 5:11–14; 6:3–6; 13:1–3; 14:23, 27; 15:1–30; 16:5; 20:28; Rom 1:7; 1 Cor 1:2; 3:16; 5:4–5; 7:17; 9:13–14; 12; Eph 1:22–23; 2:19–22; 3:8–11, 21; 5:22–32; Phil 1:1; Col 1:18; 1 Tim 2:9–14; 3:1–15; 4:14; Heb 11:39–40; 1 Pet 5:1–4; Rev 2–3; 21:2–3.

11. Best, "Church," 168.

(1) Traditional church

J. D. Payne, a Southern Baptist who claims to be "traditional to the core" uses another word for traditional church which is "*mainstream* local church" or the overwhelming majority of churches.[12] According to Payne, "Many traditional churches identify themselves primarily in terms of their services, events, structures, buildings, and organizations . . . [and as a result they] tend to be program-oriented, event-oriented, or categorically purpose-oriented in their identities."[13] In Payne's study, the term "traditional" depicts the general understanding of the local church as usually gathering every Sunday morning for two hours of worship and devoting a big bulk of its income to facilities and pastor's salaries.[14] Additionally, Payne enumerates the following propensities that can also be observed in traditional churches:

> Pastoral leadership tends to be more positional in orientation and less relational. Evangelism is, many times, one program among many programs of the church and/or is primarily accomplished through the members inviting unbelievers to a worship service where the gospel is shared. The number of members usually far exceeds the number of people who gather weekly for worship and actively use their gifts and talents to build up the church.[15]

(2) Cell church

The cell church as described by David Finnell has cell groups as the focal point of the church, and its church life revolves around the *cells* which gathers in places where members live.[16] Finnell defines cells "as the organization of the body of believers into small groups in order to worship and experience God, minister to one another, and minister to and evangelize the community."[17] Ralph W. Neighbour Jr., whose study focuses on the use of home cell groups, is one of the pioneers of cell group churches. According to Neighbour, "The Cell is the 'Basic Christian Community.' The Church is formed from them and is the sum of them. Cells never grow larger than fifteen people and multiply as

---

12. Payne, *Missional House Churches*, 3, 10. In using the label "traditional," J. D. Payne gives a disclaimer, "I am not saying that all churches that are not house churches are the same, neither am I attempting to polarize churches that are 'house' and churches that are 'traditional.'"

13. Payne, 11.

14. Payne, 10–11.

15. Payne, 11.

16. Finnel, *Cell Group Basic Training*, 9.

17. Finnel, 10.

they reach this figure. There are no other activities which exist in competition with the cells. Everything in the church is an extension of them and flows from their combined strength."[18]

Moreover, Neighbour points out that the 3Cs which encapsulates the cell group church are *cells, congregations,* and *celebrations,* with the first being the key among the three.[19] The two kinds of *cells* are called *shepherd groups* and *share groups.* The shepherd group is designed for the spiritual *feeding* and *caring* of members as they exercise their spiritual gifts to serve and support one another.[20] If the shepherd group, on the one hand, gathers for nurture, the share group, on the other hand, meets for outreach. This second type of cell only starts when three or four members from the shepherd group show the maturity and readiness to meet separately for the sole purpose of *sharing* the gospel with unbelievers.[21]

As the shepherd group or *cell* grows into five groups, a *zone servant* shepherds the five shepherd group leaders. Eventually, when it has multiplied (slowly or quickly depending on its growth rate) into twenty-five groups, the *zone pastor* shepherds the five zone servants and gathers them all together with their respective shepherd group leaders and members as a *congregation.*[22] Neighbour notes that this larger gathering on a regional basis aims to meet for the purpose of equipping or evangelism and, in some cell group churches, also for worship.[23]

Finally, as the congregation turns into 125 shepherd groups the *senior pastor* shepherds the five zone pastors and gathers them all together with their respective zone servants, shepherd group leaders and members in a *celebration.* This third gathering, as Neighbour describes, "is a mass meeting in which all the cells gather for public witness, praise, preaching, and teaching. The city-wide meeting is used for praise and worship, solid Bible teaching, evangelism, and is a vital part of the public witness of the people of God."[24]

How does a cell church differ from a traditional church? Comparing the two, Finnell presents this study in contrast between the traditional church and the cell church:

---

18. Neighbour, *Where Do We Go From Here?*, 194.
19. Neighbour, 194.
20. Neighbour, 194.
21. Neighbour, 194.
22. Neighbour, 195.
23. Neighbour, 195.
24. Neighbour, 196.

Table 3.1 A study in contrast: The traditional church and the cell church[25]

Traditional Church	Cell Church
1. Program centered	1. People centered
2. Building centered	2. Community centered
3. "Come structure"	3. "Go structure"
4. Education-based	4. Ministry-based
5. Inside-focused	5. Outside-focused
6. Professional leadership	6. Lay leadership
7. Confrontational evangelism	7. Relational evangelism

While the traditional church may have aforementioned problems, the same is also true for the cell church. Finnell cites three major weaknesses of the cell church as being doctrinal integrity, emotionalism, and experience-dependence.[26] Due to the decentralization of the cell church, there is a strong tendency for some cell groups to go to extremes doctrinally, emotionally, and experientially.[27] They need direct guidance from their pastors and to maintain proper balance and control by focusing on God's Word. These are important principles that they can learn from the traditional church.

(3) House church

Advocates of the house church movement today include Del Birkey, Lois Barrett, Robert Fitts, Rad Zdero, and Arthur Foster. In his article, Birkey states that the "'house church' refers to an indigenous and self-functioning church small enough to gather together in a home or similar surroundings."[28] Barrett defines it as "a group of people small enough to meet face-to-face, who have covenanted with God and each other to be the church under the authority of Christ and the guidance of the Spirit."[29] A house church according to Fitts can be summarized as follows: a simple church which meets in a house, a center of evangelism which makes discipleship easier and relates to the entire body of Christ, is movable, small, and is the church.[30] But Zdero simply describes

---

25. Table based on David Finnell's comparative study. See Finnell, *Cell Group Basic Training*, 2–8.

26. Neighbour, 15.

27. Neighbour, 15–16.

28. Birkey, "House Church," 70.

29. Barrett, *Building the House Church*, 18.

30. Fitts, *Church in the House*, 39–42.

a house church network in this manner, "the church *is* small groups."[31] It is Foster who gives a more extensive definition of the house church:

> Persons, usually fifteen to twenty in number, [who] form an intentional community, conceived as a small church which is part of the larger whole of the church; the community meets together for the mutual healing, sustaining and guiding of its members, for celebration, fellowship and for mobilizing energies for service beyond the house church. Thus the house church as a part shares fully in the broader aims of the Christian Church as a whole.[32]

In their work *Home Cell Groups and House Churches*, Hadaway, Wright, and DuBose cite that the two kinds of house churches are *autonomous* and *federated*, which may simply reflect different stages of growth. This is how the authors differentiates the two:

> Autonomous groups are formally unrelated to other similar-type groups or churches while federated groups form a cooperative association or committee. . . . The autonomous house may simply be at an earlier stage of maturation without the opportunity to form a second sister congregation. One cannot assume that the autonomous house church desires insulation from other groups. . . . Federated communities constitutes an aggregation of sister congregations. These are not to be confused with home cell groups. . . . [While] cell groups exist as a program of a host church . . . federated house church communities are independent collectivities which relate to each other by agreement. They typically arise outside institutional boundaries, though some may eventually attach themselves to a denomination.[33]

House churches have significant advantages or benefits when compared to other church models. Payne's description of the house church can be summarized as follows: it is more organic and less institutional, more simple and less structured, and contains more participatory worship and less passivity, more community and less acquaintance, and more ministers and less Ministers.[34] Similarly, in his book *Church Planting Movements*, David Garrison lists the following ten benefits of house churches:

---

31. Zdero, *Global House Church Movement*, 5, 127.
32. Foster, *House Church Evolving*, 27.
33. Hadaway, Wright, and DuBose, *Home Cell Groups and House Churches*, 106–107.
34. Payne, *Missional House Churches*, 38–43.

(a) Leadership responsibilities remain small and manageable.

(b) If heresies do occur they are confined by the small size of the house church. Like a leak that appears in the hull of a great ship, the heresy can be sealed off in a single compartment without endangering the whole.

(c) You can't hide in a small group, so accountability is amplified.

(d) Member care is easier, because everyone knows everyone.

(e) Because house church structure is simple, it is easier to reproduce.

(f) Small groups tend to be much more efficient at evangelism and assimilation of new believers.

(g) Meeting in homes positions the church closer to the lost.

(h) House churches blend into the community rendering them less visible to persecutors.

(i) Basing in the home keeps the church's attention on daily life issues.

(j) The very nature of rapidly multiplying house churches promotes the rapid development of new church leaders.[35]

How is a house church to be distinguished from a cell church? As Neighbour compares, "House Churches tend to collect a community of 15–25 people who meet together on a weekly basis. Usually, each house church stands alone . . . [and] they do not recognize any further structure beyond themselves. . . . In contrast, the cell group church recognizes a larger structure for church life. An assembly composed of cells which have networked under a common leader and ministry team is the norm."[36] Moreover, Payne remarks,

> The general answer revolves around the two issues of autonomy and pastoral leadership. Though a house church may be small in membership (this is not always the case), it considers itself fully autonomous, meaning that, under the headship of Christ and the Word, the church makes its own decisions regarding plans, strategies, purchases, leadership, worship expressions, missions, and so on. No overarching authoritative body or board dictates to the local congregation what the church can and cannot do. Though

---

35. Garrison, *Church Planting Movements*, 192–193.
36. Neighbour, *Where Do We Go From Here?*, 203.

many house churches network with other house churches, they still understand themselves to be independent and not dependent on the other churches for oversight.

On the other hand, a cell church may consist of many small home groups (cells), but all of the home groups together comprise the church. No group identifies itself as the church apart from the other groups. These groups are semiautonomous. Each cell makes its own decisions regarding the same aforementioned issues, but they do so in light of all the other cells. The pastoral leadership of the church oversees all of the cells; whereas in a house church network, each house church has its own leadership.[37]

To distinguish the church models from one another, Fitts likens the traditional and the cell churches to a *wheel* and the house church to a *vine*. As a wheel, according to Fitts, "they lie on the ground with spokes going out in all directions from a hub at the center;" whereas, as a vine, "it grows on the ground reaching out its branches in all directions, sending down roots at intervals, and at each interval giving birth to another plant just like itself with the same potential to send out branches which send down roots at intervals."[38] Comparing a traditional and cell church with a house church, Fitts presents their natural tendencies:

Table 3.2 A study in contrast: The traditional/cell church and house church[39]

Traditional Church and Cell Church (like a wheel)	House Church (like a vine)
1. Tends to draw unto itself	1. Tends to release outward
2. Tends to be local	2. Tends to be trans-local
3. Tends toward addition	3. Tends toward multiplication
4. Tends to build one church	4. Tends toward building many churches
5. Tends to restrict missionary vision	5. Tends to promote missionary vision
6. Encompasses the community	6. Encompasses the world
7. Envisions cell groups	7. Envisions churches meeting in houses

In addition, Rad Zdero also contrasts the three classic church models prevalent today. He describes the traditional church as a church *with* small groups and led by one person in a church building. The cell church, he

---

37. Payne, *Missional House Churches*, 13–14.
38. Fitts, *Church in the House*, 69.
39. Table based on Robert Fitt's comparative study. See Fitts, 70–71.

continues, is a church *of* small groups with a pyramid structure and leader's ladder which meets both in a church building and at home. Finally, in a house church, Zdero points out, the church *is* small groups with a flat structure and leadership teams hosted at someone's house.[40]

In his book *Missional House Churches*, Payne notes that house churches have much to teach and learn when compared to traditional churches. On one hand, "traditional churches can learn simplicity, strategies for rapid multiplication, the value of small groups, and biblical and missiological principles of indigenous church planting . . . [since] house churches have much to contribute regarding healthy expressions of fellowship, high levels of accountability and transparency, and their use of money for missions and ministry."[41] On the other hand, according to Payne, house church networks can learn from denominations and traditional churches the value of cooperation for the sake of excelling in missions, benevolence ministries, and biblical (theological) education.[42] Payne introduces the concept of a *missional house church* as a corrective to the house church movement going to the extreme.

c. Missional house church

When J. D. Payne uses the term *missional* in the title of his book, he intends "to distinguish house churches that engage the culture with the gospel, make disciples, and plant churches from those house churches that do not."[43] Payne admits that he utilizes the word quite loosely and clarifies consequently that he does "not mean to imply that the only missional churches are the house churches in [his] study."[44] Hence, it is important to note that Payne's missional house church does not belong to the house church movement. Coming from a conservative, evangelical stance, Payne has the following five-fold disclaimer:

1. He cannot disregard the traditional established local church since he loves it.

2. He does not attempt to "fix" or lead a traditional church to transition to the house church model.

---

40. Zdero, *Global House Church Movement*, 127–128.
41. Payne, *Missional House Churches*, 130.
42. Payne, 130.
43. Payne, 8.
44. Payne, 9.

3. His work is not a declaration that the house church model is the only proper expression of the body of Christ or the answer to the Church's problems.

4. His study does not intend to promote nor oppose house churches, particularly the house church movement in the United States and Canada.

5. He also qualifies that not all house churches consider themselves to be a part of the house church movement. Though it is possible that some of the churches in his study would consider themselves to be part of this movement.[45]

Furthermore, Payne also discusses in his writing the four kinds of people who are typically involved in house churches: (1) "hurting Christians" (who join for therapeutic reasons after having had a bad experience with the established church); (2) "new experience Christians" (who are seeking out the latest and greatest spiritual experience); (3) "anti-establishment Christians" (who moved the church service from a building to a house out of rebellion); and (4) "new believers" (or "missional Christians," which fits the purpose of encouraging house churches to become missional).[46] Of the Christians belonging to the last category, Payne states that many are "not satisfied with, and many do not desire, transfer growth. Not only do they know the commands of the Lord, but they also go to the fields that are ripe for the harvest."[47]

For Payne, "missional churches have within their very DNA a passion to take the gospel to their Jerusalem, Judea, and Samaria, and throughout the world. They believe if they cease to be intentionally and regularly involved in evangelism, then they cease to be a church."[48] Payne concludes that the missional house churches are already widespread in the United States, including many on the West Coast, and, interestingly, their existing house church leaders come from various regions such as the West Coast, East Coast, and the Bible Belt.[49]

The question to be raised now is this: Are the house churches of today (the house church movement and the missional house church) consistent with the New Testament's concept of house church?

---

45. See Payne, 3–4.

46. Payne, 123–125.

47. Payne, 125.

48. Payne, 8.

49. Payne, 119.

d. New Testament house church

It is apparent, as mentioned earlier, that the New Testament οἶκος was referred to in Scripture structurally as a construction, socially as a community, and spiritually as a church. Thus, the meaning of a house church in the New Testament is the regular gathering of a small Christian assembly (people) in someone's domestic residence (place) where the common practices of the early church were observed (purpose) – practices such as the sharing of leadership, shepherding of families, searching of Scriptures, and saturating of cities.

Generally, it seems that the house churches of today are more on par with the biblical concept of house church than the traditional church and the cell church. However, while the house church movement succeeds in the *shepherding of families*, if one looks closely it fails to maintain a proper balance of the other three aforementioned New Testament practices (the *sharing of leadership*, *searching of Scriptures*, and *saturating of cities*). For instance, as an overreaction to traditional church practices, today's house church begins discarding pastors who are equipped to train the laity towards leadership roles. In addition, like the cell groups of the cell church, it also tends to go to extremes doctrinally, emotionally, and experientially since its leader usually lacks biblical (theological) education. Lastly, due to being autonomous and isolated from other churches, its center of evangelism tends to be confined within the four corners of the house. Hence, the house church movement's issues with leadership, doctrinal integrity, and missions should be addressed and resolved.

What the house church movement needs is direct guidance from pastors, partnerships with other evangelical churches, and maintenance of proper balance and control by focusing on God's Word. As mentioned earlier, the house church movement can learn from traditional churches about how to cooperate in order to accomplish tasks such as missions, benevolence ministries, and biblical education. This balanced approach is exactly the one that Payne writes about in his book *Missional House Churches: Reaching our Communities with the Gospel*. Therefore, this study finds Payne's missional house church consistent with the New Testament house church concept.

Having tackled the concepts of the church and of the house church today, this study now proceeds to its discussion on the concepts of contemporary small groups.

2. Twenty-First Century Small Group

House churches were relatively small and yet strategically utilized by God in bringing tremendous growth to the early church during its first three hundred years. Today, God is using another small instrument to accomplish something big for his church: the small group. As McBride recounts,

> The house church remained the most pervasive form of church structure up until the time of Constantine about 274–337 AD – reputedly the first Christian emperor of Rome. From that time on church buildings (basilicas, cathedrals, chapels) began to displace the house church. By around 1250 AD, the Gothic cathedral had reached its pinnacle of popularity. As a result, the erroneous theological perception that the *church was a building, not a body of people* had become commonplace. Since then history has given us a variety of renewal movements that have challenged this perception. Some people, including myself, would argue that another such movement is beginning to catch fire today. The contemporary resurgence of small groups as a tool for renewal and growth is an attempt to enable the church to realize its full potential.[50]

Small groups today are remarkably plentiful and ubiquitous. They are literally everywhere within any Christian circle. The small group has become the byword of every Christian leader and has caught the attention of many. Several seminars have been conducted on small groups with corresponding textbooks and workbooks written about them. Churches today have discovered the secret that *to grow big is to go small*, and that the small gathering is as important as the large assembly. According to Ed Stetzer, "Churches that plan to grow must focus on both the large-group worship gathering and the small group. . . . A church without small groups will often struggle to connect the members of the church with one another."[51] Similarly, Howard A. Snyder cites this important truth:

> A small group of eight to twelve people meeting together informally in homes is the most effective structure for the communication of the gospel in modern secular-urban society. Such groups are better suited to the mission of the church in today's urban world than

---

50. McBride, *How to Lead Small Groups*, 19–20.
51. Stetzer, *Planting Missional Churches*, 218.

are traditional church services, institutional church programs or the mass communication media. Methodically speaking, the small group offers the best hope for the discovery and use of spiritual gifts and for renewal within the church.[52]

Though it appears that the emergence of small groups is a new and innovative phenomenon, James A. Davies reveals that this is not the case. In his article "Small Groups: Are They Really So New?," Davies contends,

> The use of small groups for religious growth and development is not a phenomenon unique to this era. Students of church antiquity know that Baptist, Moravian Brethren, Methodists, Quaker, as well as Lutherans used petite cells for religious nurturing. But church history also contains vivid examples of small conclave care-support systems which emphasized interpersonal relationships. Many current churchmen are robbing themselves of rich theological and pragmatic insights because they fail to comprehend this crucial fact.[53]

In the words of Snyder, "The small group was the basic unit of the church's life during its first two centuries. . . . In fact, the use of small groups of one kind or another seems to be a common element in all significant movements of the Holy Spirit throughout church history."[54] At present, it is important for the church to re-experience what the early Christians discovered, that gathering in small groups is vital to one's Christian life and maturity.[55] Thus, the small group is not just a fad that comes and goes in the course of time. The fact that small groups were present from the very beginning of early Christianity demonstrates that small groups are indispensable – a necessary companion for every church in every century.

Moreover, Snyder presents the eight advantages of the small group structure today: "It is flexible, . . . mobile, . . . inclusive, . . . personal, . . . can grow by division, . . . can be an effective means of evangelism, . . . requires a minimum of professional leadership, [and is] . . . adaptable to the institutional church."[56] As Snyder concludes, "the small group is not an optional method; it

---

52. Snyder, *Problem of Wine Skins*, 139.

53. Davies, "Small Groups," 43.

54. Snyder, *Problem of Wine Skins*, 139–140.

55. Snyder, 140.

56. Snyder, 140–142.

is essential structure . . . [and] the small group can become [the] basic structure in a local church if there is the vision for it and the will to innovate."[57]

a. Meaning of small groups today

A significant question to ask is how to define a small group in the context of a local church. There are various definitions of small groups today as cited by different authors. Howard Snyder simply describes the small group as "the basic church structure."[58] In the same manner, Carl George succinctly defines it as "a face-to-face meeting that is a sub-unit of the over-all fellowship."[59] According to Roberta Hestenes, a teacher in the small group field, "A Christian small group is an intentional, face to face gathering of 3 to 12 people on a regular time schedule with a common purpose of discovering and growing in the possibilities of the abundant life in Christ."[60] Likewise, Neil McBride gives a generic description: "A small group within the church is a voluntary, intentional gathering of three to twelve people regularly meeting together with the shared goal of mutual Christian edification and fellowship."[61] Lastly, Gareth Weldon Icenogle theologically depicts the small group as

> a generic form of human community that is trans-cultural, trans-generational and even transcendent. The call to human gathering in groups is a God-created (ontological) and God-directed (theological) ministry, birthed out of the very nature and purpose of God's being. God as Being exists in community. The natural and simple demonstration of God's communal image for humanity is the gathering of the small group.[62]

The best way to arrive at a correct definition of the small group is to ask the following question: What are the elements that should constitute a church-based small group today, without which a small group could not exist? Davies believes that small groups are to carry out three functions: communicating "biblical content" [focused on propositional truth], providing "community group-life and fellowship" [focused on people], and enabling "introspection

---

57. Snyder, 145, 147.

58. Snyder, 139.

59. George, *Nine Keys to Effective Small Group Leadership*, 10–11.

60. Roberta Hestenes, quoted in Coleman, *Serendipity Training Manual for Groups*, 12.

61. McBride, *How to Lead Small Groups*, 24.

62. Icenogle, *Biblical Foundations for Small Group Ministry*, 13.

and growth" [focused on personal benefits]. Davies states that "balanced groups carefully wed all three of these elements together."[63]

As with the previously discussed biblical terms "church" (ἐκκλησία) and "house/household" (οἶκος), the same three elements must also be present in a church-based small group: (1) people (the "who"); (2) purpose (the "why"); and (3) place (the "where"). First, the *people* gathering (laity and family): the small group leaders are volunteer-based and the small group learners are home-focused. Second, the *purpose* of gathering (study): the small group lessons are Bible-centered. Lastly, the *place* of gathering (city): the small group locations are Spirit-directed. Therefore, a contemporary house-sized small group in a local church setting is the regular gathering of a small Christian assembly composed of a volunteer-based leader and home-focused learners (people) for Bible-centered lessons (purpose) in a Spirit-directed location (place).

b. Models of contemporary small groups

In his Doctor of Ministry project, Jeffrey Wilson used what he calls *seeker small groups*[64] to train and mentor believers to reach those individuals for Christ who were not being reached by other evangelistic efforts. On the other hand, Blake Switzer and Gary Wayne Singleton both focused on the concept of *discipleship groups* in their own research. Switzer's dissertation seeks to show that small groups provide the best tools for discipling postmodern thinkers.[65] Similarly, Singleton's intent was to discover and implement a plan of discipleship, using small groups, which would result in people in the community making decisions for Christ and then maturing into disciples of Christ.[66]

Lyman Coleman's training manual lists the following fifteen small group models: "Study Group Model, Study/Share Group Model, Conveyor Belt Group Model, Hestenes Covenant Group Model, Classic Covenant Group Model, Cell Group Model, Basic Cho Model, Modified Cho Model, Meta Church Growth Model, Membership Class Model, Multiple Group Models, Escalator Group Model, Ministry Team Model, Discipleship Group Model, and Support Group Model."[67] Some of Coleman's small group classifications, however, do not appear to be completely distinct and may not warrant a separate type-description.

---

63. Davies, "Small Groups: Are They Really So New?," 43.
64. Wilson, "Mentoring Leaders as They Evangelize Spiritual Seekers."
65. Switzer, "Use of Small Groups."
66. Singleton, "Utilizing Neighborhood Fellowships."
67. Coleman, *Serendipity Training Manual for Groups*, 33–63.

Robert and Julia Banks, on the other hand, present only two main kinds of small groups: "interest groups" and "action groups." According to these authors, "The first kind of group draws people together around a common interest that they wish to engage in for their own benefit. . . . The second type of group brings people together around a common activity that they wish to pursue for the benefit of others."[68] Lastly, as Stetzer classifies, "Small group organizations include cell groups, home groups, Sunday school classes, and other gatherings that promote relationships in the family of faith."[69]

McBride correctly observes the following: "It seems every author of small groups has his or her list of types of small groups. Most lists are based on a description of the group's *main* activity. For example, study groups, discussion groups, support groups, fellowship groups, or evangelism groups are a few of the more common types."[70] Nevertheless, McBride suggests that models of small groups should be formed on the basis of their particular focus or orientation, which he categorizes into four groups:

> [1] *Process-oriented groups.* This type of group focuses on being a group. . . . Emphasis is placed on group identity, the dynamics of relationships, and the processes necessary to bring these about.
>
> [2] *Content-oriented groups.* This classification includes a variety of Bible study and discussion groups. The main reason for meeting is to study or discuss a biblical passage or topic of mutual relevance.
>
> [3] *Task-oriented groups.* These are "doing" groups. The primary thrust is to accomplish a defined task, job, or assignment, which the members do together.
>
> [4] *Need-oriented groups.* The primary reason underlying this type of group is a common need among the members. Sometimes called support groups or recovery groups, the members meet together for common encouragement and understanding.[71]

Moreover, McBride points out that "no one type of group is best. All serve a purpose and can be effective. Some churches elect to have only one type, such as process or content-oriented groups. But with increasing frequency, larger churches are offering all four types."[72] It is possible that all four types may

---

68. Banks and Banks, *Church Comes Home*, 122–123.

69. Stetzer, *Planting Missional Churches*, 207.

70. McBride, *How to Lead Small Groups*, 64.

71. McBride, 65.

72. McBride, 66.

simply reflect different stages or growth levels of a church-based small group as can be seen in the diagram below:

The "Stairs" Diagram of a Small Group

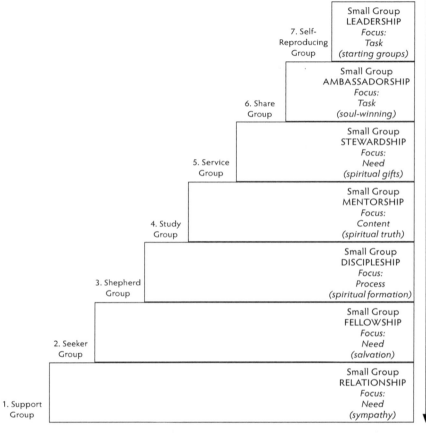

Figure 3.1 Levelling up your small group: The seven levels of a growing small group

As presented above, small groups today have various types and models depending on their focus. However, this book will not pursue models of small groups other than *home groups*. Of all types of home groups, the *growth group* will be the highlight of this study by virtue of its distinctive function in the author's present church context as a pastor of Greenhills Christian Fellowship, which uses growth groups as a church planting strategy.[73]

---

73. In fact, the figure above is what a growth group should be, levelling itself up until it becomes true to its name, a *growing group*. Just like the biological development of any living organism, every small group that is healthy should naturally grow and reproduce. Once this

1) Home groups

Sammy Elliott designed his dissertation to emphasize and encourage the deepening and strengthening of relationships through the use of "small home groups."[74] The term "home groups," sometimes called "house groups," is the generic word for small groups that are home-based, and there are various types of them. Hadaway, Wright, and DuBose accurately describe the five kinds of Christian house groups existing today (which are also summarized in the table below according to their leadership and organizational structures):

> [a] *Home Bible Study Groups* tend to be more cognitively oriented, . . . are primarily designed to instruct in doctrine and theology and thus strengthen one's *knowledge* of Scripture, . . . seek information and enlightenment rather than to foster *koinonia*, . . . may or may not be attached to a host church [and] . . . may or may not designate a leader.[75]

> [b] *Home Fellowship/Share Groups* have a much greater emphasis on the development of close, interpersonal relationships and community (*koinonia*), . . . tend to be aimed more at fellowship and mutual concern for its members, . . . may or may not be tied to a host church, [and] . . . often function without a designated leader.[76]

> [c] *Home Cell Groups* are more tightly organized versions of home fellowship/share groups, . . . are always tied to a central host church which sponsors and oversees them, . . . tend to be aimed at persons within the local church body, . . . are typically evangelistic to the extent that individuals in the group are oriented toward outreach, [and] . . . are led by house group pastors.[77]

> [d] *Base-Satellite Units* are designed to operate with a greater degree of autonomy and self-sufficiency, . . . remain small and

---

level is achieved, that is *Small Group WORSHIP* – the ultimate goal of every small group, for the glory of God. Finally, when this is attained by all individual church-based small groups, the end result is a *growing church*. See appendix 1 on page 177.

74. Elliott, "Building Community through Koinonia Home Groups."

75. Hadaway, Wright, and DuBose, *Home Cell Groups and House Churches*, 84–87.

76. Hadaway, Wright, and DuBose, 88, 90.

77. Hadaway, Wright, and DuBose, 95, 97. Similarly, Joel Comiskey also defines cell groups as "groups of people (normally between five and fifteen), who meet regularly for the purpose of evangelistic outreach and spiritual edification and are committed to participate in the functions of the local church (Acts 2:46)" (Comiskey, "Cell-Based Ministry as a Positive Factor for Church Growth," 3).

informal, must function in an urban society, [and] are tied to the host church [which] may supply a house church pastor who is a paid staff person.[78]

[e] *House Churches* are totally independent and self-contained, . . . more tightly organized, . . . see their primary if not exclusive commitment to be the house church, and membership is more costly in terms of organizational requisites and expectations.[79]

Table 3.3 Leadership and organizational structures of Christian house groups[80]

Group Type	Leadership Structure of Christian House Groups	Organizational Structure of Christian House Groups
Home Bible study	1. May be without designated pastor/leader	1. Not always tied to "host" church
Home fellowship	2. May be without designated pastor/leader	2. Not always tied to "host" church
Home cell group	3. Always with a designated pastor/leader	3. Always tied to "host" church
Base-satellite unit	4. Always with a designated pastor/leader	4. Always tied to "host" church
House church	5. Always with a designated pastor/leader	5. Not always tied to "host" church

2) Growth group

Technically, a growth group can also be classified as a home group since it is primarily home-based. When compared to the five types of home groups in the table above, the growth groups of GCF (which is a traditional church with small groups) generally best fit within the description of the *Home Bible Study*. The reason is the growth group's great emphasis on God's Word[81] (almost akin to a *study group*) which also corresponds to GCF's core value on the *centrality of the Word*. The only difference is found in the leadership and organizational structures: unlike a *Home Bible Study*, the growth group is always with a designated leader and tied to a "host" church.

---

78. Hadaway, Wright, and DuBose, *Home Cell Groups and House Churches*, 102–104.

79. Hadaway, Wright, and DuBose, 105–106.

80. This table appears in Hadaway, Wright, and DuBose, 84.

81. As noted earlier, the GROW in GCF's Growth Group means God's **W**ord, **R**elationships, **O**utreach and **W**orship.

In his book, McBride categorizes growth groups under process-oriented groups, which also includes caring groups, support groups, and covenant groups.[82] As McBride writes, "This type of group focuses on being a group. That is, the central focus is on the spiritual and/or social relationships among the members. What the group does – its meeting format – is a secondary issue. Emphasis is placed on group identity, the dynamics of relationships, and the processes necessary to bring these about."[83]

(a) **Definition.** The growth group model is an important distinctive of the author's church at GCF. What is a growth group? According to GCF's *Growth Group Manual*, "A Growth Group within Greenhills Christian Fellowship is a voluntary, intentional gathering of seven to fifteen people regularly meeting together with the shared goal of fulfilling the basic tasks of the church."[84]

(b) **Mission.** What does the Growth Group Ministry of GCF intend to do? Following every church's mission which is "to make disciples" of all nations as Jesus Christ commissioned the church in Matthew 28:18–20, GCF came up with this mission statement for its growth groups: "We will develop every member of Greenhills Christian Fellowship into maturing and multiplying disciples of the Lord Jesus Christ within the relational context of small groups where the God-given tasks of prayer, outreach, worship, education, and relationship-building are carried out."[85] Hence, based on its mission, a growth group is a combination of McBride's four orientations, combining process (maturing and multiplying disciples), content (education), tasks (prayer, outreach, worship), and need (relationship-building) in a single group.[86]

(c) **Overall Assessment.** As mentioned earlier, I have made some observations during my twenty years of ministry at GCF on the state of its growth groups, and I thereby recommended the urgent need to address certain issues that lessen the efficacy of this key strategy for church planting. In my personal assessment, the church has not developed its growth groups to their full potential in the following areas: leadership, membership, curriculum, and community. Consequently, the growth groups grow slowly and rarely multiply, thereby affecting the birth of more daughter churches.

Based on my findings, some growth groups assign their small group ministry primarily to clergy alone, which causes the scarcity of their *shepherds*.

---

82. McBride, *How to Lead Small Groups*, 65.

83. McBride, 65.

84. Greenhills Christian Fellowship, *Growth Group Manual*, 2.

85. Greenhills Christian Fellowship, 2.

86. See appendix 2 (pages 179–183) for more information on GCF's Growth Group Ministry.

Others limit their small group community to adults only, which leads to the exclusivity of their *sheep*. Still others lean towards curriculum over-dependence in their small group teaching, which brings about the superficiality of their *study*. The rest prefer meeting anywhere for their small group mission, which results in the unsuitability of their *site*. These attitudes stunt the growth of GCF's small groups and deter its new church plants locally and globally.

Having witnessed these tendencies – which are typical among contemporary small groups in the Philippines – I am committed to find ways to resolve these major problems by revitalizing the GCF growth groups in the following areas: leaders, learners, lessons, and locations. The best way to start is by looking into the context of Filipino small groups.

B. Context of Filipino Small Groups

1. Concerns of Filipino Small Groups

Forming and developing self-reproducing small groups accelerates the church planting movement. Nevertheless, small groups in the Philippines today are generally sluggish to grow and hardly multiply. As cited earlier, the common determining factors which may cause the lack of growth in small groups are the scarcity of leaders, exclusivity of members, superficiality of curriculum, and unsuitability of venue. Hence, the main goal for every Filipino small group is to meet each of these essential needs: (1) adequate and adept leaders, (2) diverse and dynamic learners, (3) textual and transformational lessons, and (4) suitable and strategic locations.

What is the root cause of these critical issues? The primary reason for all these major concerns or problems is the wrong mindset regarding the following: (1) small group leaders as *clergy only*, (2) small group learners as *limited to adults*, (3) small group lessons as *curriculum overly-dependent*, and (4) small group locations as *meeting anywhere*. Undoubtedly, such a mentality is culturally conditioned with past history at its root and the values of today as its fruit. To change one's way of thinking would require a proper appropriation of God's Word and a right perception of one's world. There is an utmost need to interpret both the Scripture and the culture. Thus, it is imperative to undergo a cultural study of small groups in the twenty-first century Filipino context.

2. Culture of Filipinos

What is culture? According to H. Richard Niebuhr's classic work, *Christ and Culture*, culture "comprises language, habits, ideas, beliefs, customs, social organization, inherited artifacts, technical processes, and values."[87] As Niebuhr further describes, "The world of culture is a *world of values*."[88] A Filipino writer, Nick Joaquin, however, simply states that "culture is itself history."[89] Additionally, Joaquin writes that "purest culture is the history attendant on the birth of nations."[90] So, history and values, as the two significant Filipino cultural factors, are given emphasis in this section of study.

a. Brief history

History, as defined in Webster's Dictionary refers to "acts, ideas, or events that will or can shape the course of the future."[91] What the Philippines is today is the byproduct of its rich historic past which this book briefly recounts as it focuses on how colonial influences shaped the future of Filipino culture. Nonetheless, it first has to be established what the pre-colonial Philippines intrinsically was.

(1) Pre-colonial Philippines

The early inhabitants of the islands – namely, the Negrito (a small minority) and the Malayan – are indispensable to the portrait of pre-colonial Philippines.[92] The ancient Filipinos were basically animistic in religion and worshipped the *anitos* or invisible beings:[93] "Their rituals were based on beliefs in a ranking deity whom they called *Bathalang Maykapál* and a host of other deities, in the environmental spirits, and in soul-spirits. The *Bathalà*, the equivalent of the Spanish *Diós*, was supposed to be the creator of the earth and man and therefore superior to all other deities."[94]

Prior to the Spaniards' advent, at the start of the tenth century AD, the Chinese came to the islands as economic men whose concern was more for profit than political power.[95] Aside from language, the Chinese influence was also commercial, encouraging "the use of umbrella, gongs, lead, porcelain, the manufacture of gunpowder, mining methods, and metallurgy."[96] Likewise, the Indians influenced the Filipinos linguistically (Sanskrit) and also religiously

---

87. Niebuhr, *Christ and Culture*, 32.
88. Niebuhr, 34.
89. Joaquin, *Culture and History*, 47.
90. Joaquin, 204.
91. Costello, *Random House Webster's College Dictionary*, 636.
92. Tuggy, *Philippine Church*, 21.
93. Tano, *Theology in the Philippine Setting*, 15.
94. Agoncillo and Guerrero, *History of the Filipino People*, 43.
95. Agoncillo and Guerrero, 27.
96. Agoncillo and Guerrero, 28.

(ancient paganism, specifically – e.g. a belief in Indra Batara, the Indian king of heaven from Vedic or Indian origin).[97] Furthermore, "the ancient Filipinos had a culture that was basically Malayan in structure and form. They had written languages that traced their origin to the Austronesian parent-stock. . . . They had music and dances for almost all occasions and a wide variety of musical instruments indicative of their ingenuity."[98] The final pre-colonial religious influence came from an Arabian missionary, Makdum, who introduced Islam in the Mindanao-Sulu area in about AD 1380 and profoundly affected the southern part of the Philippines up to this day.[99]

But what largely influenced Filipino cultural values in both a positive and negative sense were the years of colonization by both the Spanish (for centuries) and the Americans (for decades), and these, therefore, are the critical features in this segment of study.

(2) The Spanish influence

The major Spanish influence on ancient Filipino culture is religion. As Spain colonized the Philippine Islands for more than three hundred years, it resulted in the establishment of the only Christian nation in the whole of Asia. The Portuguese voyager Ferdinand Magellan, who was sailing with his men under the Spanish flag,[100] reached the Philippine Islands – particularly the Samar-Leyte region – and held the first Catholic mass in Limasawa on March 31, 1521.[101] In search of food and better accommodations, Magellan and his crew sailed to Cebu and placed its people under the Spanish Crown by converting them to Christianity – except for the chief of Mactan, Lapu-Lapu, who prevailed in resisting them and caused them to retreat.[102] Subsequent to the Magellan expedition was the voyage headed by Ruy de Villalobos. Villalobos, together with Bernardo de la Torre, also landed on the island of Leyte and "gave to the Samar-Leyte region the name *Felipinas*, in honor of Philip, the Spanish Crown prince and, later, Philip II, successor to Charles I [a name which eventually] was applied to the entire archipelago."[103] Generally, the Philippine society under Spain is depicted by Agoncillo and Guerrero in this way:

---

97. Agoncillo and Guerrero, 29–30.
98. Agoncillo and Guerrero, 52.
99. Tuggy, *Philippine Church*, 24–25.
100. Clouse, Pierard, and Yamauchi, *Two Kingdoms*, 296.
101. Agoncillo and Guerrero, *History of the Filipino People*, 70–71.
102. Agoncillo and Guerrero, 71.
103. Agoncillo and Guerrero, 72.

The Spaniards implemented a colonial policy designed not only to keep the Filipinos in political subjection, but also to exploit to the utmost the country's natural resources. This was clearly manifest in the crippling system of taxation and forced labor, the undue pre-occupation with the galleon trade and government monopolies as well as harsh agricultural and trade policies. The result was not merely an underdeveloped but a distorted and completely unbalanced economy. Spain, who lagged behind Western Europe in cultural developments, pursued a socio-cultural policy which, upon closer analysis, was intended to keep the Filipinos submissive vassals of Spain: divided, apathetic and unable to resist the iniquities of the Spanish colonial system.[104]

On February 17, 1872, three Filipino priests were falsely accused, tried in a mock trial, and publicly garroted.[105] Their unwarranted execution paved the way for the reform movement. Instead of resorting to armed struggle, the Filipino middle class campaigned for reforms in the administration of the Philippines.[106] The most educated of the reformists was Dr Jose Rizal. Unfortunately, Rizal was falsely charged with treason and connivance in the revolution which led to his execution by musketry on December 30, 1896.[107] Though the reform movement did not succeed, it "led to the founding of the revolutionary *Katipunan* with separatist aims."[108] The recognized Father of the Revolution was Andres Bonifacio. Bonifacio founded the *Katipunan* "on a radical platform, namely, to secure the independence and freedom of the Philippines by force of arms."[109] General Emilio Aguinaldo also joined the *Katipunan*. The revolution grew and many *Katipuneros* – including Bonifacio – were arrested and sentenced to death.

Consequently, the uprising against the Spanish regime escalated, but the early Filipinos could not prevail due to the Spaniards' military prowess and political organization.[110] Though there were only a few in the Philippines (not more than five thousand in number), the Spaniards were able to sustain their

---

104. Agoncillo and Guerrero, 85.
105. Agoncillo and Guerrero, 124.
106. Agoncillo and Guerrero, 129.
107. Agoncillo and Guerrero, 142.
108. Agoncillo and Guerrero, 142.
109. Agoncillo and Guerrero, 149.
110. Agoncillo and Guerrero, 104.

power in the colony through the clergy:[111] "The [Spanish] friars successfully conditioned the Filipino minds into accepting the existing arrangements of power and authority in society and through non-military but certainly more effective weapons of repression, such as threats of rebuke, excommunication and interdict, wielded great influence and exacted obedience from the Filipinos."[112]

Spanish educational institutions in the Philippines, which were run by autocratic friars, were only open to the children of Spaniards, and religion was the major curriculum.[113] When education was finally offered to native children, they were placed "in makeshift classrooms in their stables [and] were daily subjected to physical and mental tortures so that shame and fear of corporal punishment forced them to drop out of school."[114] The eventual plans to reform the educational system for the sake of Filipinos were destabilized by the reluctant Spanish friars due to their apprehension that knowledge would open the minds of natives toward rebellion.[115] Deprived of the Spanish language, the Filipinos were only partially Hispanized. Mourning on the aftermath of Hispanization, reformist Jose Rizal uttered that it constrained the mortified Filipinos to "admire and praise what was foreign and incomprehensible."[116]

(3) The American influence

It took the coming of American forces for Spanish control to be obliterated. In February 15, 1898, the Spanish-American War was triggered when Spaniards attacked the American warship *Maine* at Havana harbor and killed 246 men.[117] A few months later, America declared war with Spain on April 25. In the Battle of Manila Bay, Commodore George Dewey successfully destroyed the Spanish fleet and sank their warships.[118] On June 12, 1898, the Filipino revolutionary forces under General Emilio Aguinaldo declared Philippine independence from Spain.[119]

---

111. Agoncillo and Guerrero, 113.

112. Agoncillo and Guerrero, 113.

113. Agoncillo and Guerrero, 100–101.

114. Agoncillo and Guerrero, 101.

115. Agoncillo and Guerrero, 102.

116. Jose Rizal, "The Indolence of the Filipinos," trans. by Encarnacion Alzona, cited in Agoncillo and Guerrero, *History of the Filipino People*, 102.

117. Agoncillo and Guerrero, *History of the Filipino People*, 187.

118. Agoncillo and Guerrero, 185, 187.

119. Agoncillo and Guerrero, 197–198.

As Clouse, Pierard, and Yamauchi remark, "In 1898 the United States defeated Spain and entered the ranks of the imperial powers by taking the Philippines."[120] This lead to the Philippines coming under American occupation for almost half a century. Not long after their struggle with the Spaniards, "the Filipinos took up arms again to fight the Americans whom they had previously seen as champions of their cause against Spain."[121] What led to the outbreak of the Philippine-American War? As Agoncillo and Guerrero summarize,

> The American insistence on the evacuation by Aguinaldo's army of the strategic points along the Manila Bay area, the refusal of the American military authorities to allow the Filipino soldiers to enter the city after its surrender, and the American limitation of the areas to be occupied by the Filipino troops after the mock battle of Manila, led progressively to the deterioration of Filipino-American relations. The misunderstandings that followed these incidents climaxed in the signing of the Treaty of Paris without consultation with the Filipinos. Attempts, however, were made by a mixed commission of Filipinos and Americans to relax the tension between the two peoples, but the American members of the commission tried to prolong the sessions without trying to improve the situation because they were waiting for the American reinforcements which were then on their way to Manila. Finally, on February 4, 1899, an American sentry shot a Filipino soldier, resulting in the outbreak of the Filipino-American hostilities. The Filipinos fought at a disadvantage, for they had no sufficient arms with which to fight the enemy. But it took the Americans almost three years to conquer the Filipinos.[122]

On April 19, 1901, Aguinaldo took an oath of allegiance to the United States, officially ending the First Republic and acknowledging the sovereignty of the United States over the Philippines.[123] The war ended on July 4, 1902, upon a unilateral proclamation of general amnesty by US President Theodore Roosevelt.[124] As the Filipinos insisted on decreasing the control of the church over them, the United States Congress disestablished the Roman Catholic Church in 1902 which paved the way for Protestant missionaries to enter

---

120. Clouse, Pierard, and Yamauchi, *Two Kingdoms*, 492.
121. Tano, *Theology in the Philippine Setting*, 21.
122. Agoncillo and Guerrero, *History of the Filipino People*, 210.
123. Agoncillo and Guerrero, 224.
124. Agoncillo and Guerrero, 249.

the country and for indigenous sects to emerge, such as the *Iglesia Filipina Independiente* (Philippine Independent Church), a group that broke away from the Roman Catholic Church, and the *Iglesia ni Cristo de Manalo* (the Church of Christ founded by Felix Manalo).[125]

Meanwhile, "the American authorities established the civil government which took over the functions of the military government . . . which ushered in a new period in the struggle of the Filipinos for freedom and dependence: the era of suppressed nationalism which spanned at least the first decade of American rule, 1901–1910."[126] However, due to the quality of the educational system under the Americans –which had been absent during Spanish colonial rule – the ill feelings against their colonizers were nearly obliterated from the hearts of the Filipinos, and they readily accepted the Americans as "big brothers" to direct and support them.[127] As Agoncillo and Guerrero specify,

> The system of education introduced by the Americans was a radical departure from the highly limited, defective and religion-oriented system of education perpetuated by the Spaniards for more than three centuries. In contrast to the Spanish system of allowing only the children of the privileged classes to enjoy the educational facilities of the colony, the Americans allowed the children of the masses to take advantage of the free public school system. The government, through a law enacted by the Philippine Commission in 1903, financed the studies of deserving students and professionals in American colleges and universities. The Americans stressed citizenship training and understanding as well as practice of the democratic way of life, while the Spaniards emphasized religion and the after-life. The Spaniards denied the Filipinos the opportunity to learn the Spanish language while the Americans, in an effort to hasten the organization of the public school system, disseminated the English language.
>
> It was unfortunate, however, that the educational efforts of the Americans should later place native ideas, customs and traditions and even the national identity of the Filipinos in danger of obliteration. In the educational system established by the Americans, Filipino instructional materials were almost non-existent in the curriculum; young Filipinos were taught American

---

125. Tano, *Theology in the Philippine Setting*, 22–23.
126. Agoncillo and Guerrero, *History of the Filipino People*, 243.
127. Agoncillo and Guerrero, 305.

songs, American ideals, [and] the lives of American heroes and great men in complete indifference to Filipino patriots, ideals and culture; the use of the vernacular was prohibited and punishment was actually meted out to those who dared speak the native dialects. Until the Commonwealth was established, no Filipino was allowed to head the Department of Public Instruction.[128]

What paved the way for eventual autonomy and full Filipino independence from American dominion? In summary, Rodrigo Tano presents the five significant periods of American occupation:

[1] During the period of organization (1901–1907), the details of the new government administration were established through the Philippine Commission which was composed of Americans appointed by the United States President. [2] At the end of the constructive period (1907–1913), legislative powers were turned over to the Philippine Assembly, a body of elected Filipinos which constituted a bicameral legislature. [3] During the period of Filipinization (1913–1935), Filipinos were given the majority in the Commission until 1916 when the Jones Law dissolved the Commission, provided for a senate, and promised independence when conditions warranted it. [4] Under the Commonwealth period (1935–1946), Filipinos had complete charge of their affairs (except for the war years, 1942–1945). . . . [5] Following a period of rehabilitation and recovery from the ravages of the second world war, the Philippines was granted independence by the United States on July 4, 1946.[129]

The Commonwealth period's long progression toward final independence was disrupted when Japanese naval forces attacked the American Pacific fleet at Pearl Harbor in December 1941 and eventually invaded the Philippines.[130] For three years, under the Japanese occupation, the following took place: "Civil liberties were suppressed by the enemy, the economy was geared to the demands of the Japanese war efforts, education was revamped to re-orient Filipino thinking along Japanese lines, and political life was limited to the Japanese-sponsored Republic. Meanwhile, thousands upon thousands were

---

128. Agoncillo and Guerrero, 306–307.

129. Tano, *Theology in the Philippine Setting*, 22–24.

130. Agoncillo and Guerrero, *History of the Filipino People*, 401.

executed and imprisoned."[131] Finally, as he had promised, General Douglas MacArthur, together with the American forces, returned to the Philippines and succeeded in routing the enemy and turning over the Commonwealth Government to President Sergio Osmeña on February 27, 1945.[132] Later, the Philippines was granted its independence by the United States on July 4, 1946, and Manuel Roxas became the first president of the Republic.[133] Agoncillo and Guerrero summarize the aftermath of the nearly fifty-year American occupation of the Philippines:

> Universal education was stressed; public health and welfare was carried to the remote barrios; commerce, industry, and trade were given impetus; basic individual freedoms were respected; means of communication and transportation were greatly improved; and political consciousness was developed through the introduction of American political institutions and practices. Side by side with these positive results of the American occupation were the negative results: the general economic dependence on the United States, the partial loss of the racial heritage, the continuance of the colonial mentality, and a distorted sense of values.[134]

b. Cultural values

Filipino anthropologist, F. Landa Jocano, defines values as "shared standards on the basis of which people make judgments, interpret experiences, and guide actions."[135] The best way to understand Filipino cultural values is by studying the concept of *loob* (inside). Jocano describes *loob* as the Filipinos' way of describing their situations physically, mentally and emotionally.[136] *Loob* also has its counterpart which is *labas* (outside). Comparing the two terms, Jocano distinguishes the *loob*, which denotes the internal reality of life, from the *labas* which is its external behavioral expression.[137] As Jocano further elucidates,

> Terms like *magaan ang loob* (at ease), *masama ang loob* (feeling bad), *lakas loob* (will power), *mahina ang loob* (weak disposition), and so forth, express well the way we use the concept of *loob*

---

131. Agoncillo and Guerrero, 401.
132. Agoncillo and Guerrero, 431–436.
133. Agoncillo and Guerrero, 449.
134. Agoncillo and Guerrero, 385.
135. Jocano, *Filipino Worldview*, 85.
136. Jocano, *Filipino Value System*, 96.
137. Jocano, 97.

to describe our inner conditions. The outer conditions or *labas* are expressed in *kilos* (act), *hilig* (tendency), and *gawi* (habit). Sometimes, we put a public mask (*palabas*) to conceal our inner intentions that might prove disadvantageous if done openly. This is best expressed by such terms as *pakitang-tao* (to camouflage), *pabalatkayo* (to masquerade), *pabalat-bunga* (to fake), *kunwari* (to pretend), and *pasikat* (to show off).[138]

Moreover, the two concepts (*loob* and *labas*) are also utilized socially in differentiating *hindi ibang tao* or *taga-loob* (insider) from *ibang tao* or *taga-labas* (outsider). The former constitutes loved ones (parents and siblings) and relatives, whereas the latter comprises non-members of the family and those without kinship. Jocano points out that *loob* pertains to the implicit connotations of togetherness, like those found in the perception of "we" and "us"; whereas *labas* applies to those who don't belong to "our group."[139]

Likewise, Virgilio Enriquez argues that Filipinos have at least eight levels of social interaction under two general category levels ("outsider" and "one-of-us") which commence with *pakikitungo* (level of amenities/civility) and culminate with *pakikiisa* (level of fusion, oneness and full trust):

> *Ibang-tao* or Outsider Category Levels:
> [1] *Pakikitungo* (level of amenities/civility)
> [2] *Pakikisalamuha* (level of mixing)
> [3] *Pakikilahok* (level of joining/participating)
> [4] *Pakikibagay* (level of conforming)
> [5] *Pakikisama* (level of adjusting)
> *Hindi ibang-tao* or One-of-us Category Levels:
> [6] *Pakikipagpalagayang-loob* (level of mutual trust/rapport)
> [7] *Pakikisangkot* (level of getting involved)
> [8] *Pakikiisa* (level of fusion, oneness and full trust)[140]

Enriquez clarifies that these eight levels of collective interaction are incorporated in the ideal of *pakikipagkapwa-tao*.[141] Dindo Rei Tesoro and Joselito Alviar Jose believe that the virtue of *pakikipagkapwa-tao*, or human dealing, is a core Filipino value.[142] In their research work "A Framework for

---

138. Jocano, 97.
139. Jocano, 98.
140. Enriquez, *Pagbabagong-Dangal*, 51–52.
141. Enriquez, 52.
142. Tesoro and Jose, *Rise of Filipino Theology*, 194.

Analyzing the Filipino Character," V. P. Gapuz and C. D. Lozada Jr. explicate that "*pakikipagkapwa-tao* results in camaraderie and a feeling of closeness to one another. It is the foundation for unity as well as the sense of social justice."[143] Understanding the Filipino concept of *loob/labas* and the *ibang-tao/hindi ibang tao* category levels are the ways to a Filipino's heart and to get into it is to understand his or her mindset.

The burning issues arising from the Filipino mentality that regard small group leaders as *clergy only*, small group learners as *limited to adults*, small group lessons as *curriculum overly-dependent*, and small group locations as *meeting anywhere* are borne out of negative understandings of Filipino cultural values on *leading, grouping, studying*, and *planning*. Tracing its root from colonial influences, such a mindset needs to be probed, addressed, and transformed in order for this study to bear fruit!

(1) Leading

In his write-up on *Christian Renewal of Filipino Values,* Vitaliano Gorospe stresses that "a very significant factor in the Filipino value-system is the authority figure which [constitutes] parents, teachers, parish priest, the company boss, or the party in power."[144] A hierarchical mentality is also common among Filipinos, which could either be a Spanish or American influence. Generally, Filipinos have a high esteem for their leaders. A leader is commonly called "sir" or "ma'am" (and not by his or her first name) and is addressed in the second person plural pronoun *inyo, ninyo,* or *kayo* (you) with corresponding *po, opo,* or *oho* (yes) as a sign of respect regardless of age. Non-observance of such one would be perceived as *bastos* (rude) or *walang-galang* (disrespectful). According to Gapuz and Lozada, "Filipinos look up to their leaders as role models. Political leaders are the main models but all other leaders serve as role models as well. Thus when our leaders violate the law or show themselves to be self-serving and driven by personal interest or when there is lack of public accountability, there is a negative impact on the Filipino."[145]

In a Filipino home, parents are known for exercising absolute authority over their children. The father is regarded as the "head of the family" (*padre de familia*). He asserts his authority as the leader of the house by making decisions without consulting the children, even if it concerns their careers or lifetime

---

143. Gapuz and Lozada, "A Framework for Analyzing the Filipino Character," 1.

144. Gorospe, "Christian Renewal of Filipino Values," 45.

145. Gapuz and Lozada, "Framework for Analyzing the Filipino Character," 10.

partners.[146] Nevertheless, due to the presence of the mother, who shares in the leadership function (serving as the neck which turns the head, as commonly uttered in jest), the father "does not have enough authority to make his rule patriarchal."[147] Usually, it is the mother who manages not only the household chores and child-care, but also the finances of the family.[148] Additionally, the relationship among siblings is also not equal. As Tesoro and Jose recount, the younger ones are functionally subordinated to the first-born to the point that the eldest brother or sister can even implement discipline or assume full responsibility for the whole family when both parents die.[149]

It appears that Filipinos have a high regard for leadership but will not assume the role of leadership themselves. They like the leader but do not want to be a leader. They look up to leaders but look down on themselves. Does this have anything to do with their leadership concept or is it a mere issue of their self-esteem? As Gapuz and Lozada correctly observe,

> Filipinos are generally passive and lacking in initiative. One waits to be told what has to be done. There is a strong reliance on others (e.g., leaders, government) to do things for us. This is related to one's attitude towards authority. Filipinos have a need for a strong authority figure and feel safer and more secure in the presence of such an authority. One is generally submissive to those in authority and is not likely to raise issues or to question decision. . . . Filipinos are thus easily oppressed and exploited.[150]

The same applies to Filipino Christians. They expect leadership from the ordained minister or clergy but not from themselves. Hence, this is an issue of their mindset about the clergy, and their view of themselves, which requires examination and transformation. Since the Filipino clergy or pastors are perceived in the church as the authority figures, the highest in the hierarchy of leaders, and the spiritual "fathers" in the church, they are the only ones regarded as authorized leaders.

Being passive and lacking initiative may possibly be the natural consequences of colonialism, making Filipinos feel they are underdogs, inferior,

---

146. Agoncillo and Guerrero surmise that the tradition of arranged marriage was most likely an influence from Chinese culture. Agoncillo and Guerrero, *History of the Filipino People*, 28–29.

147. Castillo, "Church in Thy House," 105.

148. Castillo, 105.

149. Tesoro and Jose, *Rise of Filipino Theology*, 198.

150. Gapuz and Lozada, "Framework for Analyzing the Filipino Character," 4–5.

and unable to lead. When Spain colonized the Philippines, the Spanish friars were the only recognized church authorities for more than three hundred years, and Filipinos themselves were not allowed to lead. To date, Filipinos still believe that the authority to study and teach the Scripture resides in the *clergy only*, for they alone have the calling, the training, and the expertise in leading a Bible study. This extreme clerical mentality must be addressed and rectified. As Tesoro and Jose propose,

> It is evident that the Filipino mind frame as regards authority can be used in ecclesiology to explain the hierarchical nature of the Church and the authority of its pastors. However, it must be added that the "hierarchical" Filipino mentality also needs to be purified of certain shortcomings, such as the tendency to arbitrariness, or the attachment to power and rank. The Christian meaning of authority is one of service. Its function is to serve the personal freedom of God's sons and daughters, so that individuals can develop to maturity, and to foster the common good, so that the community can achieve its aspirations and goals.[151]

Another possible element that discourages a typical Filipino from leading is *hiya* or shame. They view themselves as *mahiyain* (shame-oriented). *Hiya* is commonly translated in English as "shame, embarrassment, timidity"; however, according to Enriquez, the term can also be rendered as "propriety or dignity."[152] This is possible because *hiya* has both a social and moral dimension and an external and internal aspect.[153] Hence, to properly understand *hiya* is to thoroughly examine the *labas* and *loob* dimensions of a Filipino. Bulatao gives details on the Filipino concept of *hiya*:

> To sum up *hiya* may be defined as a painful emotion arising from a relationship with an authority figure or with society, inhibiting self-assertion in a situation perceived as dangerous to one's ego. *Walang hiya* is the absence of this inhibition, such that the finer feelings of others are given offense. *Hiya* is conceived as rooted in the individuated ego, which depends upon its primary group as its normal mode of operation rather than upon its individual self. In the present state of affairs, until . . . more interior controls are developed, the culture has need of *hiya* to keep the culture

---

151. Tesoro and Jose, *Rise of Filipino Theology*, 200.

152. Enriquez, *From Colonial to Liberation Psychology*, 165.

153. Enriquez, 67–68.

from suddenly breaking apart. Meanwhile, there is need of a third type of individual who transcends the level of *hiya*, and is a mature, individuated person, sensitive to the feelings of others yet autonomous in his own right.[154]

Enriquez best defines *hiya* as "an act that is demanded by face-saving or done in order not to lose honor."[155] So *hiya* is not a cultural value that is intrinsically wrong and therefore must be absolutely denounced.[156] In fact, according to Narry Santos' book *Turning Our Shame into Honor*, "*Hiya* is a positive Filipino concept [and] when we see *hiya* as positive, we begin to discover the honor that lies behind it."[157] Moreover, Santos emphasizes that it is necessary to combine *hiya* with *dangal* in our Filipino value system and make it one's motivation in life.[158] So Gorospe is correct in saying that "Filipino values can either work *against* or *for* Christian values."[159] Filipinos can choose *hiya* to work for them. Thus, the transformation of *hiya* as an essential Filipino cultural value can actually persuade rather than dissuade a Filipino Christian to lead. As Gorospe concludes,

> The Filipino *hiya* then, when modified, can be a potential for the Christian values of chastity and modesty, self-respect and decency, and sensitivity to the feelings of others as persons. It can be the natural basis of the Christian virtue of temperance and prudence. As an external social control or sanction, it should be complemented by the interior Christian motivation of love. The Filipino who has transcended the level of *hiya* is what we mean by the mature and responsible Christian.[160]

Therefore, while *hiya* is to be affirmed when used as a positive value of a Filipino leader, clericalism or the extreme clerical mentality as a negative cultural trait among Filipinos needs to be rectified and transformed.

---

154. Jaime Bulatao, "Hiya," *Philippines Studies* 12, no. 3 (July 1964): 424–438, quoted in Gorospe, "Christian Renewal of Filipino Values," 54.

155. Enriquez, *From Colonial to Liberation Psychology*, 165.

156. Gorospe, "Christian Renewal of Filipino Values," 54.

157. Santos, *Turning Our Shame into Honor*, 229.

158. Santos, 233.

159. Gorospe, *Christian Renewal of Filipino Values*, 50.

160. Gorospe, 55.

(2) Grouping

As Tesoro and Jose explain, "The family is undoubtedly the fundamental social unit in the Philippines. This basic cell is inserted in larger social structures such as clans, groups, and communities, all of them arising from natural relations of lineage, marriage, physical proximity, or social hierarchy."[161] Castillo stresses that "as part of Indo-Malayan culture, the Filipino family is generally a bilateral extended type. This means that children are equally related to the relatives of both parents."[162] The newly married Filipino couples may stay in the house of the husband or wife's parents. The relatives of one spouse automatically become the relatives of the other. The relationship in a Filipino extended family is established in three levels: first, biologically by blood (family members); second, legally by marriage (in-laws); and third, ritually by ceremony (godparents). Jocano explains what he calls the "circle of relatives" in the Filipino setting, where the innermost circle is family (*mag-anak*), the secondary and tertiary circles of people are close and distant relatives (*kamag-anak* and *kamag-anakan*), and the outermost circle is the kin group (*angkan*).[163]

Family-centeredness has both advantages and disadvantages. On one hand, Gapuz and Lozada stress that, in the Filipino context, one gets his or her individual identity from the family, which provides emotional and physical care, and is also one's major obligation and duty.[164] On the other hand, Castillo states that "as an integral part of the family, an individual's sense of self-worth rises or falls with that of other members. The success or failure of one member affects everyone. Each member is responsible, therefore, to protect the family honor. He is also responsible to find ways and means that would increase its honor."[165] Likewise, as Jocano stresses, "Members of the family or kinship group . . . are constantly reminded to keep in mind that the shame of one member is the shame of the entire family. This is so because everyone is 'linked' to each other as *kaanak* (family member) or *kamag-anak* (kinsman)."[166]

Another downside of "familism" as a viewpoint in group orientation, according to Jocano, is the "tendencies to promote small group interests over that of the larger community. The concept of collectivity is limited to family

---

161. Tesoro and Jose, *Rise of Filipino Theology*, 192. Likewise, according to Jocano, "To a Filipino, the family is the most important social unit in the community. It is the basic building block of the national society" (Jocano, *Towards Developing a Filipino Corporate Culture*, 147).

162. Castillo, "Church in Thy House," 103.

163. Jocano, *Towards Developing a Filipino Corporate Culture*, 73.

164. Gapuz and Lozada, "Framework for Analyzing the Filipino Character," 1.

165. Castillo, "Church in Thy House," 105–106.

166. Jocano, *Filipino Value System*, 64.

members, kinship group, and friends. If ever the larger community interests are considered, these are better approached in the context of the family, kinship, and friendship (*barkada)* than through legal processes and bureaucratic contexts."[167] Similarly, these problems are seen with extreme family-centeredness:

> Excessive concern for the family creates an in-group to which the Filipino is fiercely loyal to the detriment of concern for the larger community or the common good. . . . [It] manifests itself in the use of one's office and power as a means of promoting the interests of the family, in factionalism, patronage, and political dynasties, and in the protection of erring family members. It results in lack of concern for the common good and acts as a block to national consciousness.[168]

Gapuz and Lozada believe that "our family orientation is both a strength and a weakness giving us a sense of rootedness and security, both very essential to any form of reaching out to others. At the same time, it develops in us an in-group orientation that prevents us from reaching out beyond the family to the larger community and the nation."[169]

Then, aside from being family-oriented, Filipinos are also known for being group-centered where both young and grown-up children are inclined to gather their own gang or *barkada* and exclude anyone outside the group, even their parents.[170] Castillo specifies that

> *gregariousness* among peers and kin is another Filipino trait. This desire to be part of a group meets a person's need to belong. Small groups abound, especially in urban areas where many feel lost and lonely because they are away from their families. The social behavior expressed in "our-group-only" (*tayo-tayo*) is seen wherever there is a variety of ethnic groups such as in big cities. In Metro Manila and in Mindanao churches, the membership consists of representatives of various tribes. Members tend to be concerned with the affairs of "his"/"her" tribe.[171]

Consequently, Agoncillo and Guerrero also indicate the tendency of Filipinos to be regionalistic to the point of putting down a fellow countryman

---

167. Jocano, *Filipino Worldview*, 89.
168. Gapuz and Lozada, "Framework for Analyzing the Filipino Character," 4.
169. Gapuz and Lozada, 6.
170. Gorospe, "Christian Renewal of Filipino Values," 47.
171. Castillo, "Church in Thy House," 111.

from another region.[172] During the Spanish Occupation this perennial cultural value was even used by the colonizers to "divide and conquer" the ancient Filipinos.[173] However, Gorospe concludes that "small-group centeredness can work not only for evil but also for good. . . . In the task of nation-building, the small group can play a very important role as a vehicle of change, of mutual trust, and individual responsibility."[174]

So how do average Filipinos view grouping in general and what makes them exclude children from adult group discussions? It is inherent for Filipinos to have a high regard for groups, especially their family groups (*pamilya*) and peer groups (*barkada*), due to their family-centeredness and gregariousness. Nevertheless, Filipinos have low regard for their own little children whom they perceive as unruly (*magulo*), and who are not supposed to participate in discussions involving adults. ("*Ang mga bata ay di dapat sumabat sa usapang matatanda!*") Children who do so are perceived as rude and disrespectful. As a result, Filipino children are separated from adults at home whenever their parents are dining and discussing with visitors. Filipino parents don't want to be embarrassed in front of other people when their children misbehave. ("*Nakakahiya, ano na lang ang sasabihin ng ibang tao sa atin?*") To the Filipino, the shame of one member is the shame of the entire family. This possibly explains why Filipino Christians exclude children and make small group discussions *limited to adults* only. Therefore, while small group centeredness is approved when employed as a positive Filipino value, the segregation of children from adults or the exclusivity in groupings of Filipinos needs to be addressed and worked out as a negative cultural trait.

(3) Studying

Many Filipinos believe that illiteracy is a major concern in the Philippines today due to poverty. While there are Filipino families who have the means to partake in quality education through private schools, there are still problems for parents in motivating their children to pursue their studies and aim for academic excellence. As Agoncillo and Guerrero narrate,

> The experiences of college and university professors reveal the sad fact that the average Filipino student has to be hammered and whipped into line in order to make him work hard. He will not, on his own initiative, read more than what the professor assigns.

---

172. Agoncillo and Guerrero, *History of the Filipino People*, 12–13.

173. Agoncillo and Guerrero, 13.

174. Gorospe, "Christian Renewal of Filipino Values," 49.

Why exert so much effort and spend so much time when one can pass through college with a grade of "3"? To get the white meat of a crab's legs, so the saying in Tagalog runs, you must pound those legs with a small pestle or with a big knife. And so with the Filipino student.[175]

What makes an average Filipino student, regardless of social status, have a low regard for education? Filipinos are known for complacency and mediocrity (*pwede na yan* mentality), resorting to the use of shortcuts and resulting in inefficiency. Such a negative mindset can be attributed to colonial mentality. Gapuz and Lozada explain that this undesirable cultural value can be categorized in two ways: "The first is a lack of patriotism or an active awareness, appreciation and love of the Philippines; the second is an actual preference for things foreign."[176] The two authors further state concerning Filipinos that

we are the product of our colonial history which is regarded by many as the culprit behind our lack of nationalism and our colonial mentality. Colonialism developed a mind-set in the Filipino to think of the colonial power as superior and more powerful. As a second class citizen to the Spanish and then to the Americans, we developed a sense of inferiority to the white man. We developed a dependence on foreign powers that makes us believe that we are not responsible for our country's fate.[177]

Hence the history of colonization in the Philippines has a significant impact on what a Filipino is made of today. The ugly scars seen in the present are a painful reminder of how colonialism has deeply wounded Filipinos in the past. The two major colonial masters (the Spaniards and Americans) influenced the state of education in the Philippines and affected the value Filipinos have for it. A possible negative Spanish influence on Filipinos is reflected in the existing educational system in the Philippines. As Gapuz and Lozada observe,

Schools are highly authoritarian, with the teacher as the center of focus. The Filipino student is taught to be dependent on the teacher as he attempts to record verbatim what the teacher says and give this back in original form and with little processing during examinations. Teachers reward well-behaved and obedient students and are uncomfortable with those who ask questions and

---

175. Agoncillo and Guerrero, *History of the Filipino People*, 11.
176. Gapuz and Lozada, "Framework for Analyzing the Filipino Character," 5.
177. Gapuz and Lozada, 8.

express a different viewpoint. The Filipino student learns passivity and conformity. Critical thinking is not learned in school.[178]

The American occupation in the Philippines brought a good educational system. Nevertheless, while it benefited the Filipinos to some extent, eventually it also became unfavorable to them. Agoncillo and Guerrero earlier recounted that in the desire of the Americans to educate Filipinos they *failed to contextualize* their teaching according to the customs and traditions of their students, but *succeeded in westernizing* the poor natives by having their textbooks and school curriculum written and taught primarily by foreign teachers in English.[179] Based on their observations, Gapuz and Lozada further ascertain the following consequences:

> The introduction of English as the medium of education de-Filipinized the youth and taught them to regard American culture as superior. The use of English also leads to the lack of self-confidence of the Filipino. The fact that doing well means using a foreign language, which foreigners can really handle better, leads to an inferiority complex. At a very early age we find that our self-esteem depends on the mastery of something foreign.
>
> The use of foreign language may also explain the Filipino's unreflectiveness and mental laziness. Thinking in our native language but expressing ourselves in English results not only in a lack of confidence but also in a lack of power of expression, imprecision and stunted development of one's intellectual powers. . . .
>
> Aside from the problems inherent in the use of a foreign language in our educational system, the educational system leads to other problems in us as a people. The lack of suitable local textbooks and the dependence on foreign textbooks, particularly in the higher school levels, force Filipino students as well as their teachers to face school materials that are irrelevant to the Philippine setting. They thus develop a mind-set that things learned in school are not related to real life.[180]

Therefore, the use of the American language as the primary mode of communication in schools appears to have been detrimental to the self-esteem

---

178. Gapuz and Lozada, 9.
179. Agoncillo and Guerrero, *History of the Filipino People*, 306.
180. Gapuz and Lozada, "Framework for Analyzing the Filipino Character," 8–9.

of Filipinos. It has also compelled them to rely on foreign textbooks. Instead of making their own lesson plans, many Filipino teachers are overly dependent on curriculum materials that are made in the USA. As a result, Filipinos have learned to conform to things that are foreign and alien to them which possibly explains why they are not motivated to work hard or take their studies seriously. On the other hand, Gapuz and Lozada believe that Filipinos have the aptitude for hard work once placed in suitable situations.[181] Filipinos are also intelligent and can compete with foreigners. The studies of Jose Samson show that

> the intelligence of the Filipinos is generally no different in level and range from those of foreign individuals. A survey of the intelligence of more than 500 Filipino children tested and studied at the National Coordinating Center for the Study of Youth and Children and measured by such tests as the WISC, the Stanford Revision of the Binet, the Grace Arthur Point Scale and several local tests which we have ourselves constructed for the Center, all indicate that the average intelligence of our young Filipino subjects ran between I.Q. 101 to 108.[182]

It is necessary to affirm that Filipinos have the ability (*may kakayahan*) and ingenuity (*di gaya-gaya*) to make things on their own, which are their positive traits. However, their low self-esteem (*mababang tingin sa sarili*) and mediocrity (*pwede na yan* mentality), which resulted from colonialism, demand immediate attention. Colonialism has had an adverse and lasting effect on Filipinos, to the extent of almost obliterating their identity. But while it cannot be denied that Filipinos of today are byproducts of their past, they can choose not to be affected by it anymore and sever the lingering influence of their colonial masters over them. There is a need for the Filipino Christian teachers to cease to rely too much on the works of others (*curriculum over-dependence*) and to come up with their own curricula that are truly Filipino.

(4) Planning

Generally, Filipinos have been known for having a low regard for planning and preparation. The two cultural values that may influence them to behave in this manner are the *ningas-kugon* and the *bahala na* attitude. Samson defines *ningas-kugon* as "the tendency to become over-enthusiastic at starting a piece of work and then gradually losing the enthusiasm to a point where almost no

---

181. Gapuz and Lozada, 2.
182. Samson, "Is There a Filipino Psychology," 62.

work is ever completed. . . . Like a rocket that suddenly spurts and then sputters, the individual experiences a spontaneous rise in mental energy followed by a gradual fall of energy level due to the onset of indifference or apathy."[183] Gapuz and Lozada point out that the absence of discipline among Filipinos frequently ends in unproductive and wasteful work systems.[184] They should learn to be diligent in finishing what they have started and avoiding procrastination (the *mañana* habit) – which is deferring something that should be done right away.

Likewise, Gorospe emphasizes that the *bahala na* attitude "is tantamount to the Filipino *ningas kugon* or *mañana* habit, failings which show a lack of sense of responsibility and a false trust in Providence. . . . [It] is a kind of fatalistic resignation which really represents a withdrawal from engagement or crisis or a shirking of personal responsibility."[185] However, contrary to Gorospe's stance, Jocano explains:

> *Bahala na* is to be interpreted not as fatalism or resignation. Our respondents see it as a psychological prop that Filipinos use in times of crises, especially when they have examined their resources, narrowed their options down, and are pressed for a decision they are not ready to make. All they could say is *bahala na*, then they improvised and move on. *Bahala na*, to us, is calculated risk that enables Filipinos to face the future with resiliency and strength in time of need. As one farmer has said: "I strive hard and leave my future for God to decide."[186]

In view of that, Virgilio Enriquez also rejects the interpretation that *bahala na* is escapism or fatalism which he defines as "a passive acceptance of the turns in the patterns of life, indicated by a dislike for planning and taking responsibility for one's actions."[187] So, for Enriquez, *bahala na* is not an expression of fatalism but "determinism in the face of uncertainty."[188] To rectify the misinterpretation of *bahala na*, Alfredo Lagmay presents five of its important features:

(1) It stimulates action, not inaction;
(2) It is not used in order to avoid or forget problems;
(3) It implies perseverance and hardwork;

---

183. Samson, 60.
184. Gapuz and Lozada, "Framework for Analyzing the Filipino Character," 4.
185. Gorospe, "Christian Renewal of Filipino Values," 50.
186. Jocano, *Filipino Worldview*, 92–93.
187. Enriquez, *From Colonial to Liberation Psychology*, 72.
188. Enriquez, 72.

(4) It gives a person *lakas ng loob* (courage) to see himself through hard times;

(5) It stimulates creativity.[189]

Similarly, Gapuz and Lozada stress that "the faith of the Filipino is related to *bahala na* which, instead of being viewed as defeatist resignation, may be considered positively as . . . an important psychological prop on which we can lean during hard times. This *pampalakas ng loob* allows us to act despite uncertainty."[190] Finally, Gorospe is also convinced that if humans will do their part to solve their problems, God will do his and supply whatever is deficient in their effort: "A Christian sense of responsibility and of trust in Divine Providence is the positive use of the *bahala na* attitude."[191] Thus, the *ningas-kugon* attitude among Filipinos is to be viewed as a negative Filipino value that needs transformation, whereas the *bahala na* mentality is to be affirmed when used positively.

All of the aforementioned cultural values combined together are the possible reasons why Filipino Christians do not plan and strategize for suitable and strategic locations for their small groups but rather follow a non-strategy of *meeting anywhere*.

Some cultural values and traits such as *hiya,* small group-centeredness, conformity, and the *bahala na* mentality can work either for or against Filipinos depending on how they employ them. As Gorospe concludes, "There is no reason then why Filipino values cannot become the potential for Christian values. . . . [They] can be re-oriented and mobilized not only towards nation-building but also towards a new Christian Philippines."[192] Furthermore, Filipino Christians need to be involved enough with culture to know the values and traits that should be altered. From the words of Jocano, "One of the characteristics of culture is change. No culture remains constant or static. Change is the dynamic unfolding of culture."[193] This study affirms the need to transform negative Filipino cultural values and traits. But transforming culture today is dependent on a Christian's clear understanding of two things: Christ's relationship to culture and the church's relationship to culture.

---

189. Alfredo V. Lagmay, "Bahala Na," in *Ulat ng Ikalawang Pambansang Kumperensiya sa Sikolohiyang Pilipino* (Quezon City: Pambansang Samahan sa Sikolohiyang Pilipino, 1976), 120–130, cited in Enriquez, *From Colonial to Liberation Psychology*, 73.

190. Gapuz and Lozada, "Framework for Analyzing the Filipino Character," 3.

191. Gorospe, "Christian Renewal of Filipino Values," 51.

192. Gorospe, 57, 59.

193. Jocano, *Towards Developing a Filipino Corporate Culture*, 121.

There are various positions concerning Christ and culture. In Niebuhr's classic book, he outlines five prevalent viewpoints on the issue of Christ and culture: two extreme approaches – *Christ against culture* (radicals) and *Christ of culture* (accommodationists/liberals)[194] – and three mediating positions – *Christ above culture* (synthesists), *Christ and culture* in paradox (dualists), and *Christ the transformer of culture* (conversionists).[195] This book prefers the last of Niebuhr's five models because of its "more positive and hopeful attitude toward culture."[196] However, following Craig Carter who critiqued Niebuhr's work, this study qualifies the kind of conversionist's standpoint it will support – that is

---

194. Niebuhr, *Christ and Culture*, 45–115. The first viewpoint, *Christ against culture* (the antagonist model), recognizes Christ alone as authoritative and not culture. Niebuhr states that this position "uncompromisingly affirms the sole authority of Christ over the Christian and resolutely rejects culture's claims to loyalty" (45). This is a radical view which identifies culture with "the world" as used in passages such as 1 John 2:15–16 and 5:19, where Christians are enjoined against loving "the world," since the world is "a realm under the power of evil" (48). This position asserts opposition, total separation, and an aura of antagonism towards culture. On the opposite extreme, the *Christ of culture* view acknowledges that there is good in culture and regards culture as authoritative, not Christ. Niebuhr cites that those who espouse this position (the accommodationist approach) "on the one hand interpret culture through Christ, regarding those elements in it as most important which are most accordant with his work and person; on the other hand, they understand Christ through culture, selecting from his teaching and action as well as from the Christian doctrine about him such points as seem to agree with what is best in civilization" (83). This viewpoint accommodates the gospel to what the world values most dearly. Christ is identified with the best and highest of human wisdom.

195. Niebuhr, 116–229. The *Christ above culture* view (the synthetic model) believes that Christ and culture are different and, unlike the first viewpoint (*Christ against culture*) recognizes that there is good in both. Those who take this stance are what Niebuhr calls the "church of the center" (116). The word *synthesis* is important in a broad understanding of this approach. Their aim is to correlate the fundamental questions of culture with the answers of Christian revelation. They therefore strive for a theology of synthesis, with cultural expectations subordinated to Christian concerns (120). The *Christ and culture in paradox* position is dualistic in a sense that the Christian is said to belong to two realms (the spiritual and temporal) and must live in the tension of fulfilling responsibilities to both. The dualists find "the need for holding together as well as for distinguishing between loyalty to Christ and responsibility for culture" (149). Niebuhr uses the term *paradox* to explain the fact that the dualist "is standing on the side of man in the encounter with God, yet seeks to interpret the Word of God which he has heard coming from the other side" (156). The last perspective is *Christ the transformer of culture*. Niebuhr observes that the conversionist motif is "most closely akin to dualism" (190). However, according to Niebuhr, "what distinguishes conversionists from dualists is their more positive and hopeful attitude toward culture" (191). Their more affirmative stance emanates from three theological perspectives: (1) highlighting the incarnation of the Son in creation and his coming into human culture as part of the work of redemption (191–193); (2) understanding the fall as the distortion of the good rather than equating it with physical existence (193–194); (3) seeing history as "the present encounter with God in Christ" and thus living not "so much in expectation of a final ending of the world of creation and culture as in awareness of the power of the Lord to transform all things by lifting them up to himself" (195).

196. Niebuhr, 191.

the one which rejects physical coercion or violence.[197] As mentioned by Carter, this position argues that "we should not trust ourselves to use violence. It is not our calling; our calling is to witness to the gospel of Jesus Christ. His [Jesus's] calling is to be the Lord of the cosmos, and when he returns he will do what only he can do with perfect justice."[198] Heeding the stand of the "non-violent" conversionist, this study strongly believes that the Lord has the power to change all things, and is very hopeful in the eventual transformation of human culture. There is no need for Christians, then, to seek to impose Jesus's teaching upon society by force but to simply speak the life-changing truth in love.

There is a need, therefore, for Christ to transform, through the church as his catalyst, the negative Filipino cultural values and traits such as clericalism, exclusivity, mediocrity (*pwede na yan* mentality), and the *ningas-kugon* attitude which are all largely rooted in colonialism. Nevertheless, some cultural values and traits, such as *hiya*, small group-centeredness, conformity, and *bahala na* mentality, can work either for or against Filipinos depending on how they are employed. Later, in the next section, this book will formulate a contemporary small group theology that Christ's church can use in its prophetic ministry[199] to affirm positive and transform negative Filipino cultural values connected to *leading, grouping, studying,* and *planning* as they are aligned to the Scriptures.

3. Comparison of Two Worlds

How is the Filipino world similar to or different from the Greco-Roman world? Contextually, the setting of first-century Greco-Romans and twenty-first century Filipinos are individually unique and far apart in time from each other. But this work takes up the challenge of comparing the two worlds, at least where both agree on the three-fold purpose of a typical residential space as structural (house), social (household), and spiritual (house-cult). Hence, this book establishes the idea that both the Greco-Roman and Filipino house can have a three-in-one use as a single space for domestic, public, and cultic functions.

---

197. Carter, *Rethinking Christ and Culture*, 180–196. In his review and critique of Niebuhr's book, *Christ and Culture*, Carter differentiates Christendom and non-Christendom approaches to the problem of Christ and culture and contends that the former accept violent coercion and the latter reject it. According to Carter, Niebuhr failed to make this necessary distinction, particularly between the two typologies of Christ as the transformer of culture.

198. Carter, 193.

199. The word "prophetic" is used here in the sense of "forth-telling" and not "fore-telling."

a. Greco-Roman and Filipino contexts

(1) House

The basic function of the Greek *oikos* during the first century was structurally as a house. As mentioned earlier, based on archaeological evidence that has given light to a hypothetical Roman house church, it was typical for the non-elite Pompeian craftworkers' domestic structures to be in relatively small medium-sized apartments. Despite the limited space, there was a dividing line separating the male family members from female family members – so that the women would take the private space for domestic chores, whereas the men utilized the public area of the house for work-related activities. However, the Greco-Roman houses were also very open to other people for social gathering. Could the same be said of the early Filipino house which has had a strong cultural influence on current residential structures in the Philippines?

John Leddy Phelan keenly observes that there are three early buildings in the Philippines which constitute the three strands of influence from Malayan, Spanish and American culture – namely, the nipa palm house, Roman Catholic Church or cathedral, and schoolhouse, respectively.[200] Of the three early structures, however, the nipa hut – a.k.a. the *bahay kubo* – is the typical indigenous house in the countryside. Prior to the existence of concrete houses today, the early Filipino house in rural settings was typically wooden, made of bamboo and nipa palm. Spanish jurist and chronicler, Antonio de Morga depicted the seventeenth-century Filipino house:

> The houses and dwellings of all these natives [Filipinos] are universally set upon stakes and *arigues* (i.e., columns) high above the ground. They are built and tiled with wood and bamboos, and covered and roofed with nipa-palm leaves. Each house is separate, and is not built adjoining another. In the lower part are enclosures made by stakes and bamboos, where their fowls and cattle are reared, and the rice pounded and cleaned. One ascends into the house by means of ladders that can be drawn up, which are made from two bamboos. Above are their open *batalanes* (galleries) used for household duties; the parents and children live together.[201]

---

200. John Leddy Phelan, *The Hispanization of the Philippines* (Madison: University of Wisconsin Press, 1959), cited in Tuggy, *Philippine Church*, 17.

201. Antonio de Morga, "Sucesos de las Islas Filipinas," in Blair and Robertson, *Philippine Islands, 1493–1803*, vol. 16 (Cleveland, OH: A. H. Clark Co., 1903), 117–118, quoted in Agoncillo and Guerrero, *History of the Filipino People*, 33–34.

Furthermore, due to Filipino hospitality, even strangers could easily intrude on family privacy. Visitors are highly esteemed to the extent that even the family food, bedroom, and lavatory are offered to them. The living room in daytime is converted into a bedroom at night by laying down a mat or *banig* on the floor where all the family members sleep together. The stay-in helper or *aliping sagigilid*[202] sleeps in any space available in the house. The men's work area is either below the elevated house where the farm animals are raised or within the perimeter fence where crops and vegetables are grown.

In recent years, when houses have no longer been made of wood but solid concrete, the cultural impact of the ancient nipa hut has yet remained. The togetherness of Filipino family members (both male and female) in their living quarters and their openness to family friends and neighbors (though not strangers, due to security reasons) are still evident today and kept intact, even in the urban context. Such inseparability and hospitality lingered all the more since most middle-class Filipino rented residential spaces are already adjoining others in apartments or solid-concrete medium and high rise condominiums. Moreover, as part of the American influence, the separation of residential and commercial spaces is now also required and strictly observed in the country's major cities.

Likewise, the Roman *domus* is known for its deficiency in domestic privacy. The only private space allotted for the family were the bedrooms and baths. All family members would dine together, unless guests arrived and were entertained by the male host in the atrium. The house was designed to separate public work space (for men) from domestic work space (for women) under a single roof. A segregated quarter for domestic slaves, however, was also lacking. The slaves slept anywhere close to their work areas for easy access by their masters who treated them as objects.

Therefore, while the Greco-Roman houses' lack of domestic privacy can likewise be observed in the Malayan-influenced Filipino housing, there is no dividing line separating the male family members from females in Filipino families. But Paul, having introduced a cultural transformation among Greco-Roman Christians, said, "There is neither . . . male nor female; for you are all one in Christ Jesus" (Gal 3:28).

---

202. "The *aliping sagigilid* had no property of his own, lived with the master, and could not even marry without the latter's consent. . . . The *aliping namamahay*, on the other hand, had his own family and house and served his master during planting and harvest season, rowed for him, helped in the construction of his house, and served his visitors" (Agoncillo and Guerrero, *History of the Filipino People*, 35).

The *oikos* community then and now, being almost the same in context, would provide this study a good feasibility to apply the principles of the first century Greco-Roman *oikos* to the twenty-first century Filipino house where small group gatherings are held. Regardless of the differences in structural size and partition the dynamics of being relatively small stays the same.

(2) Household

During the first century, the Greek *oikos* was also utilized socially as a household. Sociological findings depict Greco-Romans as family-centered by virtue of their high value for households, which is similarly evident among Filipinos. As Arthur Tuggy affirms, "The family is the effective center of Philippine social life. Indeed, it is the most important element in Philippine social organization."[203] To the Filipinos a family is equivalent to a home which is to be differentiated from a house. Distinguishing between the two, a house (*bahay*) refers to the building itself and a home (*tahanan*) to the people constituting the Filipino family.

Osiek and Balch presented earlier that "the family in a traditional Mediterranean society can be understood as a diachronic and synchronic association of persons related by blood, marriage, and other social conventions."[204] Interestingly, the same applies to the Filipino family which is classified generally as "a bilateral extended type."[205] Likewise, the relationships in a Filipino extended family are established biologically by blood, legally by marriage, and ritually by ceremony. Since both the Greco-Roman and Filipino families are closely knitted, the shame of one member affects the entire family.

In terms of parental control, Greco-Roman and Filipino parents are also alike. Both of them exercise absolute authority over their children. They have the proclivity to make decisions on matters pertaining to their children's education and marriage. Both Greco-Roman and Filipino parents favor a family-arranged marriage in order to find suitable partners for their children. After marriage, the male child's attachment to his mother is never severed to the extent that he is more attached to her than to his own wife. However, while Filipino and Greco-Roman parents may have similarities, they also differ in some ways especially in raising children. Gapuz and Lozada note that "child rearing in the Filipino family is characterized by high nurturance, low independence training and low discipline. The Filipino child grows up in an atmosphere of

---

203. Tuggy, *Philippine Church*, 161.

204. Osiek and Balch, *Families in the New Testament World*, 41.

205. Castillo, "Church in Thy House," 103.

affection and overprotection where one learns security and trust on the one hand and dependence on the other."[206]

Additionally, females in Greco-Roman culture were regarded as inferior to males. This was not the case, however, among early Filipinos where women were not viewed lower than men. As Agoncillo and Guerrero explicate,

> Women before the coming of the Spaniards enjoyed a unique position in society that their descendants during the Spanish occupation did not enjoy. Customary laws gave them the right to be the equal of men, for they could own and inherit property, engage in trade and industry, and succeed to the chieftainship of a *barangay* in the absence of a male heir. Then, too, they had the exclusive right to give names to their children. As a sign of deep respect, the men, when accompanying women, walked behind them.[207]

So men and women during the pre-colonial period had equal rights until Spain, and then America, invaded the Philippines. Fortunately, women's rights were eventually restored. Changes started when Filipinos were preparing for independence from their colonial masters. For instance, in September 1937, a law was passed by the National Assembly allowing women to vote and run for public office.[208] Today, equal treatment is enjoyed by both males and females and, in most families, by both parents. As Tuggy points out, "the roles of the father and mother are remarkably balanced in the Philippine family."[209] While the mother, the person in-charge of domestic work, may be functionally subordinated to the father who is the head of the family and responsible for public work, in essence they are one. As mentioned previously, both share in the leadership of the home. The Filipino father is called *haligi ng tahanan* (pillar of the home), whereas the Filipino mother is known as *ilaw ng tahanan* (light of the home). Therefore, while distinction in gender is made between the two, both the Greco-Romans and Filipinos are undeniably family-oriented.

(3) House-cult

Lastly, the Greek *oikos* during the first century also functioned spiritually as a house-cult. Klauck emphasized earlier that "the house-cult was of great importance in Greco-Roman religious practice, corresponding to the valued

---

206. Gapuz and Lozada, "Framework for Analyzing the Filipino Character," 7.

207. Agoncillo and Guerrero, *History of the Filipino People*, 35.

208. Agoncillo and Guerrero, 370.

209. Tuggy, *Philippine Church*, 161.

role of the household within the social structure."[210] This includes the private cult of Philadelphia in Lydia and Orgeones (sacrificial societies) at Athens, and the Sarapis-cult, Mithra-cult, and Dionysiac-cult in Pompeii and Rome.[211] It can be observed that the Greeks influenced the Romans religiously from the very outset as demonstrated by the Roman equivalents of the Greek gods and their interest in Greek mythology.[212]

Just like Greco-Romans, Filipinos also utilize their houses for religious purposes. In fact, as Tuggy observes, "The religious life of the family seems to center almost more in the family than in the church. . . . There are the ever-present family shrines in Philippine homes, and many wealthy families have their own private chapels."[213] It is indisputable, nevertheless, that house-cults were the effect of colonial influence. The pre-colonial Filipinos were animistic by nature and worshipped the *anitos* or invisible beings[214] until the Spaniards introduced Catholicism to the Philippines.[215] Agoncillo and Guerrero pinpoint that "Catholicism, however, did not entirely displace the pre-colonial religion. . . . Filipinos saw little distinction between magic and the Catholic belief in miracles, idolatry and the veneration of saints and images, superstitions and certain Catholic rituals."[216] Thus, in the Philippines, Catholicism is very distinct as it combines both Christian and pagan beliefs together.[217]

Consequently, the concoction of ancient Filipino animism and Spanish Catholicism resulted in folk Christianity. The aberration of people's religious concepts of Christ and his mother Mary prompted images of the Marian cult ("Mother of God") and Christ-Child (Santo Niño or "Holy Child") to be popular in every Filipino house shrine. According to Clouse, Pierard, and Yamauchi,

> The most popular of the medieval saints was the Virgin Mary. Although her cult originated in the early church, it was encouraged by the use of the term *Theotokos* ("the bearer of God") at the ecumenical church councils. The concern there was to reinforce

210. Klauck, "House Church as Way of Life," 156.

211. Klauck, 156.

212. Craig, *Heritage of World Civilizations*, 138.

213. Tuggy, *Philippine Church*, 161.

214. Tano, *Theology in the Philippine Setting*, 15.

215. Agoncillo and Guerrero, *History of the Filipino People*, 71.

216. Agoncillo and Guerrero, 97.

217. Agoncillo and Guerrero, 47.

a belief in the deity of Christ and the reality of the incarnation against Arian and Monophysite dissenters. At first the cult of the Virgin was strongest in the East, but by the ninth century it had sunk deep roots in the West as well.

She was believed to be the mediator between God and humans, in that she prayed to her Son to have mercy on sinners. Born without sin (the "Immaculate Conception"), ever virgin and sinless in her life, and taken up into heaven at her death (the "Assumption"), she was the ideal combination of purity and maternal affection. By the thirteenth century she was also known as the Queen of Heaven, and the respect given to her surpassed all previous limits. Although she was venerated with a worship higher than that offered to other saints, it was officially understood that she would not receive the worship reserved for her Son, who was God. Her miracles included helping the poor, healing the sick, and comforting the lonely.[218]

On the other hand, the devotion to the Christ-Child or Santo Niño goes back to the earliest part of the Spanish colonization of the Philippines. As Leonardo Mercado writes, "The Santo Niño was the statue which Magellan gave to queen of Cebu in 1521. Juan Camus, one [of] Legazpi's soldiers discovered it in 1565 in one of the houses spared by the fire of the fleeing Cebuanos. Legazpi enthroned the statue in the first church of the Philippines named Santisimo Nombre de Jesus."[219] Though the Santo Niño depicts an infant Jesus that has never grown into adulthood ("forever a child"), he is most recognized as a miraculous figure because he is believed to have "defeated enemies in battle, repulsed invaders, extinguished fires, provided food, and so forth."[220] This makes him one of the favorite images in homes or sometimes even in offices and public utility vehicles. The devotees pray to him for all their needs, including protection and healing, in exchange for a vow or *panata* if petitions would be granted. Later on, the devotion to this house-cult reached other parts of the country that popularly made it into a national religious icon.

The adapted Marian cult ("Virgin Mary") and the indigenous Christ-Child known as "Santo Niño" have attracted a plenitude of followers in the Philippines and have become favorite house-cults since Filipinos identify so much with these "mother and child" images. Filipinos are accustomed to being treated

---

218. Clouse, Pierard, and Yamauchi, *Two Kingdoms*, 181–182.

219. Mercado, *Inculturation and Filipino Theology*, 143.

220. Mercado, 143.

like dependent children that have never matured and are always in need of a mother's care. Consequently, like small children they looked up to their colonial masters (Spaniards and Americans) for maternal guidance and, hence, became slaves to their cultural influence. Historically, the early Filipinos were partially Hispanized for more than three hundred years (1521–1898) in terms of the Spanish *religion* and nearly Americanized for almost fifty years (1898–1946) through the English *language*. However, it should be noted that the ancient Greeks were also colonized by the Romans during the early centuries; and yet, instead of being Romanized, they Hellenized their invaders by strongly influencing them through their prominent Greek language and religion. Thus, the effects of colonization do not necessarily mean that the one colonized becomes lesser or inferior to the colonizer. It is a matter of choice.

Therefore, this study has clearly shown how the setting of the twenty-first century Filipino is parallel to that of the first-century Greco-Roman in terms of the three-fold function of a domestic space as a house (structural), household (social), and house-cult (spiritual). If the Greco-Roman domestic buildings were plausibly used for Christian house church assembly, then there is no reason why a Filipino house cannot be utilized as a venue for a Christian small group gathering. The three-fold advantage of the residential house being used for religious purposes is as follows: (1) in being domestic, the target family members are already there; (2) in being public, other families in the community can easily be invited to join; and (3) in being cultic, it is readily open to be utilized for spiritual functions just like a church building. So the parallel between the Greco-Roman and Filipino contexts makes the comparison between New Testament house churches and Filipino small groups analogous.

b. NT house churches and Filipino small groups

Is there a connection that can be established between a house church and a small group? Is it appropriate to conclude that the house church in the New Testament that Paul wrote about is also the small group as we understand it today? Prior to the introduction of basilical architecture, Snyder designates the small group, during the first two-hundred years, as the basic unit of the church's life.[221] As Meeks also points out,

> One cannot read far in the letters of Paul and his disciples without discovering that it was a concern about the internal life of the Christian groups in each city that prompted most of the correspondence. The letters also reveal that those groups enjoyed

---

221. Snyder, *Problem of Wine Skins*, 139.

an unusual degree of intimacy, high levels of interaction among members, and a very strong sense of internal cohesion and of distinction both from outsiders and from "the world." . . . The Pauline congregations belong to the category studied extensively by modern sociologists, especially American sociologists, and called "small groups" or simply "groups."[222]

Hence, Meeks refers to a house church as an "individual household-based group" which was "the 'basic cell' of the Christian movement," the nucleus of which "was often an existing household."[223] Likewise, Gehring calls it a "Christian fellowship group that [was] formed in and/or around an *oikos*."[224] The ancient *oikos* becomes a simple Christian fellowship group only if there are other church people meeting in several houses at one location which is a case of "the distribution of the local church per house."[225] So while New Testament house churches are perceived today as local churches in themselves by the house church movement, the truth of the matter is that they are not. They are only church-based, that is, they work alongside a local church and are not fully autonomous. Gehring argues that a "house church" only becomes a "local church" if there is one house church meeting at that particular locality.[226] Thus, a house church is a church (though not in the full sense) in a house setting and, at the same time, is a small group in a house context.

Moreover, both the concepts of a house church and a small group consists of the three-fold essential elements, namely, place (the "where"), people (the "who"), and purpose (the "why"), which are all derived from the Christian concept of ἐκκλησία or the New Testament church.[227] So the New Testament house church, as defined earlier, is the regular gathering of a small Christian assembly (*people*) in someone's domestic residence (*place*) where the common practices of the early church are observed (*purpose*), such as the sharing of leadership, shepherding of families, searching of Scriptures, and saturating of cities. In the same manner, the contemporary small group was described as

---

222. Meeks, *First Urban Christians*, 74.

223. Meeks, 75.

224. Gehring, *House Church and Mission*, 119.

225. Gehring, 157.

226. Gehring, 27.

227. As defined earlier, the Christian ἐκκλησία – the New Testament church – is the gathering of specific people, of *Christians only*, for the specific purpose of *worship alone*, both locally (in the place to gather people specifically at only one location) and universally (in the place to worship God generally at any one location). In short, the term ἐκκλησία in the New Testament is God's *people* meeting together for the *purpose* of worship, locally in one *place* and universally in any *place*.

the consistent meeting together of a small Christian assembly composed of a volunteer-based leader and home-focused learners (*people*) for Bible-centered lessons (*purpose*) in a Spirit-directed location (*place*).

Aside from similarities in concept, both the house church and the small group are parallel in size, which is relatively small when compared to the size of people meeting in a big church building. So while they are both church-based, they are also both house-sized. Size does matter. Rad Zdero stresses that a group's size affects the individual relationships between members and the group dynamics as a whole, as well as the process of education.[228] Likewise, McBride shares this practical principle which he adapted from Marvin Shaw, "The smaller the group, the greater the feasibility of shared leadership. Increasing group size increases the probability of a focused leader rather than shared leadership."[229] The dynamics of meeting in small numbers compared to large numbers affects not only the leaders but also other components such as the learners, lessons, and locations, as demonstrated in the table below:

Table 3.4 A study in contrast: The dynamics of meeting in small and large numbers

Components	Dynamics of Meeting in Small Numbers	Dynamics of Meeting in Large Numbers
1. Leaders	Non-professional	Professional
2. Learners	Small Diverse Group	Big Mixed Group
3. Lessons	Interactive	Lecture-type
4. Locations	Closed and Private	Open and Public

Thus, the dynamics of leading, teaching, or ministering to a small family-sized group is evidently different than the dynamics of a large church-sized group. Since both house churches and small groups meet in small numbers, their dynamics are similar, and both could expect non-professional leaders teaching a small diverse group of learners with interactive lessons in closed and private locations. Though comparable in size and group dynamics, the typical Filipino small group, however, is culturally conditioned instead of being biblically influenced, as shown in this table:

---

228. Zdero, *Global House Church Movement*, 37. Though this research does not concur with all Zdero's conjectures and conclusions, his argument here is found valid and significant.

229. Marvin E. Shaw, *Group Dynamics: The Psychology of Small Group Behavior* (New York: McGraw-Hill, 1981), cited in McBride, *How to Lead Small Groups*, 57.

Table 3.5 A comparative study of the NT church/house church and the Filipino small group

Components	New Testament Church	New Testament House Church	Typical Filipino Small Group
1. Shepherds	Usually Apostles	Usually Householders	Clergy Only
2. Sheep	Practically Many Households	Practically Few Households	Limited to Adults
3. Study	Generally Formal Biblical Learning	Generally Informal Biblical Learning	Curriculum Overly Dependent
4. Sites	Strategically in Urban Public Spaces	Strategically in Urban Domestic Spaces	Meeting Anywhere

Instead of having householders for the shepherds, a few households for the sheep, informal biblical learning for the study, and strategic urban domestic spaces for the sites, the typical Filipino small group sadly tends towards having clergy only, being limited to adults, being curriculum overly dependent, and meeting anywhere, respectively. A major contributing factor to this is the cultural context of the Filipino small group which needs transformation in terms of values in leading, grouping, studying, and planning by appropriating the New Testament house church practices (see the table below).

Table 3.6 Comparison of two cultural contexts

Components	New Testament House Church Practices	Filipino Small Group Culture
1. Leading	Involvement of Laity (sharing of leadership)	Clerical Mentality and *Hiya* (clergy only)
2. Grouping	Inclusivity of the Whole Family (shepherding of families)	Exclusivity and Small Group-Centeredness (limited to adults)
3. Studying	In-depth Bible Study (searching of Scriptures)	Mediocrity, Colonial Mentality and Conformity (curriculum overly dependent)
4. Planning	Intentional Urban Strategy (saturating of cities)	*Ningas-kugon* and *Bahala na* Attitude (meeting anywhere)

Understanding both the New Testament house church practices and the Filipino small group culture is very important to small group leaders in making their leadership and biblical teaching ministry suitable to the group members' context and reaching out to the immediate community where the small group is situated. This is essential in formulating a contemporary small group theology that will affirm positive and transform negative Filipino cultural values by using God's Word.

C. Content of Small Group Theology

So far, the areas of theological study that have already been covered in this book are biblical, historical, and doctrinal. The final stage of establishing the theological foundation for this study should then be practical – that is, appropriating New Testament house church practices by formulating contemporary small group theology. In his article "A Theology of Small Groups," Darin Kennedy forewarns that

> whenever the practical precedes the theological, a danger exists. When the foundation laid in a discussion is a "good" idea based on the experience of human beings, the discussion of God's ideas found in Scripture and in his interaction with the church is either ignored completely or used secondarily to support the original idea. Blindly following such practical ideas without giving attention to the questions and challenges of God's Word will void the idea of the life and success of God's eternal purpose. . . .
>
> If God's purposes continue throughout time and small groups fit into those purposes, then they will naturally continue when God's eternal purposes are examined and followed. However, one cannot make the connection that they did it then; therefore, God must have always wanted congregations to have small groups. The mention of small groups within Scripture simply becomes prooftexts for practicalism rather than the foundational word for the church's purpose, life, and ministry.[230]

Furthermore, Kennedy stresses that "presently, several writers are beginning to ask theological questions about the biblical concept of community and the place of small groups within it, which deserve to be recognized and discussed for what they really are."[231] The fourfold life-goal of every small group in a given area is: (1) to share its leader's life in the Lord with another potential leader

---

230. Kennedy, "Theology of Small Groups," 175.
231. Kennedy, 176.

among the laity (small group ministry); (2) to shepherd the life of each family member in the fold in every level (small group community); (3) to study the Word alone to change the group leader and each member's life (small group teaching); and (4) to strategize in sharing Christ's eternal life to the world by winning every lost life in each locality (small group mission). It is rare to find a study today on the theology of small groups dealing with these four areas – small group ministry, small group community, small group teaching, and small group mission – that results in volunteer-based leaders, home-focused learners, Bible-centered lessons, and Spirit-directed locations, respectively.

1. Small Group Leaders: Volunteer-Based Ministry

The first New Testament house church practice, discussed earlier, is the *sharing of leadership*. The transient apostles shared the local leadership of individual house churches with the householders, which even included women. This practice was made possible by the belief in the priesthood of all believers in Christ. It was also practical: since the apostles, with their very limited number and presence, could not accomplish all the tasks by themselves, they delegated or shared the leadership of the house church with trained and qualified members. The same applies to what small group leaders should be today: *volunteer-based*.

MacArthur comments, "In the New Testament church leadership belonged collectively to a group of elders who were its leaders under the Spirit of God. One man was not responsible for doing everything, and that's how it should be. The pastor is not the professional problem-solver who runs around with an ecclesiastical bag of tools, waiting for the next problem to repair or the next squeaky wheel to grease."[232] Sadly, the pastor is perceived today as a hired "trained professional," which means he should do everything in the church. This explains why even small group leadership is deemed for clergy only. Darrell Robinson labels this mindset as "The Corporate Model."[233] This is not God's design for what a church should be. The church is not a corporation and the pastor is not the CEO (Chief Executive Officer) of the church. The pastor needs to delegate and share the ministry with church volunteers. Robinson states, "No one pastor can be everything that is needed in the church."[234] As the Apostle Paul declares, "And He [Christ] gave some as apostles, and some

---

232. MacArthur, *Master's Plan*, 85.
233. Robinson, *Total Church Life*, 91.
234. Robinson, 60.

as prophets, and some as evangelists, and some as pastors and teachers, for the equipping of the saints for the work of service, to the building up of the body of Christ" (Eph 4:11–12). Thus, it is the responsibility of every believer to be a minister, while the pastor's role is to administer or be an equipper.

Donahue and Robinson suggest, "Creating a leadership culture hinges, in part, on seeing everyone in your congregation as a potential leader. Talk to these leaders by practically embedding the doctrine of the priesthood of all believers."[235] It is noteworthy that some biblical images of the church depict it as "holy/royal priesthood" (1 Pet 2:5, 9) and "the temple of the Holy Spirit/of God" (1 Cor 3:16–17; 6:19–20; Eph 2:21–22; 1 Pet 2:5). Believers, therefore, are temples and priests at the same time. As James Leo Garrett Jr. further explains:

> In "The Biblical Doctrine of the Priesthood of the People of God" the author interpreted the corporate priesthood of Israel in the Old Testament, with special reference to Exod 19:4–6a, and, after summarizing the application of sacerdotal language to Jesus, identified those New Testament texts (1 Pet 2:4–10; Rev 1:5b–6; 5:9–10) which specifically teach that all Christians are priests, and interpreted the central function of the priesthood of all Christians as being the offering of "spiritual sacrifices" to God, such as in worship, witness, stewardship, and service (cf. Rom 12:1; 15:16; Phil 2:17; 4:17–18; Heb 13:15–16).[236]

Believers have access to God the Father by virtue of their relationship with the Son and are all part of a holy priesthood: "And coming to Him as to a living stone which has been rejected by men, but is choice and precious in the sight of God, you also, as living stones, are being built up as a spiritual house for a holy *priesthood*, to offer up spiritual sacrifices acceptable to God through Jesus Christ" (1 Pet 2:4–5). Malcolm B. Yarnell III stresses, however, that "the priesthood of believers is subsidiary to the primary doctrine of the eternal priesthood of Jesus Christ. The second person of the Trinity, the Son of God, became man in order to function as both Priest and sacrifice (Heb 3:1)."[237]

William Pitts Jr. points out that the biblical teaching on the priesthood of all believers has been important in the Baptist heritage:[238] "Rejection of exclusive

---

235. Donahue and Robinson, *Building a Church of Small Groups*, 187.

236. Huber L. Drumwright and Curtis Vaughan, *New Testament Studies: Essays in Honor of Ray Summers in His Sixty-Fifth Year*, (Waco, TX: Baylor University Press, 1975), 137–149, cited in Garrett, "Priesthood of All Christians," 22.

237. Yarnell, "Priesthood of Believers," 241.

238. Pitts, "Priesthood of All Christians in the Baptist Heritage," 34.

priestly representation and affirmation of the finality of Christ's sacrifice were key theological factors in the Protestant Reformation. . . . Baptists and other evangelicals reject the claims of apostolic succession and say that every Christian is a priest. There is only one kind of Christian, and every Christian is called to ministry."[239]

With regard to the Baptist teaching that every believer in the church is a priest, Thomas Lea argues that there is no reference in the New Testament to "priest" in the singular but only to "priesthood" or to "priests" (1 Pet 2:5; Rev 5:10) which implies that the priesthood of all believers is understood by the apostles corporately rather than individually.[240] As Lea concludes, "It is much more pleasing to God when a body of individuals acts collectively rather than fiercely independently. It is much more impressive to the world to see an army moving forward in service for Christ than to catch glimpse of a few lone individuals striking out on their own. Individuals must respond to the appeal to serve the Lord, but these individuals must act together."[241]

Moreover, when we highlight the nature of the priesthood of all believers, we can recognize that this biblical teaching stresses duty rather than merely privilege.[242] As Doyle Young describes it, "in its simplest form, [it] means that the believer has been chosen and redeemed by God *for a mission.* The emphasis in being one of God's chosen priests is not one's *status,* but one's *task.* It means that every Christian is a minister and has a ministry. It means every-member ministry."[243]

That all believers are priests does not mean, however, that all believers are pastors. It is understood in the Baptist belief that while every member is a priest, not all priests in the church are the same. There should be a clear distinction between the pastoral office and the priesthood of all believers. Christians are all similar in essence in God's sight but not in function, since only some and not all are called to serve as pastors (cf. Eph 4:11–12). All are ministers but not everyone administers. So while they are essentially equal, church members are functionally subordinated to their overseers. As Young explicates,

> Now, in one sense, it *is* true. Everyone in the church is of equal *value.* The ground at the foot of the cross *is* level. God does not

---

239. Mikolaski, "Contemporary Relevance of the Priesthood of All Christians," 6.

240. Lea, "Priesthood of All Christians According to the New Testament," 15.

241. Lea, 21.

242. Lea, 21.

243. Young, "What Difference Does It Make, Anyway?," 49.

favor one group or race or gender. An oft-quoted verse is Gal 3:28 – "There is neither Jew nor Greek, there is neither slave nor free, there is neither male nor female; for you are all one in Christ Jesus." There is no special sacerdotal class that is innately higher spiritually than the rest. In this sense, everyone in the church *is* the same.

But in another sense, all church members are *not* the same. The New Testament clearly teaches that there are *different* gifts and roles in the church. And one of the roles/tasks which God appoints and gifts some to fulfil is leadership or pastoral oversight.[244]

Consequently, the wrong understanding of the functional distinction between church leaders and church members has led to the dichotomy of the clergy and the laity. Alexander Faivre states that the term *laikos* (laity) is never to be found in the Septuagint and the New Testament, but rather in some sacrilegious writings from the third century BC onward. *Laikos* was seemingly applied "to designate the local population as opposed to the administration."[245] On the other hand, Faivre points out that in the New Testament the word *kleros* (clergy) is used not merely for the ministers but for the entire believing people.[246] As Faivre further elucidates,

> In the Christian communities of the first century, there was no independent priestly function that was exercised by a special caste or minister. The laity as such was not recognized in the New Testament, which speaks only of people, a holy people, a chosen people, a people set apart, a kleros entirely responsible for carrying out a royal priesthood and calling on each one of its members to give to God true worship in spirit.[247]

Likewise, Kirby cites that any drastic division between "clergy" and "laity" was unknown in the New Testament church since each church member was prompted to render a particular service, in the same way that the whole Church is called to a work of ministry.[248] So, during the early first century, the terms clergy and laity were non-existent until distinctions gradually started between the two. Clouse, Pierard, and Yamauchi recount,

---

244. Young, 48.

245. Faivre, *Emergence of the Laity in the Early Church*, 15.

246. Faivre, 7.

247. Faivre, 7.

248. Kirby, "Church," 852.

Clement of Rome at the end of the first century introduced the term "layman," [Greek *laos*, "people"] and Clement of Alexandria was the first to use the word "clergy" (taken from the Greek word *kleros* or "lot") to refer to individuals who exercised permanent ministry in the church. . . . As time passed, the gap between the two groups widened, and eventually the Ecumenical Council at Carthage (396) formally prohibited laymen from teaching in the presence of clergymen without the latter's consent.[249]

During the third century onwards, when the early church started to transition from residential houses to basilical buildings, significant things happened concerning the development of the distinction between the clergy and the laity. As Robinson presents,

By the latter part of the third century, gradual trends had developed that elevated the position of the bishops beyond the New Testament servant/leader role. As the church joined hands with the state, specific bishops came into places of prominence. Constantine, the Roman emperor, embraced Christianity. He made Christianity the official religion of the Roman Empire.

By the fifth century AD, the bishop of Rome had gained ascendancy. This gave rise to the emergence of the Roman Catholic hierarchy, with its papal system.

Gradually, the clergy was elevated and distrust was the attitude toward the laity. The Bible was taken out of the hands of the laity. It was felt that only the clergy could adequately understand and interpret it. Only the clergy could do the spiritual work of the ministry while the laity attended meetings and gave money.[250]

Today, Robinson correctly observes that churches tend to go to extremes by either overemphasizing the clergy and minimizing the laity, or minimizing the clergy and overemphasizing the laity, when both ministry leaders and ministry servants are necessary for a church to be effective.[251] Such a situation arises from the different orientations that church people have about the clergy nowadays. Gordon Smith quotes from John Stott's book *One People* to present the classic perspectives on the role of the clergy. In *clericalism*, "the clergy

---

249. Clouse, Pierard, and Yamauchi, *Two Kingdoms*, 52.
250. Robinson, *Total Church Life*, 83.
251. Robinson, 83.

was viewed as having complete authority and responsibility in the life of the church. They spoke the Word of God; they administered Holy Communion; they were the representatives of God on earth."[252] The other extreme is called *anti-clericalism* which "believed that the church is the people, that the laity (meaning people) are the church. Therefore, authority and responsibility should lie with them."[253] The moderate position, *dualism,* "seeks to affirm both the clergy and the laity, but views them as separate and distinct callings [sacred and secular vocations]. . . . In some cases the clergy still carry great authority and responsibility in the life of the church. In other situations, the laity may have an extensive involvement in congregational life, assuming authority through a lay council and responsibility in various dimensions of the church's life."[254]

Weber comments against clericalism and anti-clericalism: "It is no secret that most churches suffer from the evil of clericalism. However, the remedy for this illness is not the anti-clericalism which characterizes so many lay movements, but the recovery of the whole people of God, the *laos,* which comprises both the laity with their ministry in the world and the office-bearers with their specific ministries."[255] If Weber takes the dualism position, would that be the best of the three? Smith concludes that none of the three perspectives is a valid scriptural or practical approach.[256] Smith, then, proposes a fourth position by viewing the pastor as a *catalyst.* By catalyst he means the person who helps others meet a desired goal, and a good example of this agent of change within a Christian community is the pastor.[257] So, as God's appointed catalyst, the pastor equips or prepares God's people "for the work of service" (Eph 4:11–12).

Hence, a correct understanding of the doctrine of the priesthood of all believers, and also the functional distinction between the clergy and the laity, is essential in formulating a theology on small group leadership. This is the essence of small group leaders appropriating the New Testament house church practice of the *sharing of leadership.* As McBride points out to group leaders,

> You may have the idea that you are responsible for all the leadership tasks within your group. On the contrary, as the designated leader

---

252. John Stott, *One People* (London: Falcon Books, 1968), 28–30, cited in Smith, *City Shepherds*, 80.

253. Smith, *City Shepherds*, 81.

254. Smith, 82.

255. Weber, "Church in the House," 24.

256. Smith, *City Shepherds*, 82.

257. Smith, 85.

your primary task is to give away the functional leadership of the group. Ideally, the group grows in its development to a point where the members – individually and corporately – share the leadership functions. Shared leadership is the ideal for most types of groups in the church. It's an outworking of the unity and functions of the body of Christ.[258]

Therefore, changing the small group's incorrect mindset on small group leaders (*clergy only*) through teaching a theology of small group ministry should result in a volunteer-based leadership that is focused on the mobilization of laity.

2. Small Group Learners: Home-Focused Community

The *shepherding of families* is the second New Testament house church practice. Robinson states that "a church as a body of Christ has a shepherding ministry to its people and community. The church must nurture, spiritually feed, and minister to a total community. The church is to pour out its life to reach and save its community."[259] More particularly, Greenway points out that urban evangelism is also aiming for the home; not a single family member disengaged from the household, but the whole family.[260] As mentioned earlier, there is plenitude of families in the New Testament which appear to be involved in house churches. These include the households of Prisca and Aquila, Aristobulus, Narcissus, Stephanas, Philemon and Apphia, Nympha, Caesar, and Lydia. This probably explains why the predominant biblical image of the church in the New Testament is a household[261] and why a church should function as a spiritual family. The household structures in the New Testament are also evident in Colossians 3:18–4:1 and Ephesians 5:21–6:9.[262] As the Christian families in the New Testament assembled in homes to study and learn from the apostles' teaching, it would be right to presume that the whole household (parents, children, and house slaves) was present and shared together in the spiritual practices. In the same manner, this is what small group learners should also be

---

258. McBride, *How to Lead Small Groups*, 40.

259. Robinson, *Total Church Life*, 57.

260. Roger Greenway, *An Urban Strategy for Latin America* (Grand Rapids, MI: Baker, 1973), 83–86, cited in Castillo, "Church in Thy House," 100.

261. For example, "the household of the faith," "the household of God," "house/household of Christ," "family of God," and "the bride of Christ."

262. Cf. the husband and wife relationship in Col 3:18–19 and Eph 5:21–33; the parents and children relationship in Col 3:20–21 and Eph 6:1–4; and the masters and slaves relationship in Col 3:22–4:1 and Eph 6:5–9.

today: *home-focused* and not only *limited to adults*. The question to ask is this: "Are small groups for families relevant nowadays?" The answer to this question relies on whether churches today value family ministry as the early church did.

In their book on *Marriage and Family Life*, Weldon and Joyce Viertel state that the home is the most significant of all social institutions because the success of the church, school, and state greatly depend on its strength.[263] So the Viertels conclude that strong families will establish strong churches, but weak families will build weak churches. While attention should be given to dysfunctional families or victims of broken homes, the future strength of the church will depend on stable homes that are grounded in the Word.[264] As John MacArthur explains, "The family is God's designated unit for passing righteousness on from one generation to the next (Deut 6:7, 20–25)."[265]

Metosalem Castillo, moreover, stresses that "the family is a winnable social unit which we should always seek to win in missionary work."[266] For this reason, Tuggy states that one of the imperatives for church growth in the Philippines is the evangelization of the household because it is a very essential unit of Philippine social organization: "The religious life of the family seems to center almost more in the family than in the church."[267] Castillo believes that this is so since the Philippines is and will continue to be a household-focused society.[268] We have heard it often said, "As the family goes, so goes the nation." But it can also be said that "as the family goes, so goes the church." Thus, it is important for every church around the world to strategically concentrate on family ministry if the global mission "to make disciples of all the nations" (Matt 28:19) is to be fulfilled: "The family belongs to God because He created it. He has designed its nature, determined its purposes, and appointed its responsibilities."[269]

Consider the doctrinal stance on "The Family" as incorporated in "The 2000 Baptist Faith and Message" where the family is depicted comprehensively in this way:

263. Viertel and Viertel, *Marriage and Family Life*, 1.

264. Viertel and Viertel, 8–9.

265. MacArthur, *Master's Plan for the Church*, 66.

266. Castillo, "Church in Thy House," 101.

267. Tuggy, *Philippine Church*, 160–161.

268. Castillo, "Church in Thy House," 98.

269. Viertel, *Marriage and Family Life*, 9.

God has ordained the family as the foundational institution of human society. It is composed of persons related to one another by marriage, blood, or adoption.

Marriage is the uniting of one man and one woman in covenant commitment for a lifetime. It is God's unique gift to reveal the union between Christ and His church and to provide for the man and the woman in marriage the framework for intimate companionship, the channel of sexual expression according to biblical standards, and the means for procreation of the human race.

The husband and wife are of equal worth before God, since both are created in God's image. The marriage relationship models the way God relates to His people. A husband is to love his wife as Christ loved the church. He has the God-given responsibility to provide for, to protect, and to lead his family. A wife is to submit herself graciously to the servant leadership of her husband even as the church willingly submits to the headship of Christ. She, being in the image of God as is her husband and thus equal to him, has the God-given responsibility to respect her husband and to serve as his helper in managing the household and nurturing the next generation.

Children, from the moment of conception, are a blessing and heritage from the Lord. Parents are to demonstrate to their children God's pattern for marriage. Parents are to teach their children spiritual and moral values and to lead them, through consistent lifestyle example and loving discipline, to make choices based on biblical truth. Children are to honor and obey their parents.[270]

Doctrinal teaching on the family should be taught both in the church and in the small group setting so that people will know and follow it. According to the Viertels, "If a church does not provide family education at every age, many will go through life without knowing what to expect as they move from

---

270. Southern Baptist Convention, "The 2000 Baptist Faith and Message." The doctrinal statement on "The Family" is based on the following Scripture references: Gen 1:26–28; 2:15–25; 3:1–20; Exod 20:12; Deut 6:4–9; Josh 24:15; 1 Sam 1:26–28; Pss 51:5; 78:1–8; 127; 128; 139:13–16; Prov 1:8; 5:15–20; 6:20–22; 12:4; 13:24; 14:1; 17:6; 18:22; 22:6, 15; 23:13–14; 24:3; 29:15, 17; 31:10–31; Eccl 4:9–12; 9:9; Mal 2:14–16; Matt 5:31–32; 18:2–5; 19:3–9; Mark 10:6–12; Rom 1:18–32; 1 Cor 7:1–16; Eph 5:21–33; 6:1–4; Col 3:18–21; 1 Tim 5:8, 14; 2 Tim 1:3–5; Titus 2:3–5; Heb 13:4; 1 Pet 3:1–7.

one stage to the next; therefore, they may experience undue anxiety and missed opportunities and happiness. Since Christian values are as significant as information on physical and social changes, a church has an obligation to provide a family-life educational program."[271] Hence, teaching that puts emphasis on the Christian home is a must for every church and for every member on every level. MacArthur forewarns, "Satan is using the immoral, lust-filled society we live in to attack the family. He has made it hard for the family to survive. The church has to help preserve the family."[272] The best way to protect the family from schemes of the evil one is through teaching sound doctrine both in big and small groups. The sample topics listed below for the family-life educational program are excellent for home discussion groups:

> The Importance of the Home
> The Basic Nature of the Home
> The Christian Ideal for the Home
> The Relationship of Husband and Wife
> The Demand for Marital Integrity
> The Relationship of Parents and Children
> Applying Christianity in the Home
> The Home's Need of Agape Love
> The Influence of Parents on Children
> The Importance of Consistent Discipline
> The Parent's Responsibility for the Spiritual Education of Their
>   Children
> Winning Children to Christ
> How Teenagers can Honor Parents[273]

With the demands of various age groups, some churches nowadays are skeptical of the home-focused small group ministry though it is correct to presume that it was a phenomenon in early Christianity as the first century church setting necessitated it. As Stott comments regarding the Roman house churches in particular, "We cannot suppose that they met according to sex or rank, so that there were different house churches for men and women, for slaves and free."[274] Since the church then was in a house setting, the mixing together of various people under one roof was inevitable. More importantly, Christ was their unifying factor (Gal 3:28). Things appeared to change when

---

271. Viertel, *Marriage and Family Life*, 234.

272. MacArthur, *Master's Plan for the Church*, 66.

273. Viertel, *Marriage and Family Life*, 230–231.

274. Stott, *Message of Romans*, 397.

large church buildings were introduced during the Constantinian period in the third century. Then down the centuries, groupings according to gender and age gradually evolved. As MacArthur correctly observes,

> There was a time when the family functioned as a unit. Every member went to church together and even sat in the same pew every Sunday. Then as the church became program-oriented, everyone went off and did his [or her] own thing. Groups were formed to counteract the loss of identity in a rapidly growing technological society. Old people became known as senior citizens. Kids became identified with youth groups that, in many cases, set the pace for the rest of the church. After a while the church began to leave the parents behind. There needs to be a balanced emphasis on all family members.[275]

A high view on family ministry is therefore essential in formulating a theology on small group ministry. Home-focused small group learning evidently includes all family members that need shepherding. However, this would likely affect the group dynamics. As McBride probes: "Are group members cross-generational, or close in age? . . . Should groups be homogeneous (same age, social status, etc.) or heterogeneous (mixed ages, social status, etc.)?"[276] Though McBride prefers homogenous groups in terms of age, he believes that both approaches are workable. McBride clarifies that "a church or organization need not limit itself to only one [approach]. With careful planning, it may be desirable to have some groups . . . be age-graded while others are cross-generational. The larger a church grows, the more it becomes necessary to provide a diversity within its groups' ministries."[277]

Moreover, McBride adds that "many churches elect to structure their entire groups' ministry around cross-generational groups. The benefits associated with such a grouping strategy are considered more important than any potential liabilities. Cross-generational groups are especially common in small churches where the numbers of people within the various age groups are not sufficient to warrant age-graded groups."[278] But big churches who are more prone to age-graded groups should also be willing to demographically divide their congregation into small groups according to household or family

---

275. MacArthur, *Master's Plan for the Church*, 111.
276. McBride, *How to Lead Small Groups*, 73.
277. McBride, 74–75.
278. McBride, 74.

in a given geographical location. Lastly, McBride shares these two practical guiding principles adapted from Shaw's book on *Group Dynamics*:

> People prefer to participate in groups where other members are similar in age, attractiveness, attitudes, personality, economic status, perceived ability, and needs. . . .
>
> Groups whose members [on the other hand] are heterogeneous with respect to sex and personality types are more conforming and perform more effectively than groups that are homogenous with respect to these characteristics. The opposite is true for age. Diversity among the members in some areas is helpful to the group's success.[279]

The efficacy of heterogeneous grouping is demonstrated according to the size of the group, which will not be a problem in a small group of ten to twelve members. It is possible, then, to open a home-focused group and invite other families to join. An example is the "Family Small Groups" of Saddleback Valley Community Church in Orange County, California. As depicted in its official website, these groups are designed to allow families to meet as a small group together with other families so that all ages can have fun as they live out God's purposes as a community.[280] Nonetheless, the common problem encountered in heterogeneous groupings with respect to age is the handling of small children. As McBride states, "I often hear the parents of young children express their frustration because they want to be in a group but can't find suitable child care. . . . What are you going to do with the children?"[281] McBride then practically suggests, "Include the children – have a group made up of family units. This can work, but be alert to the fact that having children in the group significantly changes the role and potential benefit experienced by the adults."[282] According to *The Cape Town Commitment* of the Lausanne Movement: "As we see in the Bible, God can and does use children and young people – their prayers, their insights, their words, their initiatives – in changing hearts. They represent 'new energy' to transform the world. Let us listen and not stifle their childlike spirituality with our adult rationalistic approaches."[283]

Consequently, this book makes this clarification on the matter: The theology on home-focused small group learners it formulates is not only

---

279. Shaw, *Group Dynamics*, cited in McBride, *How to Lead Small Groups*, 57, 58.
280. Saddleback Church, "Family Small Groups."
281. McBride, *How to Lead Small Groups*, 70.
282. McBride, 71.
283. *The Cape Town Commitment*.

restricted to having heterogeneous groupings with all the family members present in a given time and place. It could also mean meeting separately as homogeneous units according to age group (children, youth, and adults/ parents), provided that there is an integrated family-life educational program for all levels which, for its application, is followed up by parents at home. This study is aware of the challenges of ministering to learners of all ages as one integrated family unit. The reality according to Elizabeth Javalera, a Filipino Christian educator, is this: "Every learner is in a different stage of development. The four-year-old child, the fourteen-year-old adolescent, and the forty-year-old adult . . . are in three different stages. To help any particular age group to the fullest advantage, the teacher has to know what characterizes the stage they are in."[284] It may be difficult and very challenging to lead a heterogeneous group but doing a home-focused ministry is biblical. While it is easier to deal with homogeneous learners, the dynamics is different in handling a diverse group.

I believe, then, that small groups for families are still relevant today. In fact, some churches, especially mega-churches, are convinced that home-focused small groups are still applicable in the same manner they were in the early centuries. The bigger the church, the smaller it should get through home groups to maintain the family atmosphere, which my church, GCF is striving to sustain. Therefore, challenging the small groups' mistaken preferences for small group learners (*limited to adults*), through teaching a theology of small group community leads to a home-focused ministry that is aimed at every generation in the family.

3. Small Group Lessons: Bible-Centered Teaching

The third element in the common practice of New Testament house churches is the *searching of Scriptures*. The commitment to be faithful to the Scripture was true of both church leaders and members. Hans-Ruedi Weber cites that for believers to mature in the faith it is necessary for them to not only devote themselves to fellowship but also to the apostles' teaching.[285] As mentioned earlier, the New Testament house church teachings are based on the "Word of the Lord," or "teaching of the Lord/Christ," "apostolic letters," "gospel tradition," and "Scripture." Also noteworthy is the biblical image of the church as "the pillar and support of the truth," where the truth is directly related to

---

284. Javalera, *Training for Competence*, 38.
285. Weber, "Church in the House," 17.

the Scripture (cf. 2 Tim 2:15). Thus, in the same manner, small group lessons being taught today should also be Bible-centered.

It pays to study God's Word and know what it teaches. Teaching sound doctrine is the best antidote to any form of heresy that proliferates nowadays. One way to detect or spot the counterfeit is by knowing the real one. As Erickson concludes, "In a world in which there are so many erroneous conceptions and so many opinions, the Bible is a sure source of guidance. For when correctly interpreted, it can be fully relied upon in all that it teaches. It is a sure, dependable, and trustworthy authority."[286] Javalera asserts that the Word of God is not one among many teaching materials but the ultimate one and all the rest must be judged by it.[287] The commitment to the authority of Scripture can be traced back to the Reformation period. Robinson narrates a series of events in this period that shaped how Scripture was regarded:

> Departure from the biblical pattern of church life gave rise to a multitude of heresies. This resulted in the spiritual decline of the Middle Ages. These were the Dark Ages of human history. . . .
>
> The Renaissance was a movement that began within the universities in the late Middle Ages. There was rediscovery of the classics and a "revival of learning." A thirst for the Scriptures began to grip the minds of many who were not clergy. By the mid-fifteenth century, Gutenberg in Germany had developed moveable type. The first book printed was a Bible.
>
> Through the study of the Scriptures, spiritual restlessness led to the reformation within the Roman Catholic Church. This ushered in a climate of greater religious freedom. Everywhere little clusters of believers began to spring up. They held to the absolute authority of the Scriptures.[288]

Establishing the authority of Scripture also implies believing in the sufficiency of Scripture. If Scripture alone is authoritative then it must also be sufficient. It will be helpful to delineate the terms employed. The authority of Scripture, according to Millard Erickson, implies that "the Bible, as the expression of God's will to us, possess the right supremely to define what we are to believe and how we are to conduct ourselves."[289] Wayne Grudem, on the other hand, cites that the sufficiency of Scripture denotes that "the Scripture

---

286. Erickson, *Christian Theology*, 240.

287. Javalera, *Training for Competence*, 33.

288. Robinson, *Total Church Life*, 84.

289. Erickson, *Christian Theology*, 241.

contained all the words of God he intended his people to have at each stage of redemptive history, and that it now contains all the words of God we need for salvation, for trusting him perfectly and for obeying him perfectly."[290]

The authority and sufficiency of Scripture has implications on the theology of small group teaching. If Scripture is the final authority for faith and practice, then Scripture alone is sufficient for group Bible study. Bible-centered lessons must be the result. What kinds of biblical teaching, then, are appropriate for such? Learning how God's Word is structured or put together is critical in understanding it. Keller categorizes the two approaches in studying the Bible as *synchronic* and *diachronic*. According to Keller: "The synchronic approach is sometimes called the systematic-theological method (STM), which tends to deal with Scripture topically. It organizes what the Bible says by categories of thought."[291] Erickson, for instance, states that there are several topics within systematic theology such as *Scripture, God, man, sin, Christ, salvation, church,* and *last things.*[292] In his book *Lectures in Systematic Theology*, Henry C. Thiessen argues that "God has not seen fit to write the Bible in the form of a systematic theology; it remains for us, therefore, to gather together the scattered facts and to build them up into a logical [and harmonious] system."[293]

Subsequently, Keller describes the second approach in this way: "To study the Bible diachronically is to read along its narrative arc, and this is often called the redemptive-historical method (RHM), which tends to deal with Scripture historically. It organizes what the Bible says by stages in history or by the plotline of a story."[294] For example, in their book *How to Read the Bible Book by Book,* Gordon D. Fee and Douglas Stuart mention that the Bible's story line (which is God's own story of searching for mankind) tells us, among other things, about *Creation* (God creating mankind), *Fall* (mankind falling into sin), *Redemption* (God redeeming mankind), and *Consummation* (God restoring mankind).[295] As *The Cape Town Commitment* further states, "This overarching narrative provides our coherent biblical worldview and shapes our theology. At the center of this story are the climactic saving events of the cross and resurrection of Christ which constitute the heart of the gospel. It is

---

290. Grudem, *Systematic Theology*, 127.
291. Keller, *Center Church*, 40.
292. Erickson, *Christian Theology*, 23.
293. Thiessen, *Lectures in Systematic Theology*, 5.
294. Keller, *Center Church*, 40.
295. Fee and Stuart, *How to Read the Bible Book by Book*, 14–20.

this story (in the Old and New Testaments) that tells us who we are, what we are here for, and where we are going."[296]

But Keller warns that "failing to use both approaches invites danger. The STM, carried out in isolation from the RHM, can produce a Christianity that is rationalistic, legalistic, and individualistic. Similarly the RHM, carried out in isolation from the STM, tends to produce a Christianity that loves narrative and community but shies away from sharp distinction between grace and law and between truth and heresy."[297] Thus, to teach the whole counsel of God is to teach it both topically (synchronic) and historically (diachronic). This is the extent to which Bible-centered teaching must be done.

How should the content of God's Word in general be interpreted? In their *How to Read the Bible for All Its Worth*, Fee and Stuart elucidate the two tasks needed for understanding and teaching Scripture properly: "First, one has to hear the Word they heard; you must try to understand what was said to them back *then and there* (exegesis). Second, you must learn to hear that same Word in the *here and now* (hermeneutics)."[298] Critical to a good exegesis is asking the right questions that relate to context (historical and literary) and content. As a guide to biblical interpretation, Roy B. Zuck enumerates six basic questions to ask in approaching the Scripture:

(1) What did the words convey in the grammar of the original readers?

(2) What was being conveyed by those words to the initial readers?

(3) How did the cultural setting influence and affect what was written?

(4) What is the meaning of the words in their context?

(5) In what literary form is the material written and how does that affect what is said?

(6) How do the principles of logic and normal communication affect the meaning?[299]

Subsequently, Zuck underscores that it is important for evangelicals to keep on emphasizing the historical-grammatical interpretation as the only method which aids Christians in knowing their Bible correctly as the pattern for godly

---

296. *The Cape Town Commitment.*

297. Keller, *Center Church*, 40.

298. Fee and Stuart, *How to Read the Bible for All Its Worth*, 23.

299. Zuck, *Basic Bible Interpretation*, 66–67.

living.[300] This applies to any literary genre or form such as legal, narrative, poetry, gospel, logical discourse, and wisdom or prophetic literature.[301] Why such a variety of literary materials? Because they are all genres familiar to humanity – genres which God made use of in all sixty-six books of the Bible in order to communicate his divine Word to all human conditions. Each of these writings requires a specific set of guidelines or principles for correct interpretation (which will not be covered in this book). But regardless of their literary genre, they share enough in common that one can follow the simple process of the six Cs to produce a Bible-centered lesson: (1) content, (2) context, (3) concept, (4) connect, (5) conduct, and (6) concern.[302]

The first three Cs are essential for proper observation and interpretation of any Scripture passage. By *content* we mean the *investigation* (or observation) *of the specific text* that answers the basic question, *What do I see?* It appeals to the sense of *sight* in learners. The longer the time spent on the "investigation stage," the better the content of the text is explored. There are many observation questions that can be asked from each given verse using the five Ws (What, Who, When, Where, Why) and one H (How) regarding various subjects, people, times, places, reasons, and manners.

Second, *context* is the *interpretation according to setting* which answers this question: *What does it mean?* It is intended to appeal to the *mind* of the group members. The content of any Scripture text should only be understood in light of its context because *context rules*. The meaning or interpretation of the passage is based on its setting, which usually refers to the verses that occur before and after the passage. This is called *literary context*. The other kinds of context, such as *historical, cultural, geographical*, and *theological*, can be learned by using supplementary resources like Bible dictionaries, commentaries and atlas.

Subsequently, *concept* is the *integration* (of the content and context) *for the spiritual truth* and it answers the question, *What does it teach?* This, too, aims to appeal to the *mind* of the learners. Once the investigation and interpretation of the text are done, the next step is to summarize the study into an integrated form, in order to see how the gathered information relates to each other, and how they form a united whole. It is important to establish, however, at this point in this process that the *single meaning of the text* principle is strictly

---

300. Zuck, 58.

301. Zuck, 127–135.

302. See appendix 3 (pages 185–188) for a sample study guide lesson.

followed. The outcome, then, will be the spiritual truth or lesson that the passage is intending to teach to the original readers or hearers.

The last three Cs, on the other hand, relate the observation and interpretation of the ancient Word to its application in the present world. So *connect* links the *implication of the Scripture* to one's personal situation, and it answers the question, *What does it mean to me?* This segment is intended to appeal to the *heart* of the group members. It involves contemplation (or rumination) and imparting insights from the Word that struck or impacted one's life. Insight is the first step toward spiritual growth – insight from the text (propositional truth) to one's context (personal truth).

Consequently, *conduct* is the *implementation of a specific action* which answers this question: *How does it apply to me?* It aims to appeal to the *will* of the learners. This focuses on sharing with others (like in an accountability group) about a particular task or course of *action* to be conducted or implemented in one's life based on the deep *contemplation* of insights or implications of the Scripture. Application is the most neglected yet the most needed stage in the process. The ultimate goal is transformation (not information). So obedience to the Scripture in one's own life is a must. As James points out: "Do not merely listen to the word, and so deceive yourselves. Do what it says" (Jas 1:22). More particularly, Zuck suggests nine helpful ways in applying the Bible properly to one's personal life:

[1] Build application on interpretation.
[2] Determine what was expected of the original audience.
[3] Base applications on elements present-day readers share with the original audience.
[4] Recognize how God's working varies in different ages.
[5] Determine what is normative for today.
[6] See the principle inherent in the text.
[7] Think of the principle as an implication (or extrapolation) of the text, and as a bridge to application.
[8] Write out specific action-responses.
[9] Rely on the Holy Spirit.[303]

Lastly, *concern* is the *intercession for saints and seekers,* and it answers this question: *What should I pray for?* This calls for the "priesthood of all believers": "Therefore confess your sins to each other and pray for each other so that you may be healed" (Jas 5:16a). So, mutual confession plus mutual intercession

---

303. Zuck, *Basic Bible Interpretation,* 282–292.

equals mutual recuperation. (Thus, there will be healing!) This last stage in the process may include prayer concerns regarding one's attitude which needs to be changed and the specific action that has to be implemented in obedience to God's Word. As everyone in the group receives intercession (the "saints"), others outside the group or those of the *oikos* who need to know Christ must be prayed for also (the "seekers"). It is critical to pray for opportunities to bring them one-step-closer to the Savior and, then, to the small group.

Another issue that is noteworthy to discuss further is bridging the culture gap between today and the biblical period. How can the Bible teacher relate the ancient Scripture (particularly culturally conditioned Bible passages) to the present culture? In determining whether Bible practices are culture-bound or transcultural, Zuck gives the following guidelines: "First, see if the behavior in the biblical culture means something different in our culture. . . . Second, if the behavior does mean something different in our culture, then determine the timeless principle expressed in that practice. . . . Third, determine how the principle can be expressed in a cultural equivalent."[304] Inevitably, this opens up the controversial discussion on contextualization.

Does contextualization have a place in Bible-centered teaching? While there is the theologically liberal view of contextualization that disregards the gospel's truth, this book presents the evangelical way of doing it that is balanced, sound, and active. According to the Lausanne Movement's "Manila Manifesto": "The balance between gospel and context must be carefully maintained. We must understand the context in order to address it, but the context must not be allowed to distort the gospel."[305] Keller describes contextualization best as

> giving people the Bible's answers, which they may not at all want to hear, to questions about life that people in their particular time and place are asking, in language and forms they can comprehend, and through appeals and arguments with force they can feel, even if they reject them.
>
> Sound contextualization means translating and adapting the communication and ministry of the gospel to a particular culture without compromising the essence and particulars of the gospel itself. The great missionary task is to express the gospel message to a new culture in a way that avoids making the message unnecessarily alien to that culture, yet without removing or obscuring the scandal and offense of biblical truth.

---

304. Zuck, 96.
305. "The Manila Manifesto."

A contextualized gospel is marked by clarity and attractiveness, and yet it still challenges sinners' self-sufficiency and calls them to repentance. It adapts and connects to the culture, yet at the same time challenges and confronts it.[306]

Teaching Bible lessons is like building a bridge from the ancient Word to the present world. When Bible teachers and preachers fail in the way they contextualize the Scripture, they either created a *bridge to nowhere*, or a *bridge from nowhere*.[307] That is being biblical but not relevant (so it goes to nowhere), or being relevant but not biblical (so it comes from nowhere). Likewise, the Filipino social anthropologist Melba P. Maggay states that

> the text without context is unusable, an abstract proposition that by its very generality does not "come down," while context without the text tends to be a closed system, a windowless world trapped by its own solipsism, unvisited by the fresh burst of insight and energy the Word from outside could give. In the one we fall into the error of a false universalism, assuming that our Gospel formulations are capable of transplantation when they are actually culture-bound. In the other we fall into the error of determinism, allowing the world to set the agenda and consign us to a fairly narrow marketplace of programs and ideas.[308]

Indeed, the effective way to completely saturate the city in its unique cultural context is through contextualization. The tool for contextualizing is called "contextual theology." In his book *Foundational Issues in Christian Education*, Robert W. Pazmino suggests two processes in applying contextual theology which complement each other: *contextualization* and *decontextualization*. Contextualization requires dialogue between the urban minister and the immanent context of his ministry (so that a hermeneutic of the city in its social and cultural particularity is a must); whereas decontextualization necessitates dialogue between the urban minister and the Scripture (so that a hermeneutic of the Word is required).[309] Erickson points out that "because the message was originally expressed in a contextualized form, it must first

---

306. Keller, *Center Church*, 89.

307. John R. W. Stott, *Between Two Worlds: The Challenge of Preaching Today* (Grand Rapids, MI: Eerdmans, 1982), cited in Keller, *Center Church*, 101.

308. Maggay, *Communicating Cross-Culturally*, 11–12. Note: *Solipsism* is the philosophical belief that one's own mind alone is assured to exist and anything outside of it is unknown and uncertain.

309. Pazmino, *Foundational Issues in Christian Education*, 157.

be 'decontextualized.'"[310] So priority must be given first to the message of the gospel and the preservation of church tradition before particular attention is given to listening to the culture of the city.

For that reason, the urban minister must be able to interpret Scripture and have tools to interpret his city, so that he can let the Word of God speak to his situation. He has to study first the Word exegetically so that he may be able to know its content in the light of its context and be able to distinguish what is universal and what is cultural. After interpreting the Scripture hermeneutically in its universal principles and context, it is then the role of the urban minister to communicate homiletically the product of his study, which he chose to best fit in the context of his urban audience. In this system, the temptation to force the Jewish culture in the Bible to fit in the present urban setting will be avoided. There is indeed no shortcut in doing urban ministry. One has to be rooted in the Word before one can minister to the city.

After the Word has been decontextualized in light of its context, how then could it be contextualized in light of the present urban setting? Many evangelicals, who are faithful to the Word, tend to neglect the value of contextualization. Keller strongly believes that "churches in urban and cultural centers must be exceptionally sensitive to issues of contextualization, because it is largely there that a society's culture is being forged and is taking new directions."[311] To contextualize the presentation of the gospel is to present it in a culturally relevant way. So knowledge of the culture is important. Gene Getz describes culture as a means by which persons communicate, perpetuate, and develop their knowledge and attitude toward God.[312] Similarly, according to Pazmino: "Each person's culture serves as a lens through which he or she sees and understands other people. All information is filtered through that lens – beliefs about the world, people, life, God, and ultimate reality."[313] Hence, it is both sociology and cultural anthropology which aid contextual theology in relating the "cultured-shape truths" of the Word to the city's diverse context through a thorough analysis of the urban people's culture, customs, beliefs, folkways, and mores in a given area.

Just as Scripture was written to address its ancient context, so it must be taught today in light of the present context. As Keller points out, "Truth should not be simply declared into a vacuum – it must be delivered as a

---

310. Erickson, *Christian Theology*, 75.
311. Keller, *Center Church*, 90–91.
312. Getz, *Sharpening the Focus of the Church*, 23.
313. Pazmino, *Foundational Issues in Christian Education*, 154.

response to the questions of particular people, and this means understanding culture."[314] This is exactly what Jesus did. His incarnation is a perfect example of contextualization. What John calls the eternal Logos became flesh and dwelt among the people (John 1:1, 14). What Paul calls the preexistent God emptied Himself by taking the form of bondservant (Phil 2:6, 7). Jesus was often found with the sick, including prostitutes, and dining with sinners and tax collectors (Luke 4:40; 7:36–50; 15:1–2; 19:1–10). Indeed, Christ identified with mankind in a full and unique sense. As Charles Kraft comments in his book *Christianity in Culture*, "God in Jesus became so much a part of a specific human context that many never even recognize that he had come from somewhere else."[315] Thus, the task of contextualization does not end in merely knowing the urban culture, but it begins in being involved in its day to day life (*incarnational ministry*). It means immersing oneself in the questions, hopes, and beliefs of a culture in order to give a biblical, gospel-centered response to its questions.[316]

Additionally, there is also a need to learn how to prepare Bible-centered lesson plans. Even without curriculum material, any volunteer-based small group leader should be able to teach when given proper training on Bible study methods and biblical interpretation, which was discussed earlier. There is danger when curriculum takes the place of the Bible or someone relies too much on it. While there are many good curriculum materials, there are some which are superficial and do not have a correct view of the Scripture and others that are not Bible-centered. A careful evaluation of the curriculum is a must, but there is no substitute for developing the ability and the habit to study the Scripture by oneself.

The purpose of curriculum is to be a guide in pointing inexperienced lay teachers, or the volunteer-based small group leaders, to God's Word. The problem, however, lies when the teacher becomes overly dependent on the curriculum, neglects studying the Scripture, and makes excuses not to teach without curriculum available. As Richards explains, "Published curricula are an aid, but not the answer. All lesson materials are limited in value. When used as a crutch, even the best can stifle the freedom and spontaneity, so essential to creative Bible teaching, which the writer hopes to encourage."[317]

Preparing Bible-centered lesson plans is a difficult and serious task. It entails commitment and planning. In his book *Design for Teaching and Training:*

---

314. Keller, *Center Church*, 120.

315. Kraft, *Christianity in Culture*, 175.

316. Keller, *Center Church*, 121.

317. Richards, *Creative Bible Teaching*, 141–142.

A Self-Study Guide to Lesson Planning, LeRoy Ford comments, "Planning makes things happen which would not otherwise occur. Builders start with plans – blueprints. Teachers start with lesson plans. Good lesson plans begin with goals. However, not all teachers begin with goals! They teach – then race to move the target to where the arrow went!"[318] So learning goals must be required as the small group leader prepares the lesson plan. How then can one learn how to write them? Ford enumerates the four characteristics that must be observed in order to create well-crafted goals:

(1) Goals tell in relatively broad terms what the learners should learn.
(2) Goals tell what should happen to learners, not the teacher!
(3) Goals indicate the kind of learning or change which the learners should achieve.
(4) Goals state the subject dealt with.[319]

Richards also indicates the three kinds of lesson aims that should appeal to the learner's head (cognitive), heart (affective), and hand (psychomotor), respectively: "One is the *content aim*, in which his purpose is to communicate biblical information. Then there's the *inspiration aim*, in which his purpose is to inspire, or touch the emotions. Finally, there is the *action aim*, in which his purpose is to move to action. Each of these aims has a valid but different place in Christian teaching."[320] Worth pursuing is the last teaching aim. It must be understood that "when the teacher builds his lesson, *he must think in terms of the learner's response he hopes to achieve.*"[321] Consequently, Richards advises that the intended kind of learning must be identified first, at the very onset, before the Scripture is taught.[322]

There are five learning levels that Richards specifies in his book: rote, recognition, restatement, relation, and realization.[323] The Bible can be learned at any of these levels, but the teacher's goal is to relentlessly raise the learner's level of learning toward realization, where the biblical truths are applied in daily life.[324] The ultimate aim of Bible teaching is becoming Christlike – a changed life and not an informed mind. In his book *Teaching to Change Lives*,

---

318. Ford, *Design for Teaching and Training*, 17.
319. Ford, 17–32.
320. Richards, *Creative Bible Teaching*, 102.
321. Richards, 103.
322. Richards, 69.
323. Richards, 75.
324. Richards, 75.

Howard Hendricks stresses that "learning is change. Essentially, learning means a change in your thinking, a change in your feeling, a change in your behavior. Learning means that a change takes place in the mind, in the emotions, and in the will."[325] In the same way, Javalera also affirms: "Teaching is changing. If nobody gets changed then the teacher has not done any real teaching."[326] As declared in the Lausanne Movement's *Cape Town Commitment*: "Nothing commends the gospel more eloquently than a transformed life, and nothing brings it into disrepute so much as personal inconsistency. We are charged to behave in a manner that is worthy of the gospel of Christ and even to 'adorn' it, enhancing its beauty by holy lives."[327]

Finally, Eugene Roehlkepartain and Peter Benson assert that

> there is a clear need for effective teacher preparation and support, equipping them with the knowledge, skills, and depth of faith that allows them to be effective in their roles. Teachers are the gatekeepers for the Christian education that occurs in congregations, yet many feel inadequate and ill-equipped. Strengthening their abilities can be a key gateway to enhancing the effectiveness of all aspects of the program. . . .
>
> Christian education truly has the potential to become a pivotal strategy for nurturing a life-transforming, well-rounded faith among children, youth, and adults that will offer renewal and energy for the future of the church.[328]

Therefore, correcting the small group's wrong attitude about preparing small group lessons (*curriculum over-dependence*) through a theology of small group teaching can lead to Bible-centered studies that change lives.

---

325. Hendricks, *Teaching to Change Lives*, 85, 88. Hendricks presents seven helpful basic laws for teaching in the form of an acrostic: "[1] The Law of the Teacher – Stop growing today, and you stop teaching tomorrow; [2] The Law of Education – How people learn determines how you teach; [3] The Law of Activity – Maximum learning is always the result of maximum involvement; [4] The Law of Communication – To truly impart information requires the building of bridges; [5] The Law of the Heart – Teaching that impacts is not head to head, but heart to heart; [6] The Law of Encouragement – Teaching tends to be most effective when the learner is properly motivated; and [7] The Law of Readiness – The teaching-learning process will be most effective when both student and teacher are adequately prepared" (14, 129).

326. Javalera, *Training for Competence*, 12.

327. *The Cape Town Commitment*.

328. Roehlkepartain and Benson, "Role of Christian Education in Faith Development," 32.

4. Small Group Locations: Spirit-Directed Mission

In his comprehensive book *The Mission of God*, Christopher J. H. Wright defines mission as "our committed participation as God's people, at God's invitation and command, in God's own mission within the history of God's world for the redemption of God's creation."[329] This *mission* (derived from the Latin verb *mitto*, "to send") originates from God himself who is the Sender and at the same time the Sent One (the first missionary), where the Father and the Holy Spirit sent the Son and then the Father and the Son sent the Spirit.[330] Likewise, John Stott emphasizes that "mission arises from the heart of God himself, and is communicated from his heart to ours. Mission is the global outreach of the global people of a global God."[331]

Nonetheless, Wright qualifies that "[while] 'mission' is all that God is doing in His great purpose for the whole creation and all that He calls us to do in cooperation with that purpose . . . 'missions' is the multitude of activities that God's people can engage in, by means of which they participate in God's mission."[332] If missions refers to various programs where the church could be involved to participate in God's mission, is it then the primary aim of God's people? John Piper answers, "Missions is not the ultimate goal of the church. Worship is. Missions exists because worship doesn't. Worship is ultimate, not missions [which] is a temporary necessity. But worship abides forever. Worship, therefore, is the fuel and goal of missions. . . . The goal of missions is the gladness of the peoples in the greatness of God (Ps 67:3–4; 97:1)."[333] It is visualized vividly in the diagram below:

---

329. Wright, *Mission of God*, 23.

330. Wright, *Mission of God's People*, 210–211. It can be said, then, that just as the concept of small groups emanates from the Triune God being a community, so, too, the idea of *mission* emanates from God himself – he who did the sending yet was himself also sent as the first missionary.

331. John Stott, *The Contemporary Christian: An Urgent Plea for Double Listening* (Downers Grove, IL: InterVarsity Press, 1992), 335, cited in Wright, *The Mission of God*, 67, and in Wright, *The Mission of God's People*, 24.

332. Wright, *Mission of God's People*, 25.

333. Piper, *Let the Nations Be Glad*, 35.

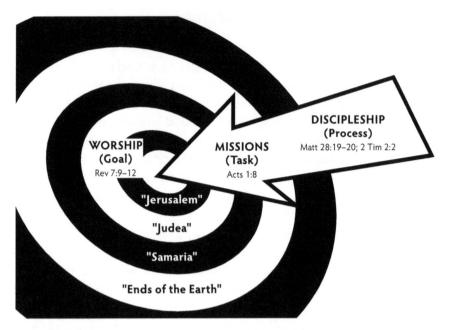

Figure 3.2 Worship as the ultimate goal of missions and discipleship

Hence, the small group mission, in being a scattered church, is not only for the purpose of evangelizing and discipling the locality but also to transform it into a community that worships God. Every maturing Christian is a soul-winner, a discipler, and a worshiper at the same time; but the primary aim of missions and discipleship is to generate the latter – a worshiper who is both witnessing and discipling for the glory of God. Missions and discipleship are merely means toward an end which is worship, so producing more missionaries and disciple-makers should be intended to culminate in producing more worshipers.[334]

Moreover, Wright also presents "the whole world (the whole of His creation) as the goal of God's mission and the scope and arena of our mission."[335] The right way to do missions is to think globally and to start locally. In their book *Discipleship Missions*, Chan and Seng state that "the mission, given to the Church at large, is to be exercised in the local church. . . . The (universal) Church in mission is fundamentally the total synergistic effort of local churches

---

334. Using the acronym GROW for the author's small group ministry, the following must be aimed for: **G**lorifying the Lord; **R**elating to the fold; **O**beying the Word; and **W**itnessing to the world.

335. Wright, *Mission of God's People*, 26–27.

faithfully engaging in their missions calling from God."[336] So the church then should be a church *in* mission and not just be a church *with* a mission.[337] As Wright further expounds in *The Mission of God*: "It is not so much the case that God has a mission for his church in the world, as that God has a church for his mission in the world. Mission was not made for the church; the church was made for mission – God's mission."[338]

Often, many churches today are found to be "too busy" in educating local church people with missions programs in far-flung countries but "too lazy" in mobilizing them to be deployed as a visible church in their respective unreached local *oikos* community. In his book *Empowered to Influence*, Ken Chua, a Singaporean marketplace minister, calls all believers to engage in a paradigm shift from doing work *in* the church (local congregation) to doing the works *of* the church (body of Christ).[339] What is the difference between the two? The former focuses on missions as a church program that is merely discussed within the four corners of the local church building, while the latter is a way of life within one's local community outreach. Chua clearly elaborates that "all we do in a local congregation are not ends in themselves: they are simply means to a larger goal of the Lord – to save *that* which was lost (Luke 19:10). What we do in the church . . . is a prologue to equip us to carry the works of the Church in the communities."[340] So to make "the church gathered the church scattered" is to change the "inward" focus of the local church constituents and make them outwardly looking towards kingdom building and global expansion. Then the heavens will be filled with "a great multitude which no one could count, from every nation and all tribes and peoples and tongues . . ." (Rev 7:9–12) – that is worship, our goal for missions!

The scope and strategy of mission has been laid down very clearly by Jesus himself in Matthew 28:18–20 and Acts 1:8. While the mission field is "all nations," the starting point is the location where the Lord of the Harvest has strategically sent or placed the missionary, which will serve as his or her own "Jerusalem." As mentioned earlier, Stark emphasizes that if the aim is to "make disciples of all nations," then the mission strategy of Paul should be followed, who went, as led by the Spirit, to major cities in his missionary journeys where

---

336. Chan and Seng, *Discipleship Missions*, 69.
337. Chan and Seng, 77.
338. Wright, *Mission of God*, 62.
339. Chua, *Empowered to Influence*, 75.
340. Chua, 75.

there were several prospective disciples.[341] In fact, the apostle claimed to have saturated the whole province with the gospel through the churches planted in just two or three centers (Rom 15:19, 23).[342] As Chan and Seng propose: "The discipling of nations – through urban missions – [is] one of our chief missions strategies."[343]

The *saturating of cities* is the fourth and last of the common practices of the New Testament house churches cited in this book, and it has already been shown from Scripture that the fastest way to saturate a whole region with the gospel is through cities. Chan and Seng point out that "we must not forget that the early church missions engaged the cities. One reason for the rapid spread of early Christianity was its movement through the cities. They are the centers of world communication and the source from where ideas spread across the country."[344] Keller also adds that "the technological revolution today has led to an unprecedented mobility of people, ideas, and capital. Because of the Internet and other forms of electronic communication, people around the world are more connected than ever before, and Western urban values in particular are spreading everywhere."[345] So what else is present in urban life that cannot be found in rural areas? Again Keller thoroughly answers:

> Along with residences, it has places to work, shop, read, learn, enjoy art and music, worship, and play, as well as public government buildings such as town halls and courts. All are mixed and compacted together within walking distance. In ancient times, rural areas and even villages could not provide all these elements; only cities could sustain them all. . . . And in modern times, the dominant arrangement – the suburb – deliberately avoids this urban pattern. Suburbs are normally dedicated to large, single-use zones – so places to live, work, play, and learn are separated from one another and are reachable only by car, usually through pedestrian-hostile zones.[346]

What are other reasons that cities are to be prioritized in terms of gospel saturation than the suburbs today? Chan and Seng further explain that "two hundred years ago, the world population was almost entirely rural. But at

---

341. Stark, *Cities of God*, 25.

342. Allen, *Missionary Methods*, 13.

343. Chan and Seng, *Discipleship Missions*, 133.

344. Chan and Seng, 123.

345. Keller, *Center Church*, 154.

346. Keller, 137.

the start of the 20th century, we witnessed a dramatic demographic shift of population from rural to urban."[347] Similarly, as *The Cape Town Commitment* of the Lausanne Movement notes: "Cities are crucially important for the human future and for world mission. Half the world now lives in cities. Cities are where four major kinds of people are most to be found: (i) the next generation of young people; (ii) the most unreached peoples who have migrated; (iii) the culture shapers; and (iv) the poorest of the poor."[348] As a strategy for world evangelization, Chan and Seng clearly see that cities

> have a critical mass of population which allows for cost-effective outreach. It thus provides us with an excellent opportunity to deploy a "saturation strategy" in these densely populated cities, such as citywide evangelistic campaigns. . . .
>
> If Christians want to reach the unreached, we must go to the cities. To reach the rising generations, we must go to the cities. To have any impact for Christ on the creation of culture, we must go to the cities. To serve the poor, we must go to the cities.[349]

Likewise, Keller asserts that "every major city is now a portal for reaching the nations of the world. In other words, one of the very best ways to reach the far parts of the world is to reach your own city!"[350] However, as Keller qualifies, he is not absolutely saying that cities are the only means. He believes that "there is still a need for Christians in every country to consider the call to relocate to distant lands to accomplish the global mission of the church. . . . [The] point is that cities – at home and abroad – are far more important now to the accomplishment of the world mission of the church than they were fifty years ago."[351] To win city-dwellers for Christ, Keller encourages believers to move into cities despite the pressures of living there. While it may indeed be very challenging to engage in urban ministry, the saturating of cities is the key to reaching the whole region, nation, and then the entire world for Christ. As Keller states, "Regardless of your particular cultural or geographical context, you will need to consider the city when forming a theological vision that engages the people you are trying to reach. In other words, because the world is on its way to becoming 70 percent urban, we all need a theological vision

---

347. Chan and Seng, *Discipleship Missions*, 124.
348. *The Cape Town Commitment*.
349. Chan and Seng, *Discipleship Missions*, 130, 162.
350. Keller, *Center Church*, 159.
351. Keller, 165.

that is distinctly urban."[352] Again, according to *The Cape Town Commitment* of the Lausanne Movement:

> We discern the sovereign hand of God in the massive rise of urbanization in our time, and we urge Church and mission leaders worldwide to respond to this fact by giving urgent strategic attention to urban mission. We must love our cities as God does, with holy discernment and Christlike compassion, and obey his command to "seek the welfare of the city," wherever that may be. We will seek to learn appropriate and flexible methods of mission that respond to urban realities.[353]

The same urban strategy must be appropriated by churches even for their small groups today. New groups should not be aimlessly opened and existing small groups should not just *meet anywhere*. The location and surrounding community are crucial and, thus, should be assessed in several ways. First, they must be conducive for learning and fellowshipping. According to Shaw, "The physical setting in which the group meets affects the members' attitudes and actions and, consequently, helps determine group process. The meeting place either positively or negatively influences members' participation in the group."[354] Most of the houses in urban settings are more ideal for Bible study than those in rural areas because they are accessible, spacious, properly lighted and well-ventilated.

Furthermore, the church must aim for strategic small group locations. Robinson suggests that it is essential "to define a specific geographic area or areas for which the church will accept primary responsibility for saturation with the gospel and sharing Christ with every person. To reach people, a church must have a specific plan for total penetration that nurtures people and wins them to Christ."[355] There is nothing more strategic than urban centers. When made the starting point of every local mission around the world, they accelerate global mission. So it is important, according to Bill Hull, that "the primary objective of every group must include mission. Most groups implode

---

352. Keller, 88.

353. *The Cape Town Commitment*. Likewise, Chan and Seng "outline the process of the church's transformation in five areas: (1) Better understanding by the Church of the city's social and economic structures; (2) The incarnation of the Church in those social and cultural realities; (3) Sensitivity, to all social levels in the city; (4) A clearer definition of the prophetic role of the Church in the city; and (5) a re-emphasis on the Church as a community of compassion by way of a Christ-centered message of hope and incarnation" (*Discipleship Missions*, 132).

354. Shaw, *Group Dynamics*, cited in McBride, *How to Lead Small Groups*, 57.

355. Robinson, *Total Church Life*, 200.

because they make their mission too small. A group that reaches only into itself becomes self-indulgent and insulated."[356] As small groups penetrate the strategic mission field and plant the seed which is God's Word sown on fertile ground, they reproduce naturally and dramatically. Hull further states that "groups won't reproduce if the expectation to do so is absent. Members of the group need a vision for reproducing and they need the will for it. If the desire to reproduce isn't in a small group's DNA, they'll delay reproduction and even resent it."[357]

Snyder is convinced that "the evangelism which will be most effective in the city will use small groups as its basic methodology. It will find the small group providing the best environment in which sinners can hear the convicting, winning voice of the Holy Spirit and come alive spiritually through faith."[358] As the church starts small in small groups in strategic urban centers it will soon grow big as it saturates the entire region. The reason why small groups should exist in cities is to form God's community that would reach out to others in society. In his article "A Theology of Small Groups," Darin Kennedy argues:

> Therefore, if developing community is not a reason for initiating small groups, or any other function of the church, then what would be a theology of small groups that would assume an existing community of God? In essence, the right question should begin with God's community, not individuals who want to be in community – not why should individuals join a small group, but why should a smaller group come out of the larger, already existing community? Why should a part separate from the whole?[359]

Finally, the small group mission should be in Spirit-directed locations. What is the Holy Spirit's role in any Christian mission? As Chan and Seng narrate, "Evangelical missions during the 19th and 20th centuries have been an epic story of the movement of the Holy Spirit as the keen director of global missions . . . [which] has been true since the beginning of the early Church."[360] *The Lausanne Covenant* states that "the Holy Spirit is a missionary spirit;

---

356. Hull, *Complete Book of Discipleship*, 231.
357. Hull, 236.
358. Snyder, *Problem of Wine Skins*, 141–142.
359. Kennedy, "Theology of Small Groups," 177–178.
360. Chan and Seng, *Discipleship Missions*, 53.

thus evangelism should arise spontaneously from a Spirit-filled church."[361] Additionally, the Lausanne Movement's "The Manila Manifesto" declares that "all the people of God are called to share in the evangelistic task. Yet without the Holy Spirit of God all their endeavors will be fruitless."[362] It is critical then to observe carefully the collaboration and interplay between the divine and human as far as missions is concerned. So praying for and obeying the Spirit's direction when it comes to small group mission is very important since apart from him our own witness is pointless and futile.

Kennedy believes that forming small groups demands vision to see where God is explicitly planting dreams in people's hearts.[363] While having small groups in strategic urban centers may be an excellent strategy, the Spirit is still the ultimate guide to the harvest field. As Snyder points out,

> The small group is not a panacea. No effort of man can bring the church to greater faithfulness in meeting the needs and problems of its day except as the Holy Spirit directs and infills. But the small group is an essential component of the church's structure and life. In order for men to be moved by the Holy Spirit there must be an openness toward God and toward others, an openness which best develops in a context of the supporting love and fellowship of other sincere seekers after God.[364]

Likewise, in their workbook *On Mission with God: Living God's Purpose for His Glory*, Avery Willis and Henry Blackaby affirm that the direction of God is vital to those who join him on mission, and it is the Holy Spirit who leads eager and submissive workers to the harvest field.[365]

Interrogating this line of thought, Allen raises the significant question of whether the Apostle Paul ever chose definite strategic areas where he planted churches.[366] Willis and Blackaby cite that "in the Scriptures recounting Paul's life are many instances of God's guidance through the Holy Spirit. One, in Acts 16:1–10, is particularly outstanding. Many elements were involved in the

---

361. *The Lausanne Covenant.* The doctrinal statement on "The Power of the Holy Spirit" is based on the following Scripture references: 1 Cor 2:4; John 15:26–27; 16:8–11; 1 Cor 12:3; John 3:6–8; 2 Cor 3:18; John 7:37–39; 1 Thess 5:19; Acts 1:8; Pss 85:4–7; 67:1–3; Gal 5:22, 23; 1 Cor 12:4–31; Rom 12:3–8.

362. "Manila Manifesto."

363. Kennedy, "Theology of Small Groups," 182.

364. Snyder, *Problem of Wine Skins*, 147.

365. Willis and Blackaby, *On Mission with God*, 25.

366. Allen, *Missionary Methods*, 8.

Lord's leading Paul in this instance. The Holy Spirit both prevented Paul from going and permitted him to go in certain directions."[367]

Examining Paul's example in detail, we see that at the very onset of the first missionary journey, "the Holy Spirit said, 'Set apart for Me Barnabas and Saul for the work to which I have called them'" (Acts 13:2). So the "work" was from the Spirit. Subsequently, in their second missionary journey Paul and Silas "passed through the Phrygian and Galatian region, having been forbidden by the Holy Spirit to speak the word in Asia; and after they came to Mysia, they were trying to go into Bithynia, and the Spirit of Jesus did not permit them" (Acts 16:6–7). Eventually, however, Paul was allowed by the Spirit to proceed to both Ephesus and Bithynia (cf. 18:19–21, 24–19:41; 1 Peter 1:1). Lastly, in his third missionary journey, "Paul purposed in the Spirit to go to Jerusalem after he had passed through Macedonia and Achaia, saying, 'After I have been there, I must also see Rome'" (Acts 19:21). As Willis and Blackaby conclude, "Paul lived a life so open to the Holy Spirit that he experienced continual guidance for His mission. . . . Even at the end of his life Paul had little doubt that God had guided him throughout his life and ministry."[368]

Since Paul's missionary journey was the work provided by the Holy Spirit, was the timing (the *when*) and the way (the *how*) to do it always determined by the Spirit, as well, with the apostle just following his instructions? How is the role of the Spirit to be distinguished from the role of the missionary, such as Paul? The Holy Spirit's role in missions is to sovereignly direct the missionary in doing the work. As Allen explains:

> He [Paul] did not start out with any definite design to establish his churches in this place or in that. He was led as God opened the door; but wherever he was led he always found a centre, and seizing upon that centre he made it a centre of Christian life.
>
> . . . To seize a strategic centre we need not only a man capable of recognizing it, but a man capable of seizing it. The seizing of strategic points implied a strategy. It is part of a plan of attack upon the whole country. Concentrated missions at strategic centres, if they are to win the province, must be centres of evangelistic life.[369]

In his book on *The Ministry of the Spirit*, Allen, speaking about the apostles in the book of Acts, qualifies that "their acts were their own acts. They were not mere will-less instruments in the hands of another. Nevertheless, the fact that it

---

367. Willis and Blackaby, *On Mission with God*, 157.
368. Willis and Blackaby, 158.
369. Allen, *Missionary Methods*, 16–17.

was possible to call the Acts of the Apostles the 'Acts of the Holy Spirit' reveals at once the truth that men have found in this book not merely the record of the acts of men, but the revelation of a Spirit governing, guiding, controlling, directing men in the acts here recorded."[370] Paul Becker, Jim Carpenter, and Mark Williams have sadly expressed that some go to the other extreme and "feel that it is 'unspiritual' to plan; they want only to be 'led by the Spirit.'"[371] Smith, similarly, observes that,

> Somehow, it is thought, ministry in the Spirit means that we do not need to give specific attention to methods of ministry, [–] administrative procedures and the nature of effective preparation or structure to leadership is somehow less spiritual.
>
> This understanding of the work of the Spirit could be called *docetic pneumatology* . . . [which] is a subtle denial of the human dimensions of the Christian ministry. Just as God revealed his glory through the Word made flesh, even so the Spirit of God conducts his transforming ministry in the church and the world through the human. . . . [Thus] the principles of effective leadership and management are not bypassed by the Spirit; they are the very structures which are filled by the Spirit.[372]

A need exists to strike a balance between the divine and human factor in missions. As Ken Gnanakan explicates, "When we give the Spirit his proper place in the missionary movement we will put the role of God's people in its rightful place alongside the divine initiative which impels mission. There is certainly a human element in mission, but it must be seen from the perspective of the Holy Spirit's function in the divine program."[373] Consider the doctrinal stance on "God the Holy Spirit" as presented in "The 2000 Baptist Faith and Message" which states that the Holy Spirit is the one who "empowers the believer and the church in evangelism."[374] Robinson stresses that "while there is abundant joy associated with the presence of the power of the Spirit, the Holy Spirit is not given for our enjoyment. Holy Spirit power is for our *employment*! It is not given to accomplish human goals. It is given to bring

---

370. Roland Allen and David M. Paton, *The Ministry of the Spirit* (London: World Dominion Press, 1960), 3, quoted in Gnanakan, *Biblical Theology of Mission Today*, 175.

371. Becker, Carpenter, and Williams, *New Dynamic Church Planting Handbook*, sec. 1.34.

372. Smith, *City Shepherds*, 97–99.

373. Gnanakan, *Kingdom Concerns*, 174.

374. Southern Baptist Convention, "The 2000 Baptist Faith and Message."

people to Jesus."[375] The power behind witnessing is divine and the human role is to simply unleash it. It cannot be denied, therefore, that "if God is not at work, even the best laid plans will fail. But if God is in a work, we can serve Him best by *prayerful planning*."[376] Eaves, in the same manner, affirms that "we are dependent upon the Holy Spirit for all wisdom and power. Therefore we should earnestly pray for the Spirit-filled life to be the daily experience of each member."[377] Finally, Manuel Ortiz is convinced that "if we continually yield our lives to the indwelling, guiding Holy Spirit, we will come to perceive what God wants us to do, and the ministry we develop will be truly of the Lord."[378] As Robinson concludes,

> Holy Spirit power is given to the church to do what God has commanded it to do. Holy Spirit power is adequate and available. When the church in faithfulness steps out under the marching orders of its Lord, it will penetrate this earth with the gospel of Jesus Christ. No barriers will stop the onward movement of the gospel. The circle of witness power will continue to extend until it encompasses the globe. *The gates of hell cannot prevail against it!*[379]

Therefore, putting forth a small group must not be incidental, but rather intentional in major strategic centers. Being deliberate entails planning both purposefully and prayerfully for the leading of the Spirit. So checking the small group's inappropriate perspective on small group locations (*meeting anywhere*) through teaching a theology of small group mission brings about a Spirit-directed strategy that is concentrated on penetration of the city.[380]

---

375. Robinson, *Total Church Life*, 183.

376. Becker, Carpenter, and Williams, *New Dynamic Church Planting Handbook*, sec. 1.35.

377. Eaves, "Effective Church Evangelism in the City," 72.

378. Ortiz, "Being Disciples," 95.

379. Robinson, *Total Church Life*, 190.

380. The acronym **WORLD** represents the mission field of the author's small group ministry: **W**orkplaces in companies, **O**ffices in the government, **R**esidential homes, and **L**earning institutions in a particular **D**istrict within a city where the local church building and small group venues are situated.

4

Research Findings and Summary

First, this book significantly finds that the word ἐκκλησία was used in the entire New Testament neither to refer to a building for public worship nor to a denomination.[1] Etymologically, the noun ἐκκλησία is derived from two Greek words ἐκ and καλέω. The common concept of the first century ἐκκλησία, as used in the Jewish sense, is an assembly or congregation of people in general. But in the Christian sense the concept of ἐκκλησία in the New Testament is a gathering of believers specifically for worship, both locally (Acts 14:23; 1 Cor 1:2; 2 Cor 1:1) and universally (Eph 1:22). So three elements are all present in the Christian ἐκκλησία: people, purpose, and place. Therefore, the New Testament church is God's *people* meeting together for the *purpose* of worship locally in one *place* and universally in any *place*.

Second, the New Testament is observed to describe the nature of the church predominantly as a house or a household (e.g. "God's house," Heb 3:6; "God's spiritual house," 1 Pet 2:5; "God's building," 1 Cor 3:9; Eph 2:22; "the pillar and support of the truth," 1 Tim 3:15; "the household of God," 1 Tim 3:15; Eph 2:19; "the household of the faith," Gal 6:10; "family of God," 1 Tim 5:1–2; 2 Cor 6:18; and "the bride of Christ," Eph 5:32; 2 Cor 11:2; Rev 19:7; 21:2).[2] The familiar metaphor for ἐκκλησία as God's house or household then refers to a spiritual (and not physical) building or a spiritual family. This was prompted by the first century domestic setting of the ἐκκλησία in someone's οἶκος (a literal house or a literal household).

Third, this study learns that the familiar concept of οἶκος and οἰκία in the Greek and Jewish sense refer to their first-century functions as structural

---

1. See pages 15–18.
2. See pages 18–19.

(domestic), social (public), and spiritual (cultic).[3] In the Christian sense, the New Testament uses οἶκος and οἰκία to refer literally to a "house," metaphorically to a "household," and, for οἶκος specifically, theologically to a "house church." Conceptually, like the first-century ἐκκλησία in the Christian sense, οἶκος in the New Testament also possesses the three basic elements of place, people, and purpose. In the structural sense, οἶκος is a construction (place); in the social sense, it is a community (people); and in the spiritual sense, it is a church (purpose). The table below compares the concept of οἶκος in the first century with ἐκκλησία in the New Testament:

Table 4.1 Conceptual comparison of *oikos* in the first century with *ekklēsia* in the NT

Biblical Images of the Church	ἐκκλησία in the New Testament	οἶκος in the First Century
"God's spiritual house" (οἶκος πνευματικός, Heb 3:6; 1 Pet 2:4–8) "God's building" (Θεοῦ οἰκοδομή, 1 Cor 3:9; Eph 2:22) "Pillar and support of the truth" (1 Tim 3:15) "Temple of the Holy Spirit" (1 Cor 3:16–17; 6:19; Eph 2:21–22)	ἐκκλησία as theologically a spiritual house	οἶκος as architecturally a literal house
"Household of God" (ἐν οἴκῳ Θεοῦ, 1 Tim 3:15; Eph 2:19) "Household of the faith" (οἰκείους τῆς πίστεως, Gal 6:10) "Family of God" (1 Tim 5:1–2; 2 Cor 6:18) "Bride of Christ" (Eph 5:32; 2 Cor 11:2; Rev 19:7; 21:2)	ἐκκλησία as theologically a spiritual household	οἶκος as sociologically a literal household

The aforementioned comparative study clearly shows how early believers, meeting in the first century οἶκος, might have utilized their domestic context and applied it to describe how the ἐκκλησία should look and function – as a spiritual house or building and as a spiritual household or family but, again, never as a literal house or building.

Fourth, the archaeological examination of the first century house (*oikos/ domus*) is a key to knowing Greco-Roman households, and studying families in

---

3. See pages 20–22.

the Greco-Roman world is foundational to understanding the house church.[4] Based on rich discoveries drawn from the Pompeian excavations, the remains of Greco-Roman houses shed light on the life of a hypothetical Roman house church. Oakes concludes that the non-elite house church model (which is limited in size, just like a small group) is the one appropriate for most study of Pauline texts. Furthermore, studying archaeological evidence gathered in the remains of Greco-Roman houses also provides some insights into the ancient Christian household's worldview and cultural practices. For instance, females in Greco-Roman culture were regarded as inferior to males; public space was the domain of men while private/domestic space was for the women. Parents could exercise authority over their children through family-arranged marriage where the transfer of property to the next generation was secured. Childrearing was largely the responsibility of mothers, whereas the homeschooling of sons during their early years belonged to the fathers. Some of the house-cults that were observed by every member of the household include the private cult of Philadelphia in Lydia, the Orgeones at Athens, and the Serapis-cult. The diagram below conceptually summarizes the three-fold function of a Greco-Roman *oikos/domus* as a house (structural function), household (social function), and house-cult (spiritual function).

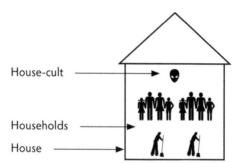

Figure 4.1 The three-fold function of a Greco-Roman *oikos/domus*

Notably, the Jewish house synagogue (as conceptually depicted in the diagram below), which was used predominantly by the early first-century Jewish community for worship and instruction, was later on utilized by the Christian community as well.

---

4. See pages 22–33.

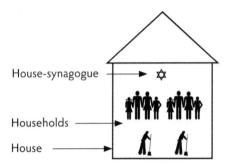

Figure 4.2 The three-fold function of a Jewish *bayit*

This study finds that the spiritual (or religious) function of a house in the Greco-Roman context, along with Jewish households, has a long history which could have influenced the origin and development of house churches. House churches were very similar to contemporary Greco-Roman house-cults except that the former prevailed over the latter in terms of showing authentic κοινωνία. The diagram below shows how the Greco-Roman *oikos/domus* is parallel to the three-fold function of a Christian *oikos* as a house (structural function), household (social function), and house church (spiritual function).

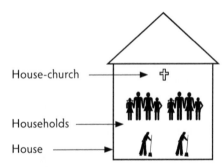

Figure 4.3 The three-fold function of a Christian *oikos*

Having investigated archaeologically the three-fold function of a house (domestic, public, and cultic) in the first-century Greco-Roman world, this study observes the following developments in the use of a house: (1) from structural (as a house construction) to social (as a household community); (2) from social to spiritual (as a house church); and eventually (3) from spiritual back to structural (though this time as a church construction). The diagram below summarizes the conception of the house church and its transition to a church house:

THE HOUSE AS A CONSTRUCTION (Structural Function)

↓

THE HOUSE AS A COMMUNITY (Social Function)

↓

THE HOUSE AS A CHURCH (Spiritual Function)

↓

THE CHURCH AS A CONSTRUCTION (Structural Function)

Figure 4.4 The conception of a house church and its transition to a church house

Fifth, historically, this research traces the three-stage structural development of the early church from a house to a basilica.[5] In the first stage (c. 50–150), owned or rented domestic residences housed the house church. Renovation of domestic structures to accommodate the early believers' needs began during the second stage (c. 150–250), which was called *domus ecclesiae* (e.g. the remains at Dura-Europos and Peter's former house at Capernaum). The third stage (c. 250–313), which White termed *aula ecclesiae*, was a departure from the use of residential houses to the use of larger buildings and halls (e.g. *Titulus Chrysogoni* or Basilica S. Crisogono in Rome). Thereafter, the church in larger public buildings eventually evolved into the church in monumental basilical buildings. Remarkably, the early church continued to use house churches throughout the first three centuries (c. 50–313), but they were pushed aside later when Constantine introduced basilical architecture and institutionalized Christianity in AD 313. The following transition was observed: (1) from the use of an unaltered house (*substructure*) in the first century to its renovation into a church (*sprouting structure*); (2) from the utilization of converted domestic residences in the second century to its subsequent transfer to public buildings with no formal features (*simple structure*); and (3) from the use of larger public buildings to the introduction of monumental basilical buildings (*superstructure*) in the third century. There is a big shift observed from the spiritual function of a house as a church to the structural function of a church as a house; thus a change in focus from believers to buildings. The flow chart below provides an overview of the structural development of the early church:

---

5. See pages 33–38.

THE CHURCH IN UNALTERED HOUSES (Substructure)

⬇

THE CHURCH IN RENOVATED HOUSES (Sprouting Structure)

⬇

THE CHURCH IN PUBLIC BUILDINGS (Simple Structure)

⬇

THE CHURCH IN BASILICAL BUILDINGS (Superstructure)

Figure 4.5 The structural development of the early church

So this study clearly shows how the architectural evolution of the early church building took place from substructure (domestic architecture) to superstructure (basilical architecture) at the time of Constantine. Such extreme transition echoes the drastic structural development of the Jewish place for worship in the Old Testament from Moses's tabernacle (a small temporary tent) to Solomon's temple (a big permanent monument). Consequently, from the initial spiritual focus of the early church gathered in a small domestic space (house church), it shifted its focus to structural development by building a huge public space (basilical church). This explains why even today a church is understood as a place (building) rather than as people (believers).

Sixth, based on the Biblical literature, Luke, other gospel writers, and Paul clearly present the spiritual function of οἶκος as a meeting place for believers during the time of Jesus and the apostles, implying the smaller size of the church then.[6] According to the Synoptic Gospels, Jesus and his disciples utilized domestic houses for ministry to the people and as a mission strategy to reach a town or city (Mark 1:29, 33; 2:1; 3:20; 9:33; Luke 10:1–12). The same applied to the apostles and first Christians in the book of Acts. Luke recounts that while they met in the temple courts, it was the gathering predominantly in domestic residences which prompted the exponential growth of the early church (Acts 2:46–47; 5:42–6:1a, 7). Additionally, there were specific Christian householders mentioned individually in the book of Acts (e.g. Cornelius, Simon the Tanner, Mary, Lydia, the Philippian Jailer, Jason, Titius Justus, Crispus, and Philip) and, most significantly, in the Pauline epistles (e.g. Philemon, Nympha, Prisca and Aquila) who all voluntarily offered their domestic spaces for spiritual use. Based on lexical study, this research looks into the possibility that the noun

---

6. See pages 39–50 .

οἶκος in Paul's expression ἡ κατ᾽ οἶκον ἐκκλησία (in 1 Cor 16:19; Rom 16:5; Phlm 1–2; Col 4:15) may refer to both the place ("house") and people ("household") as observed in various modern translations of the Bible. Grammatically, the preposition κατά with the accusative (οἶκον) may possibly be used both distributively ("the church in a houselike manner or in a series of individual houses") and locationally ("the assembly in someone's house") in the four given texts and hence should be interpreted as *a plurality of house churches within the local church as a whole.* Having critically analyzed the concept and context of οἶκος in the first-century Greco-Roman world, this study arrives at the general conclusion that the meaning of house church in the New Testament is the regular gathering of a small Christian assembly (people) in someone's domestic residence (place) where the common practices of the early church are observed (purpose).

Seventh, this study explores the content of New Testament house church practices such as the *sharing of leadership* (leaders), *shepherding of families* (learners), *searching of Scriptures* (lessons), and *saturating of cities* (locations).[7] For the sake of practicality, the transient apostles delegated the local leadership of individual house churches to ordinary volunteer workers – the trained householders who even included women. The entire household including children and house slaves was spiritually fed, led, and cared for by the appointed householder acting as undershepherd. The authoritative source of teaching came from what was written in the Old Testament and spoken by Jesus and the apostles. The house churches were strategically situated in a Greco-Roman city where there was a network of households whom God desired to redeem. So the elements that constituted the first-century house churches were trained laity as leaders, the whole family as learners, Scripture alone as the lesson, and the strategic city as the location. The table below compares New Testament house church practices with some of the biblical images of the church presented earlier. The parallels between the two clearly demonstrate that house church practices in the "literal sense" were derived from biblical images of the church in the "spiritual sense."

---

7. See pages 50–64.

Table 4.2 Conceptual comparison of the biblical images of the church and house church practices in the NT

Biblical Images of the Church	House Church Practices
• "Priesthood" (1 Pet 2:5, 9) • "Temple of the Holy Spirit" (1 Cor 3:16–17; 6:19; Eph 2:21–22)	Sharing of Leadership
• "Sheep" or "flock" (1 Pet 2:25; 5:2–4; Heb 13:20) • "Household of God" (1 Tim 3:15; Eph 2:19) • "Household of the faith" (Gal 6:10) • "Family of God" (1 Tim 5:1–2; 2 Cor 6:18) • "Bride of Christ" (Eph 5:32; 2 Cor 11:2; Rev 19:7; 21:2)	Shepherding of Families
• "Pillar and support of the truth" (1 Tim 3:15)	Searching of Scriptures
• "New or heavenly Jerusalem" (Rev 3:12; 21:2; Heb 12:22)	Saturating of Cities

Eighth, the twenty-first-century church is seen as drifting away from the New Testament church every time it overemphasizes the church building and the denomination.[8] Consequently, as a result of over-commercialism as a means to attract people, church life has become businesslike. Moreover, a sudden shift also occurred from a people-to-people setting to a program-to-people agenda. The three models of churches today (traditional, cell, and house church) have their own strengths and weaknesses. While it seems that the twenty-first century house church has more things in common with the New Testament house church than the other two, there is a corrective needed to deter it from going to the extreme. Based on his conservative and balanced perspective, Payne offers the "missional house church" which has regard for pastoral and lay leadership, family care, biblical education, and urban mission and is thus more consistent with the New Testament house church concept.

Ninth, the use of small groups is determined to not be something new in this era but common throughout church history.[9] There is a need then to rediscover what the early believers and also church fathers found regarding small groups. Up to this point, the small group is still essential; as it was before, it is still the basic structure and building blocks of a local church today. The three elements that constitute a twenty-first-century small group are also the

---

8. See pages 65–78.
9. See pages 79–82.

elements that were present in the first-century ἐκκλησία and οἶκος: people, purpose, and place. Hence, a small group today is the regular gathering of a small Christian assembly composed of a volunteer-based leader and home-focused learners (people) for Bible-centered lessons (purpose) in a Spirit-directed location (place).

Tenth, this work discovers that while there are various models of small groups today, most of them fall in one of McBride's four orientation categories (need, process, content, and task) which, when seen more closely, merely reflect different stages or levels of small group growth.[10] However, the *growth group* utilized at the author's church, Greenhills Christian Fellowship, appears to be a complete combination of each of McBride's categories in a single group (four-in-one). For example, the growth group mission states that "we will develop every member of Greenhills Christian Fellowship into maturing and multiplying disciples of the Lord Jesus Christ [*process*] within the relational context of small groups where . . . prayer, outreach, worship [*tasks*], education [*content*], and relationship-building [*need*] are carried out."[11] Furthermore, the growth group is also classified under the home group model by virtue of its being home-based. Of the five given types of home groups provided by Hadaway, Wright, and DuBose, GCF's growth group is closest to the *Home Bible Study* due to its great emphasis on God's Word (almost akin to a *study group*), except that, in terms of the leadership and organizational structures, it always contains a designated leader and is tied to the host church.

Eleventh, it has been realized in this study that the preferences of the Filipino small group for being led by clergy only, being limited to adults, being curriculum overly dependent, and meeting anywhere are culturally conditioned, with past history at its root and the values today as its fruit.[12] Historically, from the fifteenth to the nineteenth century of the Christian era, the significant Spanish and American influences on ancient Filipinos were religion and language, respectively. While the Philippines was partially Hispanized for more than three centuries by Spain through the Christian religion, it was fully Americanized for less than five decades through the English language. The colonial influences in the past have largely affected the cultural values of Filipinos today in terms of the following: leading (clerical mentality and *hiya*), grouping (exclusivity and small group-centeredness), studying (mediocrity, colonial mentality and conformity), and planning (*ningas-kugon*

---

10. See pages 82–87.

11. Greenhills Christian Fellowship, *Growth Group Manual*, 2.

12. See pages 87–111.

and *bahala na* attitude). Some of the Filipino cultural values and traits such as *hiya*, small group-centeredness, conformity, and *bahala na* mentality can work either for or against Filipinos depending on how they are employed. The rest, such as clericalism, exclusivity, mediocrity (*pwede na yan* mentality) and the *ningas-kugon* attitude, are all largely rooted in colonialism and need to be completely transformed. Transforming culture today is dependent on one's clear understanding of Christ's relationship to culture and the church's relationship to culture. This study strongly believes that *Christ is the transformer of culture.* The Lord has the power to change all things, and this study is very hopeful in the eventual transformation of human culture. However, the church should never seek to impose Jesus's teaching on all society by force but should simply speak the life-changing truth in love.

Twelfth, even if the Greco-Roman and Filipino worlds are individually unique and distant in time from each other, this research observes that in comparing them, both agree at least on the three-fold purpose of a typical residential space as structural (house), social (household), and spiritual (house-cult).[13] Structurally, though there was a boundary between public and domestic space for male and female family members in the Greco-Roman *oikos* and no dividing line separating households in the Filipino nipa hut, both were very open to other people for social gathering despite their limited space in a relatively small medium-sized house. Regardless of the differences in structural size and partition, the dynamics of being generally small stay the same. Socially, while women were discriminated against in terms of gender in the Greco-Roman world and not in the Filipino context, both cultures were/are undeniably family-oriented around the household. Spiritually, despite the fact that Greco-Romans were into paganism and Filipinos are into folk Christianity (animism and Catholicism), houses in both societies were/are used for religious purposes and therefore function as house-cults. The over-all finding, therefore, is that if the Greco-Roman house was conducive structurally, socially, and spiritually for house church gatherings, the same applies to the Filipino house for small group meetings.

Thirteenth, a connection is established between a house church and a small group, therefore deriving the conclusion that the house church which Paul wrote about in the New Testament has a lot in common with the small group that we have today.[14] Concepts of both the house church and the small group consist of the three-fold essential elements of place (the *where*), people (the

---

13. See pages 111–118.
14. See pages 118–122.

who), and purpose (the *why*), which are all drawn from the Christian concept of ἐκκλησία or the New Testament church. A house church, in a sense, is also a small group in a house setting and, at the same time, a small group is also a small church (microcosm) in a house context. Noticeably, while they are both church-based, they are also both house-sized. Both the house church and the small group are parallel in size which is relatively small when compared to the size of a group meeting in a big church building. Since the house church and the small group both meet in small numbers, their dynamics must be similar so that both could usually expect non-professional leaders of a small diverse group of learners with generally interactive lessons in typically closed and private locations.

Table 4.3 Implications of the NT house church for the contemporary Filipino small group

Components	New Testament House Church Practices		Contemporary Filipino Small Group Concerns		Small Group Theology
Leaders:	Sharing of Leadership	→	Clergy Only	=	Volunteer-Based Ministry
Learners:	Shepherding of Families	→	Limited to Adults	=	Home-Focused Community
Lessons:	Searching of Scriptures	→	Curriculum Over-Dependence	=	Bible-Centered Teaching
Locations:	Saturating of Cities	→	Meeting Anywhere	=	Spirit-Directed Mission

Fourteenth, the appropriation of New Testament house church practices to the concerns of the Filipino small group causes the formulation of a contemporary small group theology which transforms the negative Filipino cultural values.[15] The *sharing of leadership* changes the *clergy only* mentality which results in a *volunteer-based* ministry of small group leaders from the laity (theology of small group ministry). The *shepherding of families* challenges the *limited to adults* preference which leads to a *home-focused* community of small group learners at each level (theology of small group community). The *searching of Scriptures* corrects the *curriculum over-dependence* attitude which

---

15. See pages 122–157.

leads to a *Bible-centered* study of small group lessons that change one's life (theology of small group teaching). Lastly, the *saturating of cities* checks the *meeting anywhere* perspective which brings about a *Spirit-directed* strategy for small group locations in every locality (theology of small group mission). The table below presents the implications of the New Testament house church on the contemporary Filipino small group.

Hence, many important things can be learned from the practices of the early Christians who met in private homes, whose leadership task was the mobilization of laity, whose ministry target was all the generations in every family, whose teaching goal was conversion through study, and whose mission strategy was the penetration of a city as directed by the Spirit.

5

Conclusion

In this day and age where people have large dreams for themselves and glorify things that are big, small things are often overlooked. According to the Gospel of Luke, in telling his parables Jesus likened the kingdom of God to small things like mustard seeds and leaven (Luke 13:18–21). Small groups are similar: small but they eventually grow and become big. Of the two, church-based small groups are most similar to leaven or yeast. As Jesus says, "To what shall I compare the kingdom of God? It is like leaven, which a woman took and hid in three pecks of flour until it was all leavened" (Luke 13:20–21). What, then, is the connection of small groups and the church with the yeast and the flour? As Kennedy explains and concludes,

> Yeast has very distinctive properties which allow it to perform a distinctive service when mixed with flour. Yet the yeast does not stubbornly retain its independence from the flour so that it can move on to other flour mixes or explore its own possibilities apart from a particular dough mixture. Instead, the yeast is added, dispersed, and kneaded with the other ingredients until a new dough is formed and cooked, and its aroma fills the entire area and pleases the senses of the baker.
>
> Like yeast, a small group does have distinctive tasks to accomplish; but also like yeast, a small group's purpose will be fulfilled only when it loses itself within the church for the creation of a new community, who will participate in God's blessing to the entire world.[1]

Both small and large group meetings are essential for the growth of the church. However, the secret of getting bigger is going smaller. That is also true in the physical world where the great society's success is dependent on

---

1. Kennedy, "Theology of Small Groups," 183.

its small basic unit or nucleus, the family. Finding the true sense of a spiritual family in a big gathering is impossible. That explains why meeting in small numbers is important to one's Christian experience and development, and that makes the small group a necessary companion of every church in every century. So if God mightily used a small instrument like the house church to bring about big growth in the church during the first century, he can do the same with the small group in this twenty-first century. Let the church today *grow big in small groups!*

A. Recommendations for Further Research

This work can be developed further through the following recommendations for additional research. First, it is ascertained in this research that there is need for an extensive scholarly study on the words οἶκος and οἰκία. On the one hand, some scholars like Klauck attempt to differentiate the word pair (οἶκος is "house" whereas οἰκία is "household"), but Elliot ends up with opposite findings. On the other hand, a majority of exegetes contend that the two terms are simply synonymous. However, there are some instances discovered in this study regarding Luke's special use for οἶκος when pertaining to Cornelius' house/household (Acts 10:2, 22, 30; 11:12–14) and οἰκία when referring to the house of Simon the tanner (Acts 10:6, 17, 32; 11:11). In addition, Paul's consistent usage of οἶκος together with ἐκκλησία in his greetings (Rom 16:5; 1 Cor 16:19; Phlm 2; Col 4:15) but not once using οἰκία in such a context raises the question: why does he prefer one word to the other? This book, therefore, finds the need to resolve the discrepancy through new lexicographical work on οἶκος and οἰκία.

Second, aside from the house church, even the house synagogue was strategically used by Jesus in the Gospels, Paul in his epistles, and the Jewish community in general, as it has become the primary institution of Judaism. The house church that was used by the Christian community evolved through it. Additionally, further research on the extensive use of בַּיִת (house) in the Old Testament can also be conducted to establish if it has any connection with συναγωγή. "Synagogue" is often understood in biblical scholarship as not necessarily an actual building but a Jewish "place of gathering" in both private and open spaces. Therefore, a wide-ranging study on the role of house synagogues in early Christianity is also a must.

Third, a more detailed work or study on the *how* of sharing leadership, shepherding families, searching Scripture, and saturating cities today is necessary. This book merely provides an overview on these house church practices. Four comprehensive studies can still be made. For instance, specific ways should be given in terms of teaching the doctrine of the priesthood of all believers and *sola Scriptura* (biblical authority) and leading a family ministry and urban ministry in a small group context. In this way, the negative Filipino values of clericalism, exclusivism, colonialism, and fatalism will be transformed as the aspects of leading, grouping, studying, and planning in the contemporary Filipino setting are addressed. So if GCF is committed to planting satellite churches in strategic areas, then growth groups must also be strategically situated in key cities in Metro Manila, targeting families and implementing a priesthood of all believers mindset and shared leadership between pastors, elders, and other lay people, especially homeowners; and it must continue to train group leaders to handle the Scriptures properly without too much dependence on curriculum materials which are intended to be used only as a guide in pointing the learners to the Bible.

Fourth, more books such as J. D. Payne's work on *Missional House Churches* should be written as a corrective to the existing house church networks around the world. There is also a need to write about a missional small group ministry or missional growth group ministry. Hopefully, the traditional church can transform its small groups to be missional without becoming a house church movement, and thus preserve its uniqueness and difference as a traditional church.

Fifth, to conduct a survey on the concerns of Filipino small groups or, to be more specific, the GCF growth groups based on the four given areas: leaders, learners, lessons, and locations. Through the gathered data from key people in the small groups, the real issues (e.g. scarcity of leadership, exclusivity of membership, superficiality of curriculum, and unsuitability of community) can be ascertained, and the results will be more objective. In this way, the specific needs will surface (e.g. adequate and adept leaders, diverse and dynamic learners, textual and transformational lessons, and suitable and strategic locations) and goals or action points could then be set.

B. Future Plans for Project Implementation

There are many ways in which this study can be implemented in the future. In fact, the very nature of the research is such that, in order to realize its greatest benefit to the church, it must be an ongoing ministry. The author's immediate context is GCF which is located in Ortigas Center, Pasig City, Philippines. The four-fold master plan is as follows: (1) that changing the small group's mindset of small group leaders as limited to clergy, by teaching a seminar on lay leadership and the priesthood of believers, will lead to a bigger pool of effective small group shepherds among the lay leaders; (2) that challenging the preference of limiting small group learners to adults, by leading a seminar on family-based ministry and heterogeneous grouping, will result in a huge flock of interactive small group sheep as all levels are invited to join the group; (3) that correcting the attitude of curriculum over-dependence in preparing small group lessons, by facilitating seminars titled "Walk-Through the OT and NT" and "Bible Study Methods," will lead to biblical and life-transforming study of the Word; and (4) that checking the perspective of meeting anywhere in terms of small group locations, by conducting a demographic study and seminar on urban ministry, will lead to strategic sites for exponential growth in small groups and new church starts.[2]

Hence, the small group leadership task is the *mobilization* of laity; the small group ministry target is all the *generations* in every family; the small group teaching goal is *transformation* in the study; and the small group mission strategy is the *penetration* of cities as directed by the Spirit. The table below shows the end results of small group plans implemented to solve small group problems: adequate and adept leaders, diverse and dynamic learners, textual and transformational lessons, and suitable and strategic locations.

Table 5.1 End results of small group plans implemented

Categories	Small Group Plans	Small Group Problems		End Results
Small Group Task:	Mobilization of Laity	→ Scarcity of Leadership	=	Adequate and Adept Leaders
Small Group Target:	Generations in the Family	→ Exclusivity of Membership	=	Diverse and Dynamic Learners
Small Group Goal:	Conversion through Study	→ Superficiality of the Curriculum	=	Textual and Transformational Lessons
Small Group Strategy:	Penetration of the City	→ Unsuitability of the Community	=	Suitable and Strategic Locations

Therefore, the book of Acts and the Pauline epistles, which all contain the common practices of the early church that met typically in houses, point to the following: (1) a volunteer-based ministry of small group leaders from the

---

2. See appendix 4, "A Sample Action Plan," on pages 189–191.

laity, (2) a home-focused community of small group learners in each level, (3) a Bible-centered study of small group lessons that change one's life, and (4) a Spirit-directed strategy for small group locations in every locality. Such should be the case of all contemporary Filipino small groups, such as the GCF growth groups, when they appropriate the New Testament house church practices on the sharing of leadership, shepherding of families, searching of Scriptures, and saturating of cities, which will expedite the birthing of daughter churches. So why don't you *let the church meet in your house* today?

Appendix 1:
The "Stairs" Diagram of a Church

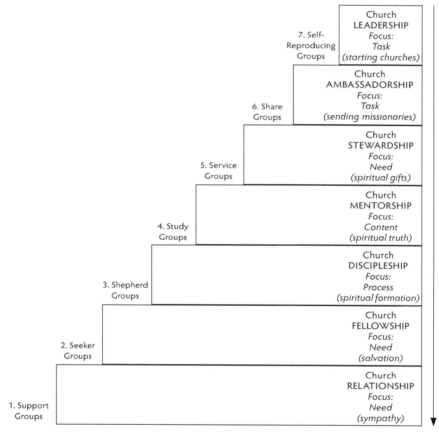

Figure A1.1 Levelling up your church: The seven levels of a growing church

Note: The figure above shows what a church should be, levelling up through its small groups (its building blocks) until it becomes a *growing church*. When this level is reached, that is *Church WORSHIP* – the ultimate goal of every church, for the glory of God.

Appendix 2:
The GCF's Growth
Group Ministry[1]

Biblical Basis

What are small groups' deepest biblical roots? Here is the biblical basis for growth groups:

1. Right at the start of Jesus's public earthly ministry, he chose key people to be part of his growth group (Matt 10:2–4).

2. Jesus spent most of his earthly ministry with his growth group. He ate with his disciples, they traveled together, and even actually lived together (cf. Acts 4:13).

3. Jesus used his growth group as the venue for leadership training (see John 17:6, 8, 12, 18).

4. It follows then that it was in his growth group that Jesus taught and modeled God's Word, spiritual values, and lifestyle. (For example, see Luke 8:10 and 11:1.)

5. Jesus kept relationships central in his ministry. It is in the context of these small groups that Jesus spent time with people – teaching, preaching, caring, healing, listening, forgiving, and encouraging.

6. Aside from large meetings, the early church met daily in small groups in homes to effectively pursue the church's mission (see Acts 2:46–47; 5:42).[2]

---

1. The material in this appendix has been lightly edited for inclusion in this publication.
2. Greenhills Christian Fellowship, *The Growth Group Manual*, 2.

Philosophy of Ministry

What does the growth group believe in and live out? The growth group's philosophy of ministry is summarized as follows:

The growth group is aptly described as the "microcosm" of Greenhills Christian Fellowship. It is like a small church. In the growth group we scale down church life to a smaller and more personal level. This is necessary because of the increasing size of our congregation. Hence, in a growth group, members get to participate in efforts geared toward building the church and winning the lost.

As a microcosm of GCF, the growth group is committed to carrying out the basic tasks of the church: prayer, outreach, worship, education, relationship-building [and service]. These are the same tasks the early church pursued as recorded for us in Acts 2:42–47. In carrying out these tasks, we could say that growth groups are at the cutting-edge of our church's development and expansion.

The church is a relational community. In the Bible we find commands such as "love one another," "encourage one another," "bear one another's burdens," and so forth. As a New Testament church, GCF is expected to obey such commands. However, obeying these "one another" commands becomes difficult, if not impossible, when people come together only for Sunday worship services and with several thousand others at that.

Logically, the growth group, as a small community of seven to fifteen people, provides the best venue for our church to obey these "one another" commands. As such, the Growth Group Ministry takes on the cudgels for enhancing Christian fellowship within GCF.[3]

Ministry Team

What constitutes a Growth Group Ministry team? Being in charge of the direction of ministry overall, the team comprises the following:

1. Growth group minister

2. At least one (1) representative from the Board of Elders

3. At least one (1) representative from the Board of Deacons

4. Seven (7) ministry team members elected by the congregation.[4]

---

3. Greenhills Christian Fellowship, 3.

4. Greenhills Christian Fellowship, 3.

Policy Statements

For a peaceful and orderly meeting, what are the guidelines to uphold in a given small group? The growth group has the following policy statements:

1. The doctrinal content of growth group materials and speakers should be consistent with the statement of faith of Greenhills Christian Fellowship.

2. As a microcosm of Greenhills Christian Fellowship, growth groups are expected to carry out the basic tasks of the church, which are:

   a. Prayer (entreating God on behalf of one another, the church, the nation, and the world)

   b. Outreach (evangelizing the lost in word and in deeds)

   c. Worship (exalting our God through singing and sharing)

   d. Education (edifying one another through the study of Scriptures)

   e. Relationship-building (encouraging one another to enrich our fellowship)

3. Growth group leaders must be members of Greenhills Christian Fellowship in good standing and must have undergone the Basic Growth Group Leaders' Training.

4. All church policies must be upheld in all growth groups.[5]

---

5. Greenhills Christian Fellowship, 4.

Table A2.1 Growth group POWER tasks[6]

Tasks	Prayer	Outreach	Worship	Education	Relationship-Building
Primary Focus	Entreat	Evangelize	Exalt	Edify	Encourage
Acts 2:42–47	"They devoted themselves ... to prayer"	"The Lord added to their number daily those who were being saved"	"They devoted themselves ... to the breaking of bread ... praising God"	"They devoted themselves to the apostles' teaching"	"They devoted themselves ... to the fellowship.... All believers were together ... [and] ate together"
Basic Human Need	Power to Live On	Profession to Live Out	Purpose to Live For	Principles to Live By	People to Live With
The Growth Group Provides	A Force for Living	A Function for Living	A Focus for Living	A Foundation for Living	A Family for Living
Emotional Benefit	Stimulation	Self-Expression	Significance	Stability	Support

Organizational Structure

How is the growth group organized? According to *The Growth Group Manual*, "The Growth Group is the basic organizational unit of the Growth Group

---

6. Greenhills Christian Fellowship, 4.

Ministry. For effective management of the ministry, these groups have been organized into clusters and districts."[7] The *Manual* goes on to explain, "a cluster refers to a unit of four Growth Groups. The number of people in a Cluster could be somewhere between 28 to 60 Growth Group members. The Cluster Supervisor provides supervision and immediate pastoral leadership to the Growth Group Leaders under his or her cluster."[8] This is better shown in the diagram below:

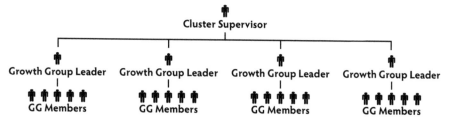

Figure A2.1 Growth group cluster supervisor chart[9]

On the other hand, "a district is a grouping of four Growth Group Clusters. The District Supervisor provides supervision and pastoral leadership to the Cluster Supervisor within a particular district."[10] This organizational set-up is parallel to the cell church's structure with its zone servants and a zone pastor. The resemblance is apparent in the diagram below:

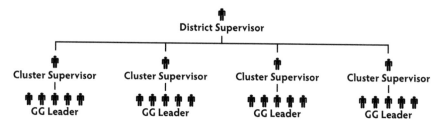

Figure A2.2 Growth group district supervisor chart[11]

7. Greenhills Christian Fellowship, 4.
8. Greenhills Christian Fellowship, 4.
9. Greenhills Christian Fellowship, 4.
10. Greenhills Christian Fellowship, 5.
11. Greenhills Christian Fellowship, 5.

Appendix 3:
A Sample Study Guide Lesson[1]

The Parable of the Prodigal Son
Luke 15:11–32

Note: Growth group is a time for *assembly, adoration, admonition,* and *accountability* and serves the following purposes: to *congregate, celebrate, communicate,* and *culminate* as a microcosm or "small church."

Objectives: By the end of this lesson, we aim for the group learners' attitude towards "sinners" to change as they:

1. Understand the Heavenly Father's steadfast love and mercy which are joyfully bestowed on any lost son or daughter who humbly returns to him.

2. Rejoice over one sinner who comes to repentance, in the same way God joyfully accepted us when we received his forgiveness from our sins.

3. Thank God for his forgiveness and joyfully celebrate in welcoming someone who was lost because of sin but is now found by a forgiving God.

→← **Assembly Time**: Introduction to *congregate* through ice breaker (about 10 minutes).

- *Ice Breaker for Starting Communication*
  Share something or someone you lost and found

↑ **Adoration Time**: Inspiration to *celebrate* through invocation, impartation of thanksgiving, and invitation to worship and read the Scripture (about 25 minutes).

- *Invocation*
  Focus your opening prayer on the Father's love and his being a Good Shepherd to us.

---

1. The material in this appendix has been lightly edited for inclusion in this publication.

- *Invitation for Adoration/Confession*
  Call to Worship: Read Psalm 23
  Suggested Songs (choose 3–4): "Forever Grateful"; "Savior Like a Shepherd"; "Shepherd of my Soul"; "Why Have You Chosen Me?"; "A Broken Spirit"; "Power of Your Love"; "Your Steadfast Love"; "All We Like Sheep"; "No Greater Love"; "Jesus Lover of My Soul"

- *Impartation of Thanksgiving*
  Allow 2–3 group members to share a testimony about the Father's love and being a Good Shepherd to them this week. Then, close it with a short prayer of thanksgiving.

- *Invitation to Read the Scripture*
  Luke 15:11–32

↓ **Admonition Time:** Instruction to *communicate* one's investigation of the specific text, interpretation according to setting, and integration for the spiritual truth (about 50 minutes).

- *Content: Investigation of the Specific Text*

  1. Who are the three major characters Jesus mentions in the story (v. 11)?

  2. What did the younger son demand from his father before leaving home (v. 12)?

  3. When the younger son left home, how did things turn out for him? What made him come home afterwards (vv. 13–19)?

  4. How did the father and the older brother receive the "prodigal son"? Compare and contrast their response (vv. 20–24, 25–32).

- *Context: Interpretation According to Setting*

  1. Among the three major characters in the story, who do you think is the focus? Father? Older son? Or younger son?

  2. What prompted Jesus to tell the parable (vv. 1–3)? Who do you think represent the father, younger and the older sons in the story?

  3. Why does the story have no concluding statement (when compared to the first two stories in this trilogy of "lostness," vv. 4–10)? What does Jesus want to tell the Pharisees in verses 25–32?

- *Concept: Integration for Spiritual Truth*

    1. What is Jesus's point in this parable? What does this story teach about sin, repentance and God's love?

    2. How have you experienced God as being similar to the father in the story? Which of the father's qualities do you most need?

    3. Whom do you most identify with? The juvenile son? The jealous brother? Or the joyful father? Why?

→ **Accountability Time**: Invitation to *culminate* in the implication of the Scripture, implementation of a specific action, and intercession for saints and seekers (about 35 minutes).

- *Connect: Implication of the Scripture*

    1. How do you respond when one of our erring brothers/sisters comes back to fellowship with us? Do you wait with open arms or do you keep him/her at arm's distance? Do you fully pardon or put him/her on probation?

    2. If you compare your spiritual journey to the younger son's, where are you right now? How would you describe it?

- *Conduct: Implementation of a Specific Action*
  Are there sins in your heart that you need to confess to God right now and ask forgiveness for? Repent and return to Him. Jesus has provided the way back to the Father (John 14:6). You can pray this prayer:

    > "Father, I have sinned against heaven and against You. I have tried to live my life on my own. Please forgive me. I'm now coming back to you – in complete surrender to the Lordship of Christ. Make me worthy to be called your child. In Jesus's name." Amen.

  If you have been a recipient of God's forgiveness for the longest time, thank Him now for His steadfast love and mercy on you. Make it a point too to joyfully celebrate in welcoming to the group someone who was lost because of sin but is now found by a forgiving God.

- *Concern: Intercession for the Saints and Seekers*

    1. How can the group pray for you? Share now your personal needs or concerns with your accountability and prayer partners. These may include attitudes that need to be changed and specific actions to be done in obedience to God's Word.

    2. As you intercede for each other ("saints"), pray also for others outside the group who need to know Jesus ("seekers"). Pray that God would give you a loving heart for the lost and cause you to rejoice for those who come to repentance.

Appendix 4:
A Sample Action Plan

Table A4.1 The disciple-making group's 2019 goal-setting worksheet

Categories	Objectives	Goals	Programs
1. **Small Group Leaders**	To mobilize a volunteer-based ministry of small group leaders from the laity which ends up producing more *maturing and multiplying disciple-makers.*	100 new members 100 new ministry servants 20 new small group leaders 1 existing group leader per month	• Membership class • Spiritual gifts class • Growth group leaders' training • One-on-one mentoring • DMG leaders' assembly • Seminars on "Lay Leadership" and "Priesthood of All Believers"
2. **Small Group Learners**	To establish a home-focused community of small group learners from each church family by shepherding group members through pastoral care and developing in them a *growing engagement in worship and prayer gatherings,* which results in producing more *worshipful and prayerful GCFers in community*	Each group visited per week Each group worshiping/praying during the weekly group meeting Each group invites one to attend the worship service and sends one representative to attend the church prayer gathering	• Home visitations • Growth group worship and prayer time/prayer walk • Growth group support for church worship services and prayer gatherings • Seminars on "Family-based Ministry" and "Heterogeneous Grouping"

3. **Small Group Lessons**	To conduct a Bible-centered study of small group lessons that change life by producing growth group study guides in tandem with sermon series, leading to the *development of integrated small group curriculum.*	1,250 printed copies of study guide material (1,000 student guides and 250 leader guides)	• Curriculum planning and writing • Seminars on "Walk Through the OT and NT" and "Bible Study Methods"
4. **Small Group Locations**	To start a Spirit-directed strategy for small group locations within the church vicinity that brings about intentional formation of Outreach Bible Studies (OBS) which eventually spin-off into growth groups.	12 new small groups	• Outreach Bible studies • Growth group express • Growth group socials • Growth group launching • Growth group testimonies • "Demographic Study" and Seminar on "Urban Ministry"

GCF'S DISCIPLE-MAKING GROUPS

"Each One, Reach One and Teach One"

We introduce this year the ministry of our Disciple-Making Groups (DMG) that aims to make our growth groups and other groups in the church intentional in disciple-making. We simply define "disciple-making" as the process of moving people from *community* to *congregation* to *core* that they might repeat the entire process in others also (2 Tim 2:2).[1] As led by the eight-person pastoral staff,

---

1. The five stages of a Disciple-Making Group are as follows: (1) Contact Stage; (2) Conception Stage; (3) Birthing Stage; (4) Growth Stage; and (5) Reproduction Stage.

the DMG structure is subdivided into four major ministry teams (with the first three being demographical and the last one geographical): (1) Children, International Christian School (ICS), and Youth; (2) Young Adults/Sports and Connect (BPO); (3) Men, Women, Couples, and Seniors; and (4) Ortigas Center, Quezon City, San Juan, and other cities.

In fulfilling their shepherding role to the flock, both pastors and elders, with the support of our ministry assistants, deacons and deaconesses, will work together in looking after the spiritual welfare of each of the Disciple-Making Groups through feeding (teaching God's Word), leading (life-on-life mentoring), and caring (visiting and praying) for them.[2] The ultimate goal of this partnership among church leaders is to produce *maturing and multiplying disciple makers* in each of the DMGs, which begins with the *pastoral care* of new small group attenders and which results in the raising of their commitment levels through *membership assimilation, ministry placement, leadership development*, and *small group reproduction*[3] so they might repeat the entire process in another new group also (which is what DMG is all about).

---

2. Shepherding is simply defined as seeking the spiritual welfare of the FLoCk by Feeding, Leading, and Caring (FLC) for them.

3. These five Key Results Areas (KRAs) are measured through five Key Performance Indicators (KPIs): (1) *New attenders shepherded* at the end of the year; (2) *New members added* at the end of the year; (3) *New ministry servants involved* at the end of the year; (4) *New leaders trained* at the end of the year; and (5) *New groups launched* at the end of the year.

Bibliography

Agoncillo, Teodoro A., and Milagros C. Guerrero. *History of the Filipino People.* Quezon City: R. P. Garcia Publishing, 1977.

Aland, Kurt, Matthew Black, Carlo M. Martini, Bruce M. Metzger, and Allen Wikgren, eds. *The Greek New Testament.* 3rd ed. Federal Republic of Germany: United Bible Societies, 1966.

Allen, Roland. *Missionary Methods: St. Paul's or Ours.* Grand Rapids: Eerdmans Publishing, 1962.

Allen, Roland, and David M. Paton. *The Ministry of the Spirit.* London: World Dominion Press, 1960.

Banks, Robert. *Paul's Idea of Community: The Early House Churches in their Historical Setting.* Australia: Anzea Publishers, 1981.

Banks, Robert, and Julia Banks. *The Church Comes Home: A New Base for Community and Mission.* Australia: Albatross Books, 1986.

Barker, Kenneth L., ed. *Zondervan NIV Study Bible.* Fully Revised. Grand Rapids: Zondervan, 2002.

Barrett, Lois. *Building the House Church.* Scottsdale, PA: Herald Press, 1986.

Becker, Paul, Jim Carpenter, and Mark Williams. *The New Dynamic Church Planting Handbook.* Oceanside, CA: Dynamic Church Planting, 2003.

Best, Ernest. "Church." In *Harper's Bible Dictionary*, edited by Paul J. Achtemeier, 168–170. San Francisco: Harper and Row, 1985.

Birkey, Del. "The House Church: A Missional Model." *Missiology: An International Review* 19, no. 1 (January 1991): 69–80.

———. *The House Church Book: Non Emerging New Testament Prototype.* 2009. Accessed 11 May 2018. https://thehousechurchbook.com/read-the-house-church-book-chapters/.

Blair, Emma H., and James A. Robertson, *Philippine Islands, 1493–1803*, vol. 16. Cleveland, OH: A. H. Clark Co., 1903.

Blue, Bradley B. "Acts and the House Church." In *The Book of Acts in Its Graeco-Roman Setting*, edited by David W. J. Gill and Conrad Gempf, 119–192. Grand Rapids: Eerdmans Publishing, 1994.

———. "Architecture, Early Church." In *Dictionary of the Later New Testament and Its Developments*, edited by Ralph P. Martin and Peter H. Davids, 91–95. Downers Grove: InterVarsity Press, 1997.

The Cape Town Commitment. The Lausanne Movement, 26 January 2011. Accessed 20 May 2018. https://www.lausanne.org/content/ctc/ctcommitment.

Carson, D. A., Douglas J. Moo, and Leon Morris. *An Introduction to the New Testament.* Grand Rapids: Zondervan, 1992.

Carter, Craig A. *Rethinking Christ and Culture: A Post-Christendom Perspective*. Grand Rapids: Brazos Press, 2006.

Castillo, Metosalem Q. "The Church in Thy House: A Study of the House Church Concept as it Relates to Christian Mission." DMiss diss., Fuller Theological Seminary, 1976.

Chan, Edmund. *A Certain Kind: Intentional Disciplemaking that Redefines Success in Ministry*. Singapore: Covenant Evangelical Free Church, 2013.

Chan, Edmund, and Tan Lian Seng. *Discipleship Missions: Getting Missional in Your Life*. Singapore: Covenant Evangelical Free Church, 2016.

Chua, Ken. *Empowered to Influence: 7 Paradigm Shifts to Impact as Salt and Light*. Singapore: Write Editions, 2012.

Clouse, Robert G., Richard V. Pierard, and Edwin M. Yamauchi. *Two Kingdoms: The Church and Culture through the Ages*. Chicago: Moody Press, 1993.

Coenen, L. "Church, Synagogue." In *A–F*, Vol. 1 of *The New International Dictionary of the New Testament Theology*, edited by Colin Brown, 291–307. Grand Rapids: Zondervan, 1975.

Coleman, Lyman. *Serendipity Training Manual for Groups*. Littleton, CO: Serendipity House, 1987.

Comiskey, Joel T. "Cell-Based Ministry: A Positive Factor for Church Growth in Latin America." PhD diss., Fuller Theological Seminary, 1997.

Costello, Robert B., ed. *Random House Webster's College Dictionary*. Revised and updated. New York: Random House, 1995.

Craffert, Pieter F. "The Pauline Household Communities: Their Nature as Social Entities." *Neotestamentica* 32, no. 2 (1998): 309–341.

Craig, Albert M., William A. Graham, Donald Kagan, Steven Ozment, and Frank M. Turner. *The Heritage of World Civilizations*. 2nd ed. New York: Macmillan, 1990.

Davies, James A. "Small Groups: Are They Really So New?" *Christian Education Journal* 2 (Fall 1984): 43–52.

Dawson, John. *Taking Our Cities for God*. Grand Rapids: Zondervan, 1987.

Donahue, Bill, and Russ Robinson. *Building a Church of Small Groups*. Grand Rapids: Willow Creek Association, 2001.

Drumwright, Huber L., and Curtis Vaughan. *New Testament Studies: Essays in Honor of Ray Summers in His Sixty-Fifth Year*. Waco, TX: Baylor University Press, 1975.

Eaves, James F. "Effective Church Evangelism in the City." *Southwestern Journal of Theology* 24, no. 2 (Spring 1982): 67–75.

Elliott, John H. *A Home for the Homeless: A Sociological Exegesis of 1 Peter, Its Situation and Strategy*. Philadelphia: Fortress Press, 1981.

———. "Philemon and House Churches." *The Bible Today* 22 (May 1984): 145–150.

Elliott, Sammy. "Building Community Through Koinonia Home Groups." DMin project, Southwestern Baptist Theological Seminary, 2004.

Enriquez, Virgilio G. *From Colonial to Liberation Psychology: The Philippine Experience*. 2nd ed. Manila: De La Salle University Press, 1994.

———. *Pagbabagong-Dangal: Indigenous Psychology and Cultural Empowerment.* Quezon City: Pugad Lawin Press, 1994.

Erickson, Millard J. *Christian Theology.* Grand Rapids: Baker Book House, 1983.

Faivre, Alexander. *The Emergence of the Laity in the Early Church.* New York: Paulist Press, 1984.

Fee, Gordon D., and Douglas Stuart. *How to Read the Bible Book by Book.* Grand Rapids: Zondervan, 2002.

———. *How to Read the Bible for All Its Worth.* 3rd ed. Grand Rapids: Zondervan, 2003.

Filson, Floyd V. "The Significance of Early House Churches." *Journal of Biblical Literature* 58, no. 2 (1939): 105–112.

Finnell, David L. *Cell Group Basic Training.* Mississauga, ON: WorldTeam Canada, 1993.

Finney, Paul C. "Early Christian Architecture: The Beginnings – A Review Article." *Harvard Theological Review* 81, no. 3 (July 1988): 319–339.

Fitts, Robert. *The Church in the House: A Return to Simplicity.* Salem, OR: Preparing the Way Publishers, 2001.

Ford, LeRoy. *Design for Teaching and Training: A Self-Study Guide to Lesson Planning.* West Broadway: Wipf & Stock, 2000.

Foster, Arthur L., ed. *The House Church Evolving.* Chicago: Exploration Press, 1976.

Gapuz, V. P., and C. D. Lozada Jr., eds. "A Framework for Analyzing the Filipino Character." In *Who and What Is the Pinoy?* Pages 1–10. Metro Manila: 24K Printing, 1990.

Garrett, James Leo, Jr. "The Priesthood of All Christians: From Cyprian to John Chrysostom." *Southwestern Journal of Theology* 30, no. 2 (Spring 1988): 22–33.

Garrison, David. *Church Planting Movements: How God Is Redeeming a Lost World.* Midlothian, VA: Wigtake Resources, 2003.

Gehring, Roger W. *House Church and Mission: The Importance of Household Structures in Early Christianity.* Peabody: Hendrickson, 2004.

George, Carl F. *Nine Keys to Effective Small Group Leadership.* Mansfield, PA: Kingdom Publishing, 1997.

George, Michele. "Domestic Architecture and Household Relations: Pompeii and Roman Ephesos." *Journal for the Study of the New Testament* 27, no. 1 (September 2004): 7–25.

Getz, Gene A. *Sharpening the Focus of the Church.* Chicago: Moody Press, 1974.

Gnanakan, Ken. *Kingdom Concerns: A Biblical Theology of Mission Today.* Leicester, UK: Inter-Varsity Press, 1993.

Goetzmann, J. "House, Build, Manage, Steward." In *The New International Dictionary of the New Testament Theology*, Vol. 2, edited by Colin Brown, 247–251. Grand Rapids: Zondervan, 1976.

Gorospe, Vitaliano. "Christian Renewal of Filipino Values." In *Split-level Christianity*, edited by Jaime Bulatao, 44–59. Quezon City: Ateneo de Manila University Press, 1966.

Greenhills Christian Fellowship Growth Group Ministry. *The Growth Group Manual.* Pasig City, Philippines: Greenhills Christian Fellowship, 1998.

Grudem, Wayne A. *Systematic Theology: An Introduction to Bible Doctrine.* Leicester: Inter-Varsity Press, 1994.

Hadaway, C. Kirk, Stuart A. Wright, and Francis M. DuBose. *Home Cell Groups and House Churches.* Nashville: Broadman Press, 1987.

Hendricks, Howard. *Teaching to Change Lives.* Portland, OR: Multnomah Publishers, 1987.

Hull, Bill. *The Complete Book of Discipleship: On Being and Making Followers of Christ.* Colorado Springs: NavPress, 2006.

Icenogle, Gareth Weldon. *Biblical Foundations for Small Group Ministry: An Integrational Approach.* Downers Grove, IL: InterVarsity Press, 1994.

Javalera, Elizabeth R. *Training for Competence.* Quezon City: Philippine Association of Christian Education, 1973.

Joaquin, Nick. *Culture and History.* Pasig City, Philippines: Anvil Publishing, 2004.

Jocano, F. Landa. *Filipino Value System.* Quezon City: Punlad Research House, 1997.

———. *Filipino Worldview.* Quezon City: Punlad Research House, 2001.

———. *Towards Developing a Filipino Corporate Culture.* Manila: Punlad Research House, 1988.

Johnson, Todd M. "Christianity at 2000: Changes Today, Challenges Tomorrow." In *Doing Member Care Well: Perspectives and Practices from Around the World*, edited by Kelly O'Donnell, 33–36. Pasadena: William Carey Library, 2002.

Keller, Timothy J. *Center Church: Doing Balanced, Gospel-Centered Ministry in Your City.* Grand Rapids: Zondervan, 2012.

———. *Loving the City: Doing Balanced, Gospel-Centered Ministry in Your City.* Grand Rapids: Zondervan, 2016.

Kennedy, Darin. "A Theology of Small Groups." *Restoration Quarterly* 38, no. 3 (1996): 175–183.

Kirby, G. W. "The Church." In *A–C*, Vol. 1 of *The Zondervan Pictorial Encyclopedia of the Bible*, edited by Merrill C. Tenney, 845–857. Grand Rapids: Zondervan, 1975.

Klauck, Hans-Josef. "The House-Church as Way of Life." *Theology Digest* 30, no. 2 (1982): 153–157.

Kraft, Charles H. *Christianity in Culture.* Maryknoll, NY: Orbis Books, 1979.

The Lausanne Covenant. The Lausanne Movement, 1 August 1974. Accessed 11 May 2018. http://www.lausanne.org/content/covenant/lausanne-covenant.

Lea, Thomas D. "The Priesthood of All Christians According to the New Testament." *Southwestern Journal of Theology* 30, no. 2 (Spring 1988): 15–21.

MacArthur, John F., Jr. *The Master's Plan for the Church.* Chicago: Moody Press, 1991.

Maggay, Melba P. *Communicating Cross-Culturally: Towards a New Context for Missions in the Philippines.* Quezon City: New Day Publishers, 1989.

Malherbe, Abraham. "The Household of God." *Mission* 3 (November 1969): 13–17.

———. *Social Aspects of Early Christianity.* 2nd ed. Philadelphia: Fortress, 1983.

Malphurs, Aubrey, and Will Mancini. *Building Leaders: Blueprints for Developing Leadership at Every Level of Your Church.* Grand Rapids: Baker Books, 2004.

"The Manila Manifesto." The Lausanne Movement, 20 July 1989. Accessed 16 May 2018. http://www.lausanne.org/content/manifesto/the-manila-manifesto.

Martin, Ralph P. *New Testament Foundations: A Guide for Christian Students.* Vol. 1. Grand Rapids: Eerdmans, 1975.

McBride, Neal F. *How to Lead Small Groups.* Colorado Springs: NavPress, 1990.

Meeks, Wayne A. *The First Urban Christians: The Social World of the Apostle Paul.* New Haven: Yale, 1983.

Mercado, Leonardo N. *Inculturation and Filipino Theology.* Manila, Philippines: Divine Word Publications, 1992.

Mikolaski, Samuel J. "The Contemporary Relevance of the Priesthood of All Christians." *Southwestern Journal of Theology* 30, no. 2 (Spring 1988): 6–14.

Mish, Frederick C., ed. *Merriam-Webster's Collegiate Dictionary.* 10th ed. Springfield, MA: Merriam-Webster, 2002.

Moo, Douglas J. *Encountering the Book of Romans: A Theological Survey.* 2nd ed. Grand Rapids: Baker Academic, 2014.

———. *The Epistle to the Romans.* Grand Rapids: Eerdmans, 1996.

Neighbour, Ralph W., Jr. *Where Do We Go From Here? A Guidebook for the Cell Group Church.* Houston: Touch Publications, 1990.

New American Standard Bible. Eugene, OR: Harvest House Publishers, 2013.

Niebuhr, H. Richard. *Christ and Culture.* New York: HarperCollins, 2001.

Oakes, Peter. *Reading Romans in Pompeii: Paul's Letter at Ground Level.* Minneapolis: Fortress Press, 2013.

O'Brien, Peter T. *Colossians and Philemon.* Vol. 44 of *Word Biblical Commentary.* Waco: Word Books, 1982.

Ortiz, Manuel. "Being Disciples: Incarnational Christians in the City." In *Discipling the City: A Comprehensive Approach to Urban Mission,* 2nd ed., edited by Roger S. Greenway, 85–98. Manila, Philippines: OMF Literature, 1992.

Osiek, Carolyn, and David L. Balch. *Families in the New Testament World: Households and House Churches.* Louisville: Westminster John Knox Press, 1997.

Patterson, Paige. *The Troubled Triumphant Church: An Exposition of First Corinthians.* Nashville: Thomas Nelson, 1983. Reprint, Eugene, OR: Wipf & Stock, 2002.

Payne, J. D. *Missional House Churches: Reaching Our Communities with the Gospel.* Colorado Springs: Paternoster, 2007.

Pazmino, Robert W. *Foundational Issues in Christian Education.* Grand Rapids: Baker Book House, 1988.

Petersen, Joan M. "House-Churches in Rome." *Vigiliae Christianae* 23, no. 4 (1969): 264–272.

Piper, John. *Let the Nations Be Glad: The Supremacy of God in Missions.* 3rd ed. Grand Rapids: Baker Academic, 2010.

Pitts, William L., Jr. "The Priesthood of All Christians in the Baptist Heritage." *Southwestern Journal of Theology* 30, no. 2 (Spring 1988): 34–45.

Richards, Lawrence O. *Creative Bible Teaching.* Chicago: Moody Press, 1970.

Roberts, Bob, Jr. *The Multiplying Church.* Grand Rapids: Zondervan, 2008.

Robinson, Darrell W. *Total Church Life: How to Be a First Century Church in a 21st Century World.* Nashville: Broadman & Holman, 1997.

Roehlkepartain, Eugene C., and Peter L. Benson. "The Role of Christian Education in Faith Development." *Southwestern Journal of Theology* 38, no. 2 (Spring 1996): 24–32.

Saddleback Church. "Family Small Groups." Small Group Life Media Center. Saddleback Media Center, 22 May 2017. Accessed 11 May 2018. http://saddleback.com/mc/m/eee9e/.

Samson, Jose A. "Is There a Filipino Psychology." In *Filipino Psychology: Theory, Method, and Application,* edited by Rogelia Pe-pua, 56–63. Quezon City: University of the Philippines Press, 1982.

Santos, Narry F. *Turning Our Shame Into Honor: Transformation of the Filipino Hiya in the Light of Mark's Gospel.* Quezon City: Lifechange Publishing, 2003.

Schaub, Marilyn M. "House." In *Harper's Bible Dictionary,* edited by Paul J. Achtemeier, 409–410. San Francisco: Harper and Row, 1985.

Selman, M. J. "House." In *New Bible Dictionary,* 3rd ed., edited by I. Howard Marshall, A. R. Millard, J. I. Packer, and D. J. Wiseman, 487–490. Downers Grove: InterVarsity Press, 1962.

Singleton, Gary Wayne. "Utilizing Neighborhood Fellowships to Implement the Biblical Mandate to the New Testament Church to Make Disciples." DMin project, Southwestern Baptist Theological Seminary, 1991.

Smith, Gordon T. *City Shepherds: The Challenge of Urban Pastoral Ministry.* Manila, Philippines: Alliance Publishers, 1991.

Snyder, Howard A. *The Problem of Wine Skins: Church Structure in a Technological Age.* Downers Grove: InterVarsity Press, 1975.

Southern Baptist Convention. "The 2000 Baptist Faith and Message." Southern Baptist Convention, 14 June 2000. Accessed 11 May 2018. http://www.sbc.net/bfm2000/bfm2000.asp.

Stark, Rodney. *Cities of God: The Real Story of How Christianity Became an Urban Movement and Conquered Rome.* New York: HarperCollins, 2006.

———. *The Rise of Christianity: How the Obscure, Marginal Jesus Movement Became the Dominant Religious Force in the Western World in a Few Centuries.* Princeton: Princeton University Press, 1996.

Stetzer, Ed. *Planting Missional Churches.* Nashville: Broadman & Holman, 2006.

Stott, John R. W. *Between Two Worlds: The Challenge of Preaching Today.* Grand Rapids, MI: Eerdmans, 1982.

———. *The Contemporary Christian: An Urgent Plea for Double Listening.* Downers Grove, IL: InterVarsity Press, 1992.

————. *The Message of Romans*. Leicester: Inter-Varsity Press, 1994.

Switzer, Blake E. "The Use of Small Groups for Making Disciples of Postmodern Thinkers in Contemporary American Culture." PhD diss., Southwestern Baptist Theological Seminary, 2002.

Tano, Rodrigo D. *Theology in the Philippine Setting*. Quezon City: New Day Publishers, 1981.

Tesoro, Dindo Rei M., and Joselito Alviar Jose. *The Rise of Filipino Theology*. Pasay City: Daughters of St Paul, 2004.

Thiessen, Henry C. *Lectures in Systematic Theology*. Rev. ed. Grand Rapids: Eerdmans, 1979.

Thomas, Robert L., ed. *New American Standard Exhaustive Concordance of the Bible with Hebrew-Aramaic and Greek Dictionaries*. Nashville: Holman Bible Publishers, 1981.

Tuggy, Arthur. *The Philippine Church: Growth in a Changing Society*. Grand Rapids: Eerdmans, 1971.

Verner, D. C. *The Household of God: The Social World of the Pastoral Epistles*. Chico, CA: Scholars Press, 1983.

Viertel, Weldon, and Joyce Viertel. *Marriage and Family Life*. Makati City, Philippines: Church Strengthening Ministry, 1978.

Vine, W. E., Merrill F. Unger, and William White Jr. *Vine's Complete Expository Dictionary of Old and New Testament Words*. Nashville: Thomas Nelson, 1985.

Wallace, Daniel B. *Greek Grammar Beyond the Basics: An Exegetical Syntax of the New Testament*. Grand Rapids: Zondervan, 1996.

Weber, Hans-Ruedi. "The Church in the House." *Concern* 5 (June 1958): 7–28.

Willis, Avery T., Jr., and Henry T. Blackaby. *On Mission with God: Living God's Purpose for His Glory*. Nashville: LifeWay Press, 2001.

Wilson, Jeffrey. "Mentoring Leaders as They Evangelize Spiritual Seekers through Seeker Small Groups." DMin project, Southwestern Baptist Theological Seminary, 2000.

Wright, Christopher J. H. *The Mission of God: Unlocking the Bible's Grand Narrative*. Downers Grove, IL: InterVarsity Press, 2006.

————. *The Mission of God's People: A Biblical Theology of the Church's Mission*. Grand Rapids: Zondervan, 2010.

————. *Old Testament Ethics for the People of God*. Leicester: Inter-Varsity Press, 2004.

Yarnell, Malcolm B., III. "The Priesthood of Believers: Rediscovering the Biblical Doctrine of Royal Priesthood." In *Restoring Integrity in Baptist Churches*, edited by Thomas White, Jason G. Duesing, and Malcolm B. Yarnell III, 221–244. Grand Rapids: Kregel, 2008.

Young, Doyle L. "What Difference Does It Make, Anyway? The Priesthood of All Christians Applied to the Local Church." *Southwestern Journal of Theology* 30, no. 2 (Spring 1988): 46–54.

Young, Robert. *Young's Analytical Concordance to the Bible*. Peabody, MA: Hendrickson, 2014.

Zdero, Rad. *The Global House Church Movement.* Quezon City: Navigator Ministries, 2004.

Zuck, Roy B. *Basic Bible Interpretation.* Colorado: Chariot Victor Publishing, 1991.

Langham Literature and its imprints are a ministry of Langham Partnership.

Langham Partnership is a global fellowship working in pursuit of the vision God entrusted to its founder John Stott –

> *to facilitate the growth of the church in maturity and Christ-likeness through raising the standards of biblical preaching and teaching.*

Our vision is to see churches in the majority world equipped for mission and growing to maturity in Christ through the ministry of pastors and leaders who believe, teach and live by the Word of God.

Our mission is to strengthen the ministry of the Word of God through:
- nurturing national movements for biblical preaching
- fostering the creation and distribution of evangelical literature
- enhancing evangelical theological education

especially in countries where churches are under-resourced.

Our ministry

Langham Preaching partners with national leaders to nurture indigenous biblical preaching movements for pastors and lay preachers all around the world. With the support of a team of trainers from many countries, a multi-level programme of seminars provides practical training, and is followed by a programme for training local facilitators. Local preachers' groups and national and regional networks ensure continuity and ongoing development, seeking to build vigorous movements committed to Bible exposition.

Langham Literature provides majority world preachers, scholars and seminary libraries with evangelical books and electronic resources through publishing and distribution, grants and discounts. The programme also fosters the creation of indigenous evangelical books in many languages, through writer's grants, strengthening local evangelical publishing houses, and investment in major regional literature projects, such as one volume Bible commentaries like *The Africa Bible Commentary* and *The South Asia Bible Commentary*.

Langham Scholars provides financial support for evangelical doctoral students from the majority world so that, when they return home, they may train pastors and other Christian leaders with sound, biblical and theological teaching. This programme equips those who equip others. Langham Scholars also works in partnership with majority world seminaries in strengthening evangelical theological education. A growing number of Langham Scholars study in high quality doctoral programmes in the majority world itself. As well as teaching the next generation of pastors, graduated Langham Scholars exercise significant influence through their writing and leadership.

To learn more about Langham Partnership and the work we do visit **langham.org**